COLLECTION

Eli, Eli, lamma sabacthani?

Volume IX

CREATIO

Creation

Atila Sinke Guimarães

ISBN: 0-9819793-8-6
Library of the Congress Number: 2015958651
First edition 2016 by Tradition in Action, Inc.
Printed and bound in the United States of America

On the front cover is the mosaic *Creation of Heavens and Stars* from the late 12th century, in Monreale Cathedral, Sicily, Italy / Granger Historical Picture Archive

Cover by the TIA art desk

Tradition in Action, Inc.
P.O. Box 23135
Los Angeles, CA 90023
www.TraditionInAction.org

Other Books by the Same Author

From the Collection *Eli, Eli, Lamma Sabacthani?*

In The Murky Waters of Vatican II - Volume I - Demonstration of the ambiguity in the official texts of Vatican II

Animus Injuriandi I (Desire to Offend I) - Volume II - The spirit of Vatican II reflected in the desire to offend the Church

Animus Injuriandi II (Desire to Offend II) - Volume III - Exposes the offenses made against the honor due to the Catholic Faith

Animus Delendi I (Desire to Destroy I) - Volume IV - The spirit of Vatican II, expressed in the desire to destroy the Church

Animus Delendi II (Desire to Destroy II) - Volume V - How Secularization and Ecumenism express the spirit of Vatican II and act to destroy the Church

Will He Find Faith? (Inveniet Fidem?) - Volume VI - How the foundations of the Catholic Faith changed radically after the Council

Destructio Dei (The Destruction of God) - Volume VII - The principal conciliar theologians defend a notion of God at variance with Catholic doctrine

Fumus Satanae (The Smoke of Satan) - Volume VIII - The background thinking of Progressivism on God and eternity

Ecclesia (The Church) - Volume XI - The new progressivist ecclesiology confirmed by the Council, completely at variance with Catholic doctrine

Special Editions to the Collection

Quo Vadis, Petre? (Where are you going, Peter?) – An analysis of the ecumenical initiatives planned for the passing of the Millennium

Vatican II, Homosexuality & Pedophilia – A complement to *In the Murky Waters* to cover the effects of these vices on the clergy, mainly in the U.S.

Previews of the New Papacy (co-author) – A photographic confirmation of the desire to destroy the Papacy

Other Works of Interest

We Resist You to the Face (co-author)

An Urgent Plea: Do Not Change the Papacy (co-author)

War, Just War

Booklets

- The Universal Republic Blessed by the Conciliar Popes -The Biblical Commission on the Jews - Curious Affinities between the Thinking of JP II and Marxism - Petrine Primacy Challenged - The Return of the Muslin Threat The End of the Galileo Myth - A Cordial Invitation to 171 Rabbis and Jewish Scholars - Resistance versus Sede-Vacantism - We Are Church: Radical Aims, Dangerous Errors

---

TABLE OF CONTENTS

* * *

INTRODUCTION

§ 1 In this Volume we will study the progressivist conception of Creation. According to its thinking, there would be no essential difference between God and Creation; the Former, therefore, would be immanent in the latter.

§ 2 We will study the evolution of the cosmos, which would be for Progressivism the *princeps legem* of the universe. A divine immanence present in all created beings would free itself by means of evolution; this process would generate a step by step ascension from the state of brute matter to the human stage; afterward, a new level would be achieved, that of the "new man" or the "new Creation." In this future step, spirit would govern matter causing man and the cosmos to become glorious and divinized. Thus, Creation would merge into the Divinity, and the redemptive cycle of an initial "disaster," which would have engendered it, would be completed.

§ 3 As we consider this initial "disaster," as well as a "disaster" in man, we see that we are facing the notion of evil and sin. Therefore, we will also turn our attention to the progressivist conception of original sin in the next Volume X.

§ 4 What could the original sin be, according to the progressivists, except the rupture of an initial equilibrium, which allowed the divine immanence to gradually free itself and evolution to freely develop?

§ 5 According to this conception, through this "sin" Adam consciously introduced into the universe a negative and anti-immanentist force that opposed the process of evolution: Such a 'sin' would be individualism, individualization. With individualism, the notions of mine and yours came into being and, with it, the notions of property, law, justice and rigor. From these disruptive elements came disputes and wars. This was the kingdom of evil, which generated the "structures of sin."

§ 6 In order to redeem such "sin," a New Adam appeared in History. He is Jesus, a man united to the universal and the archetypical notion of the cosmos – the *Logos* – in such a way that, through His very existence He made the "narrow-minded" and "sinful" conception of individualism obsolete. His life, passion and death were testimonies to the abolition of the kingdom of evil.

§ 7 Through love He diluted the boundaries of the "mine" and "yours"; through communion He dispersed property; through participation He eliminated the contours of the law. His mercy made a *tabula rasa* of justice, and with His inexhaustible forgiveness He wiped out any idea of rigor. Thus, the historic Jesus reopened the obstructed road of immanence, the pathway of evolution. In His Resurrection He anticipated the final stage in which all of mankind will become glorious and divine. This is the progressivist thinking.

Creation, sin and Redemption are the three subjects dealt with in this Volume and in the following Volume X.

*

§ 8 In other parts of this Collection we have already mentioned the progressivist doctrine of evolution.[1] Someone could think, therefore, that we are merely repeating the same topic.

This is not the case, however, because when we dealt with the topic in other Volumes, we generally did so only with the aim of offering the Reader an overview that would facilitate the understanding of another topic under analysis. The principal concern was not evolution, but some other subject related to it. In those overviews, we usually mentioned that the matter of evolution would be addressed *ex professo* in another place of this Collection. That mentioned place is the present Volume.

For polemical purposes, we have already demonstrated and documented parts of the evolutionary doctrine in several places of this Collection.[2] We will not analyze these parts again here, but we will simply refer to them when necessary.

---

[1] Cf. Vol. I, *In the Murky Waters of Vatican II* (Los Angeles: TIA, 2008), Chap. IV Note 5f, Chap. VII §§ 10-19; Vol. III, *Animus Injuriandi II*, (Los Angeles: TIA, 2011), Chap. II §§ 7, 8, Note 10, Chap. IV §§ 23, 35, 37, 43, Chap. V §§ 9-11, 13-16, Note 9, Chap. VII §§ 4, 27, Note 7. Vol. IV, *Animus Delendi I* (Los Angeles: TIA, 2000), Chap. III § 16, Chap. IV §§ 3, 5; Vol. VI, *Inveniet Fidem?* (Los Angeles: TIA, 2007), Chap. III §§ 209-221, 244-246, Chap. IV §§ 23-36, 83-85, Note 1; Vol. VII *Destructio Dei* (Los Angeles, TIA, 2012), Chap. II, §§ 62, 63, 74, Note 6,f, n, Chap. III, §§ 73-74, 77, 128, Chap. IV §§ 5, 6, 20-24, 68, 84, 90, 91, 111-113, 332-335; Vol. VIII, *Fumus Satanae* (Los Angeles. TIA, 2015), Chap. I §§ 64, 67, 71, 104, Chap. III §§ 29, 30, 32, 35, Note 19, Chap. IV §§ 46-48, 60, 61, 64, 160, 161, Chap. VI § 3.

[2] * Regarding the progressivist doctrine of evolution in History, see Vol. I, *In the Murky Waters of Vatican II*, Chap. VII §§ 14,.18; Vol. III, *Animus Injuriandi II*, Chap. V §§ 10, 11; Vol. IV, *Animus Delendi I*, Chap. III, § 16; Vol. VIII, *Fumus Satanae*, Chap. IV §§ 60, 61.

§ 9 Someone who read the previous Volume VIII, in which we expounded the Trinitarian doctrine of Progressivism, could object that the original matrixes of the thinking behind evolution were set out there. It would be superfluous, then, to dedicate more space for a detailed exposé of the progressivist doctrine on Creation.

This objection does not seem pertinent since the goal we have pursued in this Collection since Volume VI is to present the balance of the fruits of Vatican Council II and a full exposition of its thinking. Thus, after the presentation of the progressivist Trinitarian doctrine, we must analyze its consequences.

§ 10 Strategically speaking, to analyze these consequences, taking into consideration the general procedure of the progressivists, is still very opportune. Indeed, the less elevated their doctrine, the more numerous the statements of their authors. Thus, the documents that expose the less elevated doctrine are clearer and more numerous. Consequently, at these lower levels, the fruits of the Council and expressions of its thinking are more plentiful. If we were to omit presenting them, we would not achieve our objective.

§ 11 According to the progressivist conception, the study of Creation, sin and Redemption is very important. It is a very high perspective – although inferior to that which we analyzed in Volume VIII, *Fumus Satanae* – from which proceeds the progressivist protology or etiology and, subsequently, its soterology and eschatology.[3]

*

* Regarding the evolutionary conception of grace and sanctification, see Vol. III, *Animus Injuriandi II*, Chap. VI §§ 1, 2, Chap. VII, §§ 5-7 Vol. V, *Animus Delendi II*, Part II Chap. III §§ 5-11; Vol. VI, *Inveniet Fidem?* Chap III, §§ 222-228, 232, 233; Vol. VII, *Destructio Dei*, Chap. III §§ 13, 20, 77, 81, 82, Chap. IV, § 33; Vol. VIII, *Fumus Satanae*, Chap. VI § 3; Vol. XI, *Ecclesia*, Chap. I §§ 179-186, Chap. II §§ 7-17, 62-66, Chap. VI §§ 12-17.

[3] **Protology** is the study of the first beginnings of mankind (from the Greek: *protos* = first); **etiology** is the study of man's origins (from the Greek: *aitia* = cause, origin); **soterology** is the study of salvation or redemption and its fruits (from the Greek *soteria* = salvation); **eschatology** is the study of the realities that will precede the end of the world (from the Greek *eschata* = final things).

§ 12 From Volume VI on, this Collection is analyzing the fruits and the thinking of the Council. Here we remind the Reader to what degree these objectives are inseparable.

§ 13 When we analyzed the destruction of the presuppositions of the Faith[4] and the various ways employed to demolish the dogma of the Triune God,[5] the preponderant note was the presentation of the fruits of the Council. In parallel, however, countless aspects of its thinking also appeared. When we studied the progressivist Trinitarian dramaturgy,[6] the tonic note was the thinking of the Council. Collaterally, however, the fact of bringing to light this doctrine exposes one of the most deleterious fruits of Vatican II.

§ 14 In this Volume IX and in the following Volume X, what are the tonic notes?

Insofar as these works will develop the already presented doctrine and offer an encompassing visualization of many progressivist themes, it will be a manifestation of its thinking.

Insofar as this thought is contrary to Catholic doctrine, it will manifest how, as a fruit of the tolerance of the Council, error and heresy undermine and destroy orthodoxy.

§ 15 This twofold objective is explicable since the more efficacious method to destroy Catholic doctrine is not to attack it directly, but rather to replace it with another doctrine that is gradually introduced.

§ 16 *In a first phase*, the progressivists look for points that are not completely explained in Church teaching that allow them to plant the seeds of a new doctrine.

In the case of evolution, for example, they scrutinized the still unfinished interpretation of the six days of Creation. They introduced the hypothesis that the days referred to in Scripture were allegories used by Moses to symbolize eras, each of which could have extended to thousands or millions of years.[7] With this they sowed the seed of the evolutionary conception.

---

[4] Vol. VI, *Inveniet Fidem?* (Los Angeles: TIA, 2007). *passim.*

[5] Vol. VII, *Destructio Dei* (Los Angeles: TIA 2013), *passim.*

[6] Vol. VIII, *Fumus Satanae* (Los Angeles: TIA 2015), *passim.*

[7] The allegoric or historic interpretation of the first chapters of Genesis was condemned by St. Pius X. Discussion on this matter was presented in Vol. III, *Animus Injuriandi II*, Chap. IV §§ 28-31, Note 42; see in this Vol. IX *Creatio*, Chap I, Note 2.

§ 17 *In a second phase*, shielded by the supposed orthodoxy of their hypothesis, the progressivists shape the tree of the new theory that sprang from that seed. This tree already has branches different from those supporting Catholic doctrine. In order to elide the imputation of heterodoxy, the progressivists shield themselves with sophistic interpretations or conform themselves to the occasional trimming of this or that branch of their tree, all the while keeping their progressivist doctrine alive and healthy.

In the case of the evolutionary theory, the progressivists turned deaf ears to the condemnation of St. Pius X. They set forth the idea that man would be a product of the process of evolution, with the ape as his nearest ancestor, and other animals more remotely, going back finally to a hypothetical protozoa – an original cell that would constitute the most elementary form of life from which man would have proceeded.

One of the consequences of such a conception that frontally collided with Catholic doctrine was that, following the coherence of evolution, there was not only an original couple – Adam and Eve – from whom all of mankind proceeded, but countless apes gave origin to countless couples. This Polygenism, sophistically defended by many, was condemned in the Encyclical *Humani generis* by Pius XII.[8] For a while the progressivists conformed to that trimming. They took great care, however, to keep their evolutionary theory intact.

§ 18 In a *third phase*, they abandon that initial caution and become bold. In this phase they do not fear to draw, from that initial theory, consequences that are clearly against Catholic doctrine. They defend the argument that the Church must change her "obsolete" thinking to others more in accordance with the imperatives of science, the modern world, the union of religions or the dignity of the human person.

In the case of evolution, the consequences were numerous. Let us illustrate this phase with just one example. Based on the supposition that the creation of inanimate beings began millions of years ago and that of man one or two million years in the past,[9] the progressivists claimed that it would be probable

---

[8] Cf. Pius XII, Encyclical *Humani generis* of August 12, 1950 (Petrópolis: Vozes, 1961), n. 36.

[9] When Joseph Ratzinger was still a priest, he endorsed criticisms against the Catholic doctrine regarding the time and age of man on earth. He wrote: "But we all know today that, before this phase was

that countless human beings existed during that long time span. All this would have taken place before the episodes reported in Scriptures and, of course, the foundation of the Catholic Church.

So, they continue, given that God in His infinite goodness could not have created men without giving them the possibility of salvation, the latter existed outside the context of Sacred History and the institution of the Catholic Church. Therefore, by an imperative of the discoveries of science, it is convenient today for the Church to modify the dogma that outside of the Church there is no salvation.

§ 19 In a *fourth and last phase*, they pass from boldness to arrogance. They imagine that they can "dogmatically" condemn the Catholic doctrine that is opposed to their new teaching.

In the mentioned case of the salvation of the millions of men who would have existed without knowing the true Faith, the progressivists explicitly attack the dogma *extra Ecclesia nulla salus*. They argue that such a dogma could only be admitted when the Church was still in an "infantile stage."

Today with the contributions of the Enlightenment, the Church would have become "adult," and it is no longer possible to imagine that outside of her bosom there is no salvation. They demand the modification of dogmatic theology on this point. Whoever disagrees with them is anathematized as primitive and obscurantist, as one who wants to re-commit the same "error" the Church would have committed when she condemned Galileo.[10]

§ 20 Thus, the indirect method of destruction used by the progressivists reveals itself to be much more efficient than the direct attack. If someone were to limit himself to analyzing only the direct assaults against Catholic doctrine, he most probably would not apprehend the amplitude of the maneuver being employed.

The objectives of this and the next Volumes are, therefore, twofold and cumulative. As we describe the progressivist thinking about Creation, sin and Redemption, we will be simultaneously indicating the method used to destroy the Catholic dogmatic theology on these matters.

---

reached [the biblical report about the appearance of man], hundreds of thousands of years of life and human effort had already run their course, which were not taken into consideration by the biblical picture of history" (*Fé e Futuro,* Petropolis: Vozes, 1971, p. 11-12; see context in the excerpt quoted in Chap. I § 52)

[10] On the supposed error of the Church in the case of Galileo, see our refutation in Chap.IV Note 88.

As far as the thinking of Progressivism is concerned, this Volume IX is a continuation of the previous Volume VIII. As for exposing a maneuver of auto-demolition, this Volume is the description of the fruits of the Council that destroy Dogmatic Theology.

*

§ 21

The subject matter of this Volume IX is divided fundamentally into two parts: the analysis of Evolution and the study of Historicism. Both subjects are approached as basic elements to change the doctrine of the Church on Creation. As much as possible, we will try to show the immanentist content of these progressivist conceptions and explain their links to Vatican II.

* * *

CHAPTER I

BATTLES *A PROPOS* THE DOCTRINE OF CREATION; VICTORY OF PROGRESSIVISM AT VATICAN II

§ 1 Among the behind-the-curtain fights that paved the way for Vatican II, perhaps the most important was the battle over the notion of Creation.

It was *a propos* this fight that Progressivism introduced historical criticism of Scriptures, the biblical movement and *ressourcement* – the return to the sources, the Fathers of the Church – in order to find a legitimization for its theses. As a consequence of their attempt to adapt the interpretation of Genesis to the theory of evolution, they introduced a conception that Creation was not made by God in six days as a completed and accomplished reality,[1] as the Church has always taught;[2] rather, it would be a

---

[1] According to Catholic doctrine, the work of Creation was completed on the sixth day: "Thus the heavens and the earth were finished, and all the furniture of them. And on the seventh day God ended his work which He had made: and He rested on the seventh day from all the work which He had made. And God blessed the seventh day, and sanctified it: because in it He had rested from all His work which God created and made" (Gen 2:1-3). The work of Creation was complete regarding the genres and species created, although not regarding the government, conservation and production of new individuals, which continues to the present (cf. Cornelius a Lapide, *Commentaria in Genesim*, chap. 2:2).

[2] To assist our Reader, we repeat here Note 42 in Chap. IV of Vol. III, *Animus Injuriandi II*, which reports the position of the Church on Creation:

a. Faced with the growing modernist tendency to allow an "historic" interpretation of the first chapters of Genesis, the Biblical Commission under the Pontificate of St. Pius X issued the following condemnation on June 30, 1909, in the form of questions and answers:

"Concerning the historical character of the first three chapters of Genesis:

"***Question 1***: Do the various exegetical systems, which have been designed and defended under the guise of science to exclude the literal historic meaning of the first three chapters of Genesis, rest on solid foundations?

"***Answer*** - No.

"***Question 2***: Notwithstanding the historical nature and form of Genesis, the special connection of the first three chapters with one another

---

and with the following chapters, the multiple testimonies of the Scripture both in the Old and the New Testaments, the almost unanimous opinion of the Fathers and the traditional interpretation – transmitted by the Israelite people – always upheld by the Church, is it permitted to teach that the aforesaid chapters of Genesis do not contain accounts of events that really occurred and that, therefore, do not correspond to objective reality and historical truth, but are fables derived from the mythologies and cosmogonies of ancient peoples which – after being purged of any polytheist error – were adapted by the sacred author to the monotheistic doctrine? Or are they allegories and symbols without any foundation in objective reality, proposed to inculcate religious and philosophical truths under the appearance of history? Or, still, are they legends, in part historical and in part fictitious, freely composed for the instruction and edification of souls?

"***Answer*** - No to all the parts of the question.

"***Question 3***: Can the literal historical sense in particular be called into doubt when dealing with facts narrated in the same chapters which touch the foundations of the Christian religion, such as the creation of all things by God in the beginning of time; the special creation of man; the formation of the first woman from the first man; the unity of the human race; the original felicity of our first parents in a state of justice, integrity and immortality; the command given by God to man to test his obedience; the transgression of the divine command at the instigation of the Devil in the form of a serpent; the degradation of our first parents from that primeval state of innocence, and the promise of a future Redeemer?

"***Answer*** - No." ... (DS 3512-3514)

"***Question 7***: Supposing that it was not the intention of the sacred author, as he wrote the first chapter of Genesis, to teach in a scientific way the inner formation of things visible and the complete order of Creation, but rather to give his people an accessible narration adapted to men's senses and capacities, such as was the current language of the time, should one, in the interpretation of these things, seek to adhere always and exactly to the rigor of scientific language?

"***Answer*** - No." (DS 3518)

b. This clear and peremptory statement oriented the teaching of the Magisterium for several decades. On January 16, 1948, however, a letter of the Secretariat of the Biblical Commission addressed to Cardinal Emmanuel Suhard, Archbishop of Paris, came to light (cf. DS 3862-3864). Although we will not analyze here the intentions behind this letter, it was utilized by the progressivists to try to circumvent the decisions of St. Pius X. Indeed, they alleged that that new letter introduced the possibility of a "scientific" reinterpretation of the literary style of the first chapters of Genesis, stating: "It is necessary ... to examine closely the literary procedures of ancient peoples of the East, their

divine process in motion, which would be completing itself as History unfolds.[3]

§ 2 The notion of human nature itself was modified. It would no longer be a metaphysical reality that defines the immutable essence of mankind, but an existential or phenomenological reality capable only of a provisory "definition" in each stage of its evolution. Better said, it could be defined only in comparison with its final stage, still not attained.

It would be better neither to speak of human nature – a static concept – nor look for abstract definitions. Rather, such notions should be abolished and man should be analyzed only as he presents himself *hic et nunc* (here and now).

---

psychology, their ways of expressing themselves and their particular notion of historic truth" (DS 3864).

Progressivists were, thus, able to claim that this letter from the Secretariat of the Biblical Commission relativized the concept of historical truth and paved the way for the historical method of interpreting Scripture.

Their liberalizing efforts were cut short very soon, however, when Pius XII issued the Encyclical *Humani generis* of August 12, 1950. In it, he affirmed: "One should particularly deplore a certain excessively free interpretation of the historical books of the Old Testament. Those who favor this system in order to defend their cause, wrongly refer to the Letter which was sent not long ago to the Archbishop of Paris by the Pontifical Biblical Commission" (January 16, 1948: AAS, vol. 40, pp. 45-48, n. 37).

After summarizing the letter's contents, Pius XII reaffirmed the infallible nature of the truths contained in the first chapters of Genesis. He wrote: "If, however, the ancient sacred writers have taken anything from popular narrations ... it must not be forgotten that they did so with the help of divine inspiration, which protected them from any error whatsoever selecting and evaluating those documents. Therefore, by no means can anything of the popular narrations inserted in the Sacred Scripture be considered on a par with myths or other such things" (*ibid.*, n. 38).

Thus, the precepts of St. Pius X remain valid.

See also in this Vol. IX, Chap. I § 82, Note 98.

[3] That is to say, there would not be defined angelic, human, animal, vegetal and mineral natures separate from the divine nature. Rather, there would be a process of continual mutation by which each nature would tend toward the immediately higher one, and all would tend toward the divine.

§ 3 To suppose that creation is a dynamic reality *in fieri* (in continuous motion) profoundly changes the notion of Divine Providence, which, according to Catholic doctrine, is God governing, sustaining and maintaining the Creation that He made.

§ 4 The progressivist concepts of grace and revelation, understood according to the evolutionary theory, replace this concept of Providence. On the one hand, "grace" becomes a divine element that would propel human ontology itself to ascend gradually in the process of evolution. It is a new concept of grace.[4] On the other hand, such "grace" acting over man's consciousness, would produce "revelation," that is, a divine communication that would show to each man in his present phase of evolution the better way to unite himself to God.

§ 5 Thus, the very notion of Religion is changed. Through "grace" and "revelation" man would gradually attain in History the eschatological plenitude to which he was called. In this way, the "history of salvation" replaces the traditional notion of the Catholic Religion.

These are the serious consequences of the progressivist notion of Creation being incubated in certain ecclesiastical milieus before they were partially accepted by Vatican II.[5]

§ 6 The defenders of the ensemble of these notions could not be at ease in face of traditional Catholic doctrine and Perennial Philosophy. They needed, then, to attack them and replace them with something else. This was the mission of the *Nouvelle Théologie*.

On the opposite side, there were some who defended the true Catholic doctrine.

We see, therefore, that is very important to know what happened with the clash of these two currents, which took place in the period between Vatican I and Vatican II.

*

---

[4] Cf. Vol. X, *Peccatum – Redemptio*, Chap. VIII, 2, C-F.

[5] These would include, for example, the theologians of the movement *Nouvelle Théologie*: among them, namely, Pièrre Teilhard de Chardin, Hans Urs von Balthasar, Henri de Lubac, and Joseph Ratzinger, as we will see in this Chap. I §§ 45-62; Chap. III §§ 2-31; Chap. V. §§ 11-21.

1. From Vatican I to Vatican II: Disputes about the Concept of Creation

§ 7 When Vatican I was interrupted by the invasion of Garibaldi's troops into the Eternal City, the ensemble of theological teaching about Creation followed the same line of the traditional doctrine ministered by the Church since time immemorial.

An opposing tendency, however, was taking root in many minds. This shift in teaching followed the desire to adapt the Church to the modern thought introduced by the Enlightenment, the modern culture born from the French Revolution and the imperatives of modern science, an emerging Scientificism. This mentality inclined scholars and theologians to contest the perennial Church doctrine and gave rise to the birth of pioneer theories, which made that liberal tendency explicit.[6] Anton Günther in Austria and Antonio Rosmini in Italy wrote essays developing this new thinking, which soon would be vigorously condemned by Pius IX. [7]

§ 8 Pius IX, however, was not eternal. The *ralliement* of Leo XIII, which aimed to legitimate the new French political regime, had a corollary: the desire to adapt Catholic thinking to Modern Philosophy. Some progressivist authors, who describe the genesis of their current, point to Leo XIII as the one who started the process that has led to the present day situation. One commentator, Fr. Giuseppe Colombo, notes:

§ 9 "The philosophical problem becomes prominent at the moment that Leo XIII became the propeller for the restoration of Thomism.[8*] The Pontiff proposed to achieve unity in theology by renewing its philosophical structure. This became necessary because of theology's contact with a 'separated' philosophy or, more precisely, with the separated philosophers of the modern epoch."[9]

---

[6] On the difference between revolutionary actions in the realms of tendencies, ideas and facts, see Plinio Corrêa de Oliveira, *Revolution and Counter-Revolution* (São Paulo: Diário das Leis, 1982), part I, chap. V, p. 23.

[7] For outlines of the principal doctrines of these two priests, see Vol. VI, *Inveniet Fidem?* Chap. III §§ 128, 129, 132; Vol. VII, *Destructio Dei*, Chap. II, Note 41; Chap. IV, §§ 143-149. The Church Magisterium condemned the thinking of both (cf. DS 2828-2831, 3201-3241).

[8*] Cf. Encyclical *Aeterni Patris*, 1879.

[9] Giuseppe Colombo, "La Création," in V.A., *Bilan de la Théologie du XXe. Siècle* (Tournai-Paris: Casterman, 1970), vol. 2, p. 271.

§ 10 When Colombo attributes this desire to Leo XIII, he seems to be referring to the following excerpts of the Encyclical *Aeterni Patris* in which the Pontiff describes a philosophy that is separated from the faith:

"Moreover, to the old teaching a novel system of philosophy has succeeded here and there, in which we fail to perceive those desirable and wholesome fruits which the Church and civil society itself would prefer. Under the impulse of the innovators of the 16th century, men started to philosophize without any consideration for faith and granted each other full license of allowing their thoughts to run according to their own caprice and bent."[10]

After criticizing such philosophers and their followers, the Pontiff employs words that could be interpreted as an appeal to unite Modern Philosophy with Scholastic Philosophy. He asserts:

"In saying this **we have no intention of discountenancing the learned and able men who bring their industry and erudition, and, what is more, the wealth of new discoveries to the service of philosophy**. **For, of course, we understand that this tends toward the development of learning**. But one should be very careful lest all or his chief labor be exhausted in these pursuits and in mere erudition. **The same thing is true of sacred theology, which, indeed, may be assisted and illustrated by all kinds of erudition, though it is absolutely necessary to approach it in the grave manner of the Scholastics in order that, thanks to the united forces of revelation and reason, it may continue to be 'the invincible bulwark of the faith.'**"[11]

§ 11 Thus, for the liberals, modernists and progressivsts, according to their own interpretation, Leo XIII would have legitimated the union of Scholastic Theology with Modern Philosophy, or at least with some of its presuppositions and concepts. Leo XIII would have made this opening, therefore, in the very encyclical in which he encouraged Thomism.

§ 12 The practical and immediate result of *Aeterni Patris* was a split among theologians. In other words, it gave a right to speak and contest to those who until then had lacked such an advantage. Cardinal Yves Congar writes:

---

[10] Leo XIII, Encyclical *Aeterni Patris* of August 4, 1879 (Petrópolis: Vozes, 1956), n. 31.

[11] *Ibid.*, n. 32.

"The fruit [of *Aeterni Patris*] was to break theology, which thus fell into a profound crisis after the rebirth of the second Scholasticism."[12]

§ 13 Indeed, parallel to those who cheered the new stimulus given to Scholasticism appeared those who defended the adaptation of theology to Modern Philosophy and science. Colombo describes the situation:

"The restoration of Thomism did not take place without difficulties. First, it clashed with the positivist orientation of the second half of the last century [of the 19th century], which tended to affirm itself as the proper representation of science and which, in its more radical manifestations, implied the decline of all speculative science.

"Once this harmful opposition was overcome, it [the rebirth of Scholasticism] found another more explicit obstacle, which emerged straightforwardly against the restoration of Scholasticism and, more specifically, of Thomism. This was founded essentially on the objection that philosophy must be contemporary to be valid; it cannot exist only by the force of authority that calls for a return to the past.

"The party [favoring Scholasticism] responded to this objection with the assertion that the truth is always valid; therefore, the philosophy that expresses it is also valid. It is not the case to create a truth or invent a philosophy that expresses it, but simply to recognize its [Scholasticism's] value and update it.

"Today, in light of the developments that have followed, it seems we can say that, consciously or unconsciously, those two positions were based on two conceptions of philosophy. For one, philosophy is history, an invention of the created mind. The immanent risk of this position is relativism, that is, to abandon the profession of the truth under the pretext that it must be constantly perfected and, consequently, does not exist. For others, philosophy is the truth definitively acquired in a scholastic way. In this case, the risk is to materialize and transform the truth into a thing."[13]

---

[12] Yves Congar, *Théologie*, in DTC (Paris: Letouzey et Ane, 1946), p, 241, *apud* Colombo *La Création*, p. 271

[13.] G. Colombo, *La Création*, pp. 271-272.

§ 14 Fr. Giuseppe Colombo mentions the philosophical *ralliement*, a "third position," or a "third Scholasticism,"[14] which, according to him, would be what Leo XIII intended:

"No one [neither the neo-Thomists nor the historicists] drafted with the necessary consciousness and objectivity the outlines that the 'third Scholasticism,' which originated from the Encyclical *Aeterni Patris*, should have had. Therefore, the possibility for this initiative remains open."[15]

The admission of a philosophical contestation of Thomism constituted a powerful precedent inside the Church to start the theological "re-reading" of the Bible and the doctrine of Creation.[16]

§ 15 The tendency to adapt theology to science and evolution, along with the assimilation of historic criticism, generated the Biblical Movement.[17] Even then, this movement already clearly denied the doctrine of Creation taught by the Church, as described by Colombo:

"The theology at the beginning of the [20th] century was already sensitive to the scientific question. This was, in fact, the pressing question of the moment. … It was, thus, that a theology inspired by concord appeared. …

---

[14] Colombo speaks here of a "third Scholasticism," referring to the neo-Thomism encouraged by *Aeterni Patris*, Congar, above, employed the expression "second Scholasticism," referring to the same phenomenon.

It seems to us that Colombo's expression is more precise, since in the 16th century there was already a "second Scholasticism" (cf. Vol. VI, *Inveniet Fidem?* Chap. III §§ 6-21). Nevertheless, we prefer the expressions neo-Scholasticism or neo-Thomism.

[15] G. Colombo, *La Création*, p. 272

[16] Cf. *ibid*. See also Vol. VI, *Inveniet Fidem?*, Chap. III §§ 140-142, 154, 157, 191.

[17] When we speak of the Biblical Movement, we are referring exclusively to the movement of modernist origin that later was taken up and spread by the progressivists. We do not refer to the healthy reaction against this movement taken under the initiative of St. Pius X, which gave birth to the foundation of the Pontifical Biblical Institute of Rome in 1909. Incidentally, it was not long before this Institute was also infiltrated and, finally, dominated by the progressivist current. In 1927, the Institute opened a Jerusalem campus, which encouraged more autonomy and experimentation in exegesis and the modern methods.

"At the start of the century, science was particularly an adept of the hypothesis of evolution.[18] It contested Catholic doctrine on the origin of the world and, therefore, the theology of Creation. From this was born an apologetic that, by fidelity to a certain spirit of concord, tried to avoid a rupture with science. But, this did not happen without great difficulties, both because of the profoundly positivist ideological context in which the hypothesis of evolution was presented and because of contestations that were made against the biblical datum. It was in this oblique way that the scientific problem provoked the appearance of the biblical problem.

"In reality, the biblical problem had presented itself autonomously to early 20th century theology, generated by the development of the historical sciences.[19] History, as already noted, is the great contribution of the 19th century to our cultural patrimony with the method of historical criticism and its application to solve problems. Fatally, it was also applied to the study of Christianity. The School of Tübingen and, then, the one in Munich had already applied it to the study of Christian thought and dogma. Inevitably it was also applied to the study of the Bible. On the Catholic side, this application was made by [Alfred] Loisy. Then, the modernist crisis exploded with a loud bang."[20]

§ 16 With the definitive condemnation of Modernism by St. Pius X, who called it the "synthesis of all heresies,"[21] the spirit of "concord" that had gradually taken over the Church during the long pontificate of Leo XIII, was shaken. The fervor for sound teaching reignited, the reaction against the modernist innovations became stronger. The intransigence proper to the militant character of the Church reared up again. The demands made on the behalf of science and history were rejected. The tradition of dogmatic teaching prevailed. Colombo records this development:

"In the 20th century, the modernist crisis weighed heavily over all of theology. Thus, it carried with it … a strong current that favored the restoration of Thomism – a current that was not just constructive but also promoted a radical and systematic

---

[18] In Chapter II we will study the alleged scientific character of evolution.

[19] In Chapter IV §§ 127-136, we will discuss the alleged scientific character of Historicism.

[20] G. Colombo, *La Création*, p. 272.

[21] Cf. St. Pius X, Encyclical *Pascendi Dominici gregis* of September 8, 1907 (Petrópolis: Vozes, 1959). n. 39.

rupture with Modern Philosophy. Consequently it firmly closed the door on the new demands, from both science and the biblical exegesis.[22*] As long as this climate lasted, the theology of Creation had no alternative but to hold firmly to the positions it had established at the beginning of the century before other problems appeared. It could only consolidate its positions."[23]

§ 17 However, that militant spirit gradually and slowly waned in the pontificates of Benedict XV and Pius XI:

"It is difficult to mark the moment when the anti-modernist intransigence ended and a new surge began in theology."[24]

As the militant spirit died, the spirit of "concord" re-established itself, its fruit ready for harvesting. Progressivism, which is a form of neo-Modernism, prevailed:

"Gradually and almost unnoticed, a new situation in Catholic theology burgeoned and became strong, a situation that – speaking in a schematic and objective way – seemed to define itself as the antithesis of the anti-modernist period."[25]

§ 18 According to Colombo, the opening to biblical criticism assumed its official character with Pius XII:

"The most salient mark of the new theological situation was an openness to the biblical problem. ... Although the Church Magisterium held firmly to its prerogative of authentic interpreter of Revelation, it did not intend to redress the reading of the Bible with easy interpretations; on the contrary, it encouraged every means possible to find the true meaning of the Scriptures.[26*]"[27]

§ 19 Thenceforth, the immutable truths of Dogmatic Theology and, in parallel, the metaphysical principles of Scholastic Philosophy left center stage and entered into oblivion. They were replaced by other conceptions – among them a new notion of Revelation – in which we no longer find the majestic coherence of the interpretation of Scripture with the ensemble of Catholic dogmas. On the contrary, a certain exegetic liberty was installed, whereby each one could attempt his own interpretation of the

---

22* Cf. Encyclical *Pascendi*.

23 G. Colombo, *La Création*, p. 273.

24 *Ibid*.

25 *Ibid*.

26* Cf. Pius XII, *Divino afflante Spiritu*, 1943.

27 G. Colombo, *La Création*, p. 273.

Sacred Letters, disregarding Dogmatic Theology. One could say that Protestant free-examination of Scriptures entered Catholic exegetics. In this regard, Colombo observes:

"It should be stressed that this process of replacement was simultaneously a process of demystification. In effect, it supposes not only acknowledging the limits of Dogmatic Theology, but also consequently leads to the denouncement of its undue pretension to consider itself as a theology *sic et simpliciter* [thus and simply]."[28]

§ 20 Such "demystification" was only possible because of a change of atmosphere: The anti-modernist militancy was on the decline; ecumenism and openness to the world had begun.[29]

§ 21 As the ecclesiastical milieus opened themselves to this tendency, many in them were overcome by an "inferiority complex" with regard to the world. Here and there foreboding complaints were raised affirming that the Church was no longer convincing, that her dogma, morals, habits, customs, missiology and liturgy were outdated. Everything had to be reformed to enter with a new face the pursuit of the novelties of the modern world.

This position of spirit was more or less inevitable, given that the ambience of sacrality that must exist *de pleno jure* (enjoying full rights) in the Holy Church was rejected. Such a sacrality should exist not only in the Church, but it must also overflow from her into the temporal sphere. Once the fundamental principle of the primacy of the sacral over the profane is denied, the poles of influence between the spiritual and the temporal spheres are inverted. This produces *mutatis mutandis* a type of caesaropapism, which caused so much harm to the Church in the East with the Schism, and in the West with Anglicanism and Gallicanism.

In the final analysis, this progressivist position implies the glorification of human respect and the subservience of the religious to the profane. From this erroneous position proceeds every possible obliteration in the relationship of the Church with different peoples. It is an attitude that opens the door to all defections, apostasies and heresies.

§ 22 Among the obliterations that came in the wake of the new openness to historical criticism, ecumenism and the modern world was the notion that pretended that the Church could only

---

[28] *Ibid.*, p. 274.

[29] Cf. *ibid.*

reach a minority of people because of her antiquated positions. From this erroneous thinking came new demands, as we can deduce from this excerpt by Colombo:

"Post-modernist theology is characterized not only by an openness to the biblical problem, but also by a real openness to other problems that appeared at the beginning of the century – such as the scientific and philosophical problems. In fact, thenceforth these problems increasingly overlapped … to the point of creating a cultural context in which Christian thinking constituted a stain, marked by its singularity and, thus, revealing its lack of influence and reach. It was inevitable that Christianity's situation as a minority in the world would be expressed on the cultural level.

"Consequently, as people became aware of this situation, a reaction to make Christian thought leave its isolation and reengage with the modern culture became imperative. Theology reencountered under new forms the need to face the philosophical and scientific problems that it wanted to ignore at the beginning of the century.

§ 23

"That demand, which circumstances made increasingly urgent, began to be met after two cultural movements that facilitated an openness. The first, a positive one, came after theology opened itself to the biblical problem: It was established that one could dissociate the biblical problem from the other questions, in particular the scientific problem. After that, the conclusions of science that were considered pernicious to the teaching of the Bible at the beginning of the century and, therefore, demanded rejection, now became acceptable because they were recognized as compatible with the biblical teachings. Such conclusions, in fact, regarded another aspect of reality, different from the Bible.[30]

---

[30] Although Pius XII's *Divine afflante Spiritu* had, in a certain way, given the right of citizenship to historical criticism of the Scripture, as Colombo observes, it seems to us exaggerated to affirm that the document legitimized "conclusions of science that were considered pernicious to the teaching of the Bible at the beginning of the century and made them compatible with the Scripture." Among these legitimizations, the most important, according to the author, would be the theory of evolution.

In fact, in the encyclical there are references to archeological discoveries (nn. 11, 22, 23), to the need to study the biblical languages (nn. 12, 23) and, in various places, to the study of history. However, it is impossible to apply the generalization made by the author to archeology, philosophy and history – certainly sciences that have seen major

"The second movement, on the contrary, was a negative one that took place in the wake of the restoration of Thomism. It marked the end of the hope that had illuminated that movement at its start, as the number of its convinced supporters grew smaller and the skeptics simultaneously increased. Moreover, many were convinced of the essential futility of that attempt and declared that, from then on, theology must resolutely open itself to Modern Philosophy and, more generically, to modern culture. This demand, which naturally spread, would grow stronger and form its own theological current that took the name *Nouvelle Théologie* [New Theology]."[31]

§ 24 The traditional doctrine on Creation – undermined, as we have seen, by the introduction of historical criticism in the analysis of the texts of Revelation and by its opposition to Thomism – suffered a new frontal attack with the apologia of the theory of evolution put forth by the Jesuit Pierre Teilhard de Chardin.

In his synopsis, Colombo bases himself on some errors or improprieties in order to defend the progressivist current. We will point them out as they appear. He continues his description:

"When the War started, the *Nouvelle Théologie* became for theology an invitation to rethink the traditional theses that expressed the theology of Creation. Teilhard de Chardin belongs to this current. He is one of its best known representatives and, perhaps, the element that catalyzed and propelled it forward.

---

developments in recent times. For the principal "scientific" problem he is addressing is evolution, and it cannot be included in the three sciences mentioned in the encyclical.

Not even the following phrase by Pius XII could be adduced to support evolution: "This true liberty of the children of God, which adheres faithfully to the teaching of the Church, and welcomes and gratefully uses the contributions of profane science, this liberty, upheld and sustained in every way by the confidence of all, is the condition and source of all lasting fruit and of all solid progress in Catholic knowledge" (n. 48).

This comment in the encyclical, undoubtedly generic, should be understood as a conclusion about the mentioned sciences – archeology, philosophy and history. It seems to us abusive to interpret it as referring to approval of the theory of evolution introduced into the progressivist doctrine of Creation, as Colombo assumes.

If *Divino afflante Spiritu* is not the base for Colombo's affirmation that the Church opened the door to evolution, it is gratuitous, since he presents no other proof.

[31] G. Colombo, *La Création*, p. 275

His fundamental contribution was to realize a synthesis between Christian thinking and the current scientific representation of the world in all its implications.

"In particular, taking into account the intense controversies raised by his thought, there is a certain unanimity in considering the ensemble of the work of Teilhard de Chardin as an attempt to give a direction to evolution. He considered it the mechanism that engenders the universe – 'creative evolution' – through its successive leaps forward. Its ***direction*** is found in Christification and, therefore, in the unification with God that comes straight from Christian revelation, without denaturizing the reality of evolution.

"In this overview Teilhard de Chardin thinks that the theology of Creation, based on the metaphysics of the participative being, must maintain its conceptual value, but also must transcend itself if it wants to take into account the new vision of the universe in evolution.

"The result is, *first*, a shift in the center of interest in the Creation question: the fact of Creation clearly descends to a second plane, leaving the direction in first place. On the one hand, the fact of Creation goes to a second place because it is considered 'incontestable' in the eyes of science, given that evolution transcends its own horizon. The dilemma between Creationism and Evolutionism posed at the beginning of the [20th] century thus reveals itself to be a pseudo-dilemma because, if the scientific view demands Evolutionism, it can propose nothing against Creationism and can, therefore, coexist with it.[32] In this regard,

---

[32] a. When he defends the origin of Creation as transcending the horizon of science, Colombo seems to falsify the dilemma between Creationism and Evolutionism.

It seems elementary to us that if science pretends to explain the universe, it must analyze its origin and not just the way it develops. This is clearly evident in the efforts of Astrophysics in the last decades to elaborate various theories about the origin of the cosmos. Further, one of the principal aims of Biology, and especially Micro-Biology, is to discover the origin of life. By denying that the origin of the universe lies within the horizon of science, Colombo commits the *first error* of his argumentation.

b. However, independent of this reason, let us suppose *argumentandi gratia* (for the sake of the argument) that the origin of the universe did

Teilhard de Chardin could propose that his evolutionary perspective encompassed the totality of the doctrine of Creation.

"On the other hand, once the fact of Creation presents itself as 'incontestable' for science, it necessarily and definitively places itself out of the ambit of science's competence. Thus situated outside its range, it cannot be combated by science or raise its interest. On the contrary, once the evolutionary conception is admitted, all interest is turned toward the end of evolution, because from this comes its direction.

"Theology is, thus, invited to consider Creation not at its beginning, as it did in the past, but at its end. From this perspective, where man is now the pivotal point of evolution, *Cosmo-*

---

lie outside the limits of science and was established only in the realm of Philosophy.

The description of evolution as a process of gradual liberation of a nobler life, supposes an initial element immanent in the entire universe. Such an element should be God himself since evolution in its march makes the universe tend toward the divine. Now then, if God were immanent in the universe, the necessary corollary is that the universe at a certain moment should have emanated from God. Thus, from the philosophical point of view, Evolutionism necessarily supposes the denial of the Catholic doctrine on Creation (cf. DR 31, 235, 421, 428, 706, 1701, 1782-1783, 1893-1805m 2074).

Therefore, discussion about the "direction" of Creation did not objectively shift attention from the "fact" of Creation because it is by its "direction" that evolution reveals itself to be immanentist and emanatist. That is, the discussion is re-directed to the way God created – if He created *ex nihilo* or by emanation. This is equivalent to returning to the "fact" of Creation.

Thus, the dilemma of Creationism vs. Evolutionism remains as acute – or even more so – as it was at the beginning of the 20th century. This is the *second error* of Colombo's argumentation.

c In addition to these errors, his prejudice also manifests itself: When he aims to attack Thomism, he affirms that philosophy and science are "thenceforth increasingly overlapping" (cf. *La Création*, p. 275, excerpt quoted in § 22). Here, however, when he tries to "baptize" evolution and shield it from the deserved accusation of immanentist, he makes his reader believe that philosophy and science have no link whatsoever with one another.

Notwithstanding his errors and prejudice, we continue to follow his quite lucid and surprisingly encompassing synopsis.

genesis leads to *Noogenesis*, Creation is unified, and the dualism or opposition between the world and man – established by the old paralyzed mentality – disappears.[33]

"Still from this perspective, the difference between the theology of Creation and the theology of man loses its *raison d'être*. The latter, by breaking the impulse of evolution or, more precisely, by ignoring it, reduces the theology of Creation to the question of its origin; thus it cannot address, except in an exterior way, the question of its end.[34] Can we say that we know the reality of something without knowing its direction? Can we know a direction without knowing its end? Suddenly, the theology of Creation discovered the poverty of its own traditional concepts."[35]

Thus, we have the progressivist position: From the moment it assumed the evolutionary theory of Teilhard de Chardin, Progressivism accepted a doctrine of Creation adapted to the new ideas and different from traditional Catholic doctrine.

§ 25 Colombo stresses the need for these adaptations born from the theses of Teilhard:

---

[33] That is, the notion of human nature as substantially different from the rest of the universe disappears. According to the un-paralyzed or evolutionary mentality, there would be a permeation of the essences of all beings in the universe that would prevent them from becoming differentiated. Man would be the pole of convergence of all the cosmic energies, which would be concentrated in him to prepare the new phase of evolution.

[34] Colombo's lack of seriousness is surprising in this regard. Does he not know that – parallel to the doctrine on the creation of man – the Church has the treatise *De Novissimi*, which analyzes his last ends, as well as a treatise on grace, which studies the principal means through which man reaches his end? What is the purpose, then, of Colombo's accusation of poverty launched against traditional Catholic doctrine? His accusation only becomes consistent when we adopt his immanentist point of view. Indeed, if we were to consider that there is a divine immanence in man that would be liberated through the process of evolution, then, the beginning, the means and the end of Creation would be contained in a single "moment" of human life. In this case, the doctrine about the end of man would appear to be a question placed "in an exterior way." However, it is also true that this immanentist perspective is no longer Catholic doctrine. Therefore, to have any coherence in his criticism, Colombo is obliged to leave the ambit of Catholic orthodoxy. Otherwise, his critique lacks seriousness on this point.

[35] G. Colombo, *La Création*, pp. 275-276.

"For Teilhard's aims to be met, Christian thinking had to find its significance and importance in modern culture. Teilhard made an effort to achieve this, not only moved by a basic intuition that consisted in interpreting evolution in a Christic sense, but also by means of an original re-reading of the Christian theses on Creation, in which he replaced matters that had an incontestable meaning, but lacked importance and significance in the eyes of the modern world."[36]

§ 26

This was the state of affairs when Pius XII published the Encyclical *Humani generis*, with the official objective of blocking the progress of the *Nouvelle Théologie*.

As a matter of fact, we can find in this document many obstacles to the development of this current. To wit, the principal ones seem to be:

- Some noteworthy restrictions made against Evolutionism;[37]
- A damaging attack against the Existentialist Philosophy;[38]
- Some mentions of Historicism that serve to discredit it;[39]
- A censure against the movement of a return to sources of the ancient Fathers because of its independence from the Magisterium;[40]
- Some indirect criticisms of ecumenism;[41]
- A general warning against the dangers of dogmatic relativism;[42]
- An alert to the danger of denying the dogma of Original Sin and the consequent doctrine of the Redemption of Our Lord Jesus Christ.[43]

§ 27

There is no doubt that *Humani generis* was inspired by a healthy reaction against the mounting tide of Progressivism inside the Church. However, it was not clearly condemnatory; it

---

36 *Ibid.*, p. 277.

37 Cf. Pius XII, *Humani generis*, nn. 5-6, 34-36.

38 *Ibid.*, nn. 6, 14, 31.

39 *Ibid.*, nn. 7, 20-21, 37.

40 *Ibid.*, nn.17.

41 *Ibid.*, nn. 11-12, 26, 42.

42 *Ibid.*, nn. 14-15.

43 *Ibid.*, n. 25.

was a warning. It was a breakwater that offered some protection from the full force of the waves, but did not stop the tide from continuing to rise.

§ 28 Although taking a viewpoint opposite to ours, Colombo confirms this opinion regarding Creation:

"Today, after sufficient time has passed, it is necessary to say that the Encyclical [*Humani generis*] was a filter more than a brake to the doctrine of Creation.[44*] On the one hand, it limited itself to reject once again the positions that questioned the liberty of God in Creation. But, on the other hand, it admitted the principle that scientific evolution can have a place in Christian thought,[45*] thus officially putting a closure to reservations and suspicions present for almost a century."[46]

§ 29 From this affirmation, the progressivist author goes on to draw consequences that seem disproportionate to us:

"After Evolutionism is considered more as a general principle than as a particular doctrine,[47*] there is no longer opposition between theology and the scientific question as it presents itself, with its own terms and demands, despite the counsels of moderation and prudence that accompany it.[48*] From that point onward, theology could tread this road without encountering insuperable obstacles."[49]

It seems to us that Colombo simplifies the position of *Humani generis* regarding Evolutionism and draws excessive consequences on this matter.

§ 30 In effect, Pius XII does not approve the general principle of evolution as Colombo affirms. He only admits that the subject can be discussed, reserving the final word to the Magisterium:

"It remains for us now to speak about those questions which, although they pertain to the positive sciences, are nevertheless more or less connected with the revealed truths of the Christian faith. In fact, not a few insistently demand that the Catholic Religion take these sciences into account as much as

---

44* DS 3890.

45* DS 3896-3897.

46 G. Colombo, *La Création*, pp. 277-278.

47* Cf. P. Teilhard de Chardin, *Le Phénomène Humain*, pp. 236-243.

48* DS 2897.

49 G. Colombo, *La Création*, p. 278.

possible. This certainly would be praiseworthy in the case of clearly proved facts. But caution must be used when there is rather question of pure hypotheses, having some sort of scientific foundation, in which the doctrine contained in Sacred Scripture or in Tradition is involved. If such conjectural opinions are directly or indirectly opposed to the doctrine revealed by God, then they in no way should be admitted."[50]

§ 31

It is in this cautious and balanced context that we should understand the admission of a debate on Evolutionism, which is expressed in these words:

"For these reasons, the Magisterium of the Church does not forbid that, in conformity with the present state of human sciences and sacred theology, research and discussions on the part of men experienced in both fields take place with regard to the doctrine of Evolutionism, in as far as it inquires into the origin of the human body as coming from pre-existent and living matter – for the Catholic Faith obliges us to hold that souls are immediately created by God. However, this must be done in such a way that the reasons for both opinions, that is, those favorable and those unfavorable to Evolutionism, be weighed and judged with the necessary seriousness, moderation and measure, and provided that all are prepared to submit to the judgment of the Church, to whom Christ has given the mission of interpreting authentically the Sacred Scriptures and of defending the dogmas of Faith.[51*]

"Some however, recklessly transgress this liberty of discussion when they act as if the origin of the human body from pre-existing and living matter were already completely certain and proved. They only argue based on certain data that have been discovered up to now and by reasoning on those data and as if there were nothing in the sources of divine revelation that demands the greatest moderation and caution in this question."[52]

§ 32

It seems to us that Colombo, whose analysis we offer as a sample of the progressivist current, directly incurs the accusation of recklessness that Pius XII points out in the Encyclical. For, although 20 years had passed from the publication of the Encyclical (1950) to the publication of Colombo's work (1970),

---

[50] Pius XII, *Humani generis*, n. 34.

[51*] Cf. Pius XII, *Pontifical Allocution to the Members of the Academy of Sciences* of November 30, 1941, in AAS, vol. 33, p. 506.

[52] Pius XII, *Humani generis*, n. 35.

in that period scientific evidence for the evolutionary theory did not make any significant advance. Even up to the moment of the publication of this work (2015), that is, 45 years later, no scientific evidence has been discovered that can transform the hypothesis of Evolutionism with certainty, as we will see later in this Volume.[53]

This recklessness or lack of seriousness of the author in the above-cited excerpts is present in two baseless generalizations: *first*, he assumes as demonstrated what is simply a scientific hypothesis, which he calls "a particular doctrine." *Second*, he amplifies this "doctrine" to the level of a general principle.

Further, to reach his conclusion – "there is no longer any opposition between theology and the scientific question as it presents itself, with its own terms and demands" – Colombo bases himself on the authority of Teilhard de Chardin. Now then, Teilhard, for both doctrinal and political reasons, cannot be used to interpret the intentions of *Humani generis*.

§ 33 The *doctrinal reason* is that the Evolutionism of the French Jesuit is clearly immanentist, as we have already demonstrated in this Collection.[54] And the Encyclical combats the pantheist consequences of such immanentism:

"If anyone examines the state of affairs outside the Christian fold, he will easily discover the principal paths that not a few self-called learned men are entering. **Some imprudently and without discernment hold that the evolutionary system**, which has not been indisputably proven even in the domain of natural sciences, **can be extended to the origin of all beings, and with reckless audacity support the monistic and pantheistic hypothesis of a universe in continual evolution**."[55]

§ 34 The *political reason* is that Teilhard de Chardin, as leader of the *Nouvelle Théologie* and especially as a preeminent defender of Evolutionism, was one of the targets of the censures in *Humani generis*. It was due to the sanctions issued in the wake of that Encyclical[56] that Teilhard was obliged to leave France

---

[53] Cf. Chap. II of this Volume.

[54] Cf. Vol. III, *Animus Injuriandi II*, Chap. V §§ 8-14, Note 9, Chap. VI Note 12, Chap. VII Note 7; Vol. VI, *Inveniet Fidem?,* Chap. I §§ 4-7, Chap. III §§ 2, 153, 154, Note 117, Chap. V §§ 81-89, 111-116, 152-161, Note 92; Vol. VII, *Destructio Dei*, Chap. II §§ 12, 13, 19, 20, 37, 57,Chap. III § 229, Chap. IV §§ 5, 6, 13, 68, 69, 98-103, 210-215, 329-334, Note 302; Vol. VIII, *Fumus Satanae,* Chap. I §§ 55-58, 61-69, Note 55, Chap. III §§ 32-36, Chap. IV, §§ 161-163, 174-178, Chap. V §§ 113-114, Chap. VII §§ 102, 103, 121.

[55] Pius XII, *Humani generis*, n. 5.

[56] Cf. Vol. IV, *Animus Delendi I*, Chap. III § 9 Note 4b.

and move to the United States in 1951, where he would die in 1955. Therefore, it is absolutely absurd to use the authority of Teilhard to interpret the intentions of Pius XII in the mentioned Encyclical.

§ 35 In view of the great dissemination made of the works of Teilhard de Chardin, on June 30, 1962, the Congregation of the Holy Office published the following *Monitum* (admonition) regarding the writings of the French Jesuit:

"Various works of Fr. Pierre Teilhard de Chardin, some of which were published posthumously, are being edited and are gaining considerable support.

"Refraining from a judgment about those points that concern the positive sciences, it is quite evident that in philosophical and theological matters the mentioned works abound in ambiguities and even serious errors that offend Catholic doctrine.

"For this reason, the Most Eminent and Most Reverend Fathers of the Supreme and Sacred Congregation of the Holy Office exhort all Ordinaries as well as the Superiors of Religious Institutes, Rectors of Seminaries and Directors of Universities, to protect minds, particularly of the youth, against the dangers of the works of Fr. Teilhard de Chardin and his associates."[57]

§ 36 Notwithstanding such a censure, Teilhard was defended by Cardinal Henri de Lubac and others; further, his work was publicly praised in a letter by the then Secretary of State Cardinal Agostino Casaroli, writing on behalf of Pope John Paul II.[58]

§ 37 Despite the observations we made about Colombo's weak foundations for his conclusions on Pius XII's Encyclical, the consequence pointed out by him with regard to the progressivist theology of Creationism and Evolutionism is unfortunately quite true:

"From that point onward [the publication of *Humani generis*], theology could tread this road without encountering insuperable obstacles."[59]

§ 38 In summary, the tendency to adapt the thinking of the Church to Modern Philosophy – encouraged by the *Aeterni Patris* of Leo XIII – would jeopardize the perennial concepts of Thomist Philosophy, which established the basis for the traditional doctrine on Creation.

---

[57] *L'Osservatore Romano*, July 1, 1962.

[58] Cf. *L'Osservatore Romano*, June 12, 1981, letter transcribed in Vol. IV, *Animus Delendi I*, Chap. III.Note 8d, see also 8b, c.

[59] G. Colombo, *La Création*, p. 278; see the context of the quote in § 29.

After this adaptation was admitted, Historicism and Evolutionism entered the Catholic ambit in the name of the demands of science. In the case of Historicism: historical criticism introduced the possibility of changing the interpretation of the Scriptures; this would be legitimated by the Encyclical *Divino afflante Spiritu* of Pius XII. In the case of Evolutionism: the interpretation of Genesis on the six days of Creation was reformed to adapt to the "certainties" of natural science; this would be endorsed by the Encyclical *Humani generis,* also by Pius XII.

§ 39 Thus, the three questions – philosophical, biblical and scientific – strongly assisted one another, each preparing the ground for the next, and resulted in challenging Catholic Dogmatic Theology.

§ 40 Regarding the doctrine of Creation, how did the question stand at the end of Pius XII's pontificate?

Certainly there were still defenders of true Thomism: apologists of the Biblical Movement as conceived by St. Pius X as an initiative to oppose the introduction of neo-Protestant and modernist relativism in the interpretation of the Sacred Letters, as well as partisans of the traditional doctrine of the Church, who were opposed to the theological consequences of the scientific hypothesis of Evolutionism.

However, the general climate was no longer one of doctrinal cohesion. Far past were the times of Vatican I, in which Pius IX and, then, St. Pius X adopted the language of "yes, yes, no, no" regarding the errors of the modern world.

As dusk fell on the Constantine Church, Pius XII – despite some good cautionary measures against various errors – seemed to be already *de facto* admitting theological pluralism. And in such pluralism, the progressivists had the advantage of their initiative, courage, intelligence, capacity for an agile and skillful articulation and clarity of goals. The conservatives and traditionalists, although still in the majority, did not have a great love for Catholic doctrine. They accepted it, taught it and defended it as if by atavism. Doctrinal tolerance undermined what zeal they had.

In the twilight of the kingdom of Pius XII it was not hard to conjecture what the future would bring.

*

2. Confirming this Overview: Outline of the Progressivist Doctrine of Creation

§ 41 So far, we have described the genesis of the battles on the doctrine of Creation. Based on the synopsis of Giuseppe Colombo, it was possible to establish some landmark gains for the progressivist doctrine on Creation. However, regardless of the usefulness of this overview, *per se* it is insufficient to prove either that the ensemble of progressivists agrees with its affirmations or that Vatican II represented a victory for this current. Let us dedicate, then, this Item 2 to prove the first fact, and Item 3, the second.

As we present such confirmations, other important concepts that orient the progressivist thinking will appear. We will transcribe them without special analysis, but in Letter D we will synthesize them to allow the Reader a convenient overall view of this topic.

A. Generic Confirmations of Item 1

§ 42 It is from the progressivist theogony, its singular conception of God – the "God for"[60] – that the deepest foundations of the progressivist cosmology proceed and, consequently, its vision of Creation. According to this view, the "God for" would have had the "need" to create. Such Creation would have been effected by the Trinity, in which a feminine element is included.[61]

From that Trinitarian sphere would have proceeded another one, also eternal, the "Jerusalem that is above." In this sphere Christ, Mary, Adam and Eve would exist.[62] Creation would have been brought into being caused by a disaster in these spheres.[63]

§ 43 From a less profound perspective, we find Evolutionism as the base of the progressivist conception.

Agreeing with Colombo, Fr. John O'Donnell, S.J., describes the basic conception of "many exegetes and theologians" of our times in an article on the thinking of von Balthasar:

---

60 Cf. Vol. VII, *Destruction Dei*, Chap. III §§ 58-60, Chap. IV §§ 14-18.

61 Cf. Vol. VIII, *Fumus Satanae*, Chap. I §§ 51-111; Vol. VI, *Inveniet Fidem?*, Chap. V §§ 152-158.

62 Cf. Vol. VIII, *Fumus Satanae*, Chap. IV §§ 1-8, 97-103, 141-151.

63 Cf. *ibid.*, Chap. V, *passim*, Chap. VI §§ 1-6.

"Accepting an evolutionary world-view, they would understand the full realization of humanity, not as something that happened in the beginning of History, but as the goal to be achieved, as the eschatological fulfillment of History. According to this interpretation, Christ's work is not to restore the primeval state, but to make possible the eschatological state. This final state of fulfillment is not a restoration of the primeval state, but something more. The Omega is more than the Alpha."[64]

§ 44 Fr. Anthony Fernando, O.M.I., also speaks generally when he attributes the acceptation of Evolutionism to the ensemble of theologians:

"When the theory of evolution was first proposed, Christians believed it was difficult to reconcile this theory with their traditional notion of Creation. But the theologians took advantage of the occasion to re-think the meaning of the Genesis narrative and eventually found forms to expound the doctrine of Creation so that it could shelter even the theory of evolution.

"This theological problem and the way it was resolved help us considerably to understand Buddhist illumination from a Christian perspective. … God continues to be the Creator even if the universe is the result of evolution; this is because it was He who implanted this evolving force in the elements. In the same way, God could be the Revealer even if the ideas come from the minds of man."[65]

These are general confirmations. Next we will present specific confirmations of Colombo's synopsis.

B. Specific Confirmations: Symbiosis of Evolutionism & the Doctrine of Creation

§ 45 Pope Benedict XVI, when he was just a priest, confirms the progressivist doctrine on Creation and offers us various components of their thinking. He writes:

"When Charles Darwin developed the idea of the evolution of all living beings in the middle of last [19th] century, thus radically questioning the traditional representation of the stability of the species created by God, he started a revolution in the eyes of the world, similar in its depth to that which we link to the name of Copernicus. …

---

[64] John O'Donnell, "Man and Woman as 'Imago Dei' in the Theology of Hans Urs von Balthasar," *Clergy Review* (London), n. 78, p. 126.

[65] A. Fernando, "Revelação Cristã e Iluminação Budista," *Concilium*, 2/1976, pp. 54-55.

"The examples referred to here are sufficient to demonstrate the narrowness of the horizon in which, until 100 years ago, our images of the world and history moved. How paralyzed was the tradition, taken from the Bible, of a thinking totally projected from the Judeo-Christian history of salvation! What an enormous revolution in the fact that, beyond the immense amplification of space that had already occurred, an analogous toppling of frontiers regarding time and history was imposed!

"In many aspects, the consequences of that step were as dramatic as those of the Copernicus revolution. Because the dimension of time affects man's being in an incomparably more profound way than that of the space. Because now, for the first time, the representation of space itself became relative and changed, losing its perfectly defined form to become subject to history and temporality. Man appeared as a being formed by infinite transformations. The great constants of the biblical image of the world, the primitive and final stage, receded to the unpredictable. The fundamental understanding of reality changed: Becoming took the place of being, evolution replaced Creation, and ascension replaced the Fall. …

"We try to resolve … the problem of knowing whether the basic concepts of creation and evolution – contradictory at first glance – can be reconciled. But this does not mean that the theologian has to make a dishonest compromise and tactically declare that the terrain, already unsustainable, is futile, when shortly before he solemnly presented it as an inalienable part of the faith."[66]

§ 46

Ratzinger stresses that, for him, Creationism is unsustainable:

"First of all, there is an aspect of this question that is relatively important and only partially of a theological nature. The idea of the immutability of the species, which dominated before Darwin, had been legitimated backed by the concept of Creation. It saw each species as a datum of Creation, which since the beginning of the world maintained itself as something singular and different from the other species, thanks to the creative action of God. It is evident that the idea of evolution contradicts this form of faith in Creation and that this type of faith has become unsustainable today."[67]

---

[66] Joseph Ratzinger, "Fé en la Creación y Teoria Evolutiva," in V.A., *Es Esto Dios?* (Barcelona: Herder, 1973), pp. 231-232.

[67] *Ibid.*, pp. 232-233.

§ 47 Further on, he reiterates:

"The form in which the creationist idea became concrete in practice was swept away by the evolutionary theory. Here, the believer must be taught by science, because the way he had imagined Creation corresponded to a pre-scientific conception of the world, which is unsustainable today."[68]

§ 48 After reaffirming that the "creationist faith" has become "unsustainable" and "useless,"[69] Ratzinger goes on to present the "solution": to stitch together the progressivist faith with the evolutionary theory. The principal defenders of Evolutionism normally do not mention from where the universe proceeded or where it is directed. They only speak about how the universe develops. So, the progressivist current offers the evolutionary process a beginning and an end. This is what Ratzinger calls "meaning" in the following texts:

"In face of the fundamental problem – which the theory of evolution does not resolve – that is, whether absurdity or coherence should prevail, this [progressivist] faith expresses the conviction that the whole world, as the Bible says, proceeds from the *Logos* or the Creator Thinking, and represents the temporal form of His self-realization."

He explains this further:

"Creation should not be conceived following the model of an artisan who makes all types of objects, but rather as that of a Creator Thinking. … To believe in Creation is to include in the faith the changing world discovered by science, as a world full of meaning that proceeds from a creating *Logos*."[70]

He goes on to indicate the final point toward which evolution is directed:

"The recognition of a world in evolution as the self-realization of a Creator Thinking includes its return to the creating action of the Spirit, to the *Creator Spiritus*."[71]

§ 49 By presenting the beginning and end of the process, Ratzinger imagines he has resolved the problem between a materialist Evolutionism and the faith. For, it seems, the *Logos* would be immanent in matter from its initial rudimentary stage.

---

68 *Ibid.*, p. 234.

69 *Ibid.*, p. 235.

70 *Ibid.*, p. 241.

71 *Ibid.*

§ 50 Evolutionism pretends that the spirit is just a more developed stage of matter. Now, Ratzinger tries to reconcile this evolutionary pretension with the Catholic faith in the creation of the human soul by God. Doing this, he seems to admit a divine immanence in matter in a way that makes the spirit spring up from matter. These are his words:

"It is evident that the spirit cannot appear as a random product of material evolution, but rather, matter would be an integral element of the history of the spirit. However, this is just another way to affirm that the spirit was created and is not a mere product of evolution, even when it appears as if it were evolution. …

"According to this, the appearance of the spirit signifies that a movement forward reached the objective that had been targeted. Finally, we must say that the formation of the spirit can absolutely not be represented as an artisan action of God, which would have begun to act in the world suddenly."[72]

§ 51 From these notions Ratzinger arrives at a completely relativist interpretation of the creation of man:

"Also, in what concerns man, Creation does not signify a remote beginning; rather, when we say 'Adam' we are referring to each one of us; each man is directly related to God. The faith does not affirm more about the first man than about each one of us. And, inversely, it does not affirm less of us than of the first man."[73]

§ 52 In his work *Faith and Future,* Ratzinger also directly attacks the traditional interpretation of the first chapters of Genesis, seemingly incurring the condemnation of St. Pius X on this matter.[74] Dealing with the objections the positivists make against the Catholic Faith, Ratzinger endorses their criticisms:

"They are asking if the Christian Faith has any future, or if it is not being made more and more obsolete by intellectual evolution. …

"Let us take a look at the general pictures and see where the critical points are to be found. The difficulty begins with the first page of the Bible. The concept presented there of the origin of the world is in direct contradiction of everything we know to-

---

[72] *Ibid.*, p. 242.

[73] *Ibid.*

[74] Cf. DS 3512-3519; cf. above Note 2 of this Chapter.

day about the origin of the universe. … And, thus, the questions continue, almost on each page as we read the Bible. The figure of clay molded into man by the hands of God is largely inaccessible to us, as well as, after, the figure of the woman taken out of the side of the sleeping man, recognized by him as his own flesh. …

"This continues after the report of the fall with the biblical chronology of history, which describes Adam in a cultural period set in about the year 4000 BC. This date does in fact accord with the biblical counting of time … but today, everyone knows that before this event, many hundreds of thousands of years of human life and effort had already run their course, which find no place in the biblical historical picture, which is set strictly within the framework of the ancient Eastern notion of time."[75]

These texts of Benedict XVI confirm the initial overview of this Chapter and proffer various points of the progressivist conception of Creation.[76]

C. Other Confirmations: Important Theologians Attack Catholic Doctrine on Creation & Embrace Progressivist Evolutionism

§ 53 There are many other confirmations that the theory of evolution defended by Progressivism aims to destroy the doctrine of Creation as the Catholic Church has always taught it.

Fr. Schoonenberg defends the mutability of the dogma and the change in the traditional interpretation of the Scriptures, exemplifying such a change with the doctrine of Creation:

"It follows that the affirmations of the ecclesiastic Magisterium, as well as those of the Sacred Scripture and of Jesus himself, are human affirmations [sic] and, consequently, situated

---

[75] Joseph Ratzinger, *Fé e Futuro*, pp. 10-12.

[76] Cf. Letter D, below.

If science were to admit that Evolutionism is not true (cf. Chap. II), it would be very interesting to know the response of the "progressivist faith" as described by Benedict XVI, since it would, then, become "pre-scientific," "unsustainable" and "futile." Would Ratzinger apply the same implacable rigor against Evolutionism that he uses against the Catholic faith in Creationism?

historically and conditioned by the language and culture of the time when they where formulated and by the problems for which they furnished an answer.

"Thus, the first hermeneutic principle is that the texts (including the inspired and infallible texts) do not provide an answer to questions that were not present at the time they were posed. For example, the words of Genesis (1:26, 2:7. Rom 5:12-21 and the expression *origine unum* of the Council of Trent) say nothing about the possibility of the evolutionary origin of man from an animal. The question of evolution only appeared in the 19th century."[77]

§ 54

Fr. Hans Küng agrees with Ratzinger and Schoonenberg, extending the same criterion to the texts of the Scripture regarding the end times. In the following excerpt, we see that science is established as the fundamental standard of biblical exegesis, which is tantamount to introducing a scientific free-examination into the interpretation of Scripture. Küng writes:

"The six days of creation and the narrative of man's creation are images – this we know today – that do not describe scientifically the evolution of the creation of the world, but rather announce – also to today's man – the glory and sovereignty of the Creator. …

"Analogously, the synoptic descriptions of the end times received from the Prophets, especially Isaiah and Daniel, and the contemporary interpretation of the Apocalypse, in which stars fall from heaven, the sun darkens and the angels sound trumpets, cannot be attributed *per se* to Jesus. Nor do they pretend to depict a scientific picture of the end of the world, but rather they serve solely to announce the final and definitive plenitude and revelation of the Kingdom God as an event that surpasses our knowledge and can only take place by God's power.

"In these various synoptic or Pauline descriptions, which by the way do not agree among themselves, we should differentiate between image and meaning, the form of expression and the content of the affirmation."[78]

---

[77] J.A.M. Schoonenberg, no title, in V.A., *Cinco Problemas que Desafiam a Igreja de Hoje* (São Paulo: Herder, 1970), p. 66.

[78] Hans Küng, *A Igreja* (Lisbon: Moraes, 1969), vol. 1, pp. 94-95.

§ 55 Cardinal Yves Congar, in his turn, endorses the notion of a Creation co-extensive with time and history similar to that defended by Ratzinger, and not a Creation made by God at a determined moment:

"Creation must not be placed in a moment of time at the beginning, when God would have made His Creation, leaving it to develop afterward outside His presence. His creative act is co-extensive with time. Creation continues just like human action – progress, scientific research, discovery, medicine, sports, enjoyment, artistic creation – all human activity is the creation of God."[79]

§ 56 Fr. Marie-Dominique Chenu defends the same notion of Creation as he deals with the progressivist conception of tradition, which is not so different from the notion of evolution:

"This transformation of the world is Creation in act. Creation is not a capricious operation of God at the beginning of History that continues to unfold in mediocrity. It is the today of the Creator. The concept of Creation became weak in Christian consciousness. It is reinvigorated since we comprehended that the building up of the world is Creation in act, a work to which God calls man to be His collaborator."[80]

§ 57 In a deeper way, Chenu returns to the same topic, now alluding to an immanence of God in Creation:

"Creation is not an a-temporal phenomenon; it lies in the flux of time. And History is a reality homogenous to Creation. Creation is always in action. And, if God is immersed in History – the Council says 'the Word became flesh and entered History' – then my representations of God are not eternal, static and a-temporal. God is in time, He is a God who is coming, and not a God who created in the past, according to an elementary imagery."[81]

§ 58 Cardinal Henri de Lubac says more or less the same, confirming the "meaning" of Evolutionism already asserted by Ratzinger. De Lubac writes:

"There is a genesis, an effective growth, a maturing of the universe. There is a Creation that is not merely maintained,

---

[79] *Jean Puyo Interroge le Père Congar* (Paris: Centurion, 1975), p. 180.

[80] *Jacques Duquesne Interroge le Père Chenu* (Paris: Centurion, 1975), p. 72.

[81] *Ibid.*, p. 82.

but is continuous. Once the world has an objective, it thus has a sense, that is, simultaneously a direction and a meaning."[82]

§ 59 Fr. Teilhard de Chardin also sees Creation as a reality co-extensive with the world and history, as an evolving divine immanence in the universe:

"We often hear of a first instant of the world: This is a false expression and a vain quest!

"The creative act is not interlaid in the chain of antecedents. It is placed in the universe in all of its extension and duration. It is impossible for the element of the world to leave the world, to arrive only at some lower boundary of the world. It is impossible for it to soundly conceive a physical limit for the world, or even to reasonably imagine Creation isolated from an element of the world, separated from the world or outside of the world."[83]

§ 60 The progressivist doctrine of Creation could be summarized in this synthesis of Teilhard, which essentially corresponds to that of Benedict XVI:

"As it develops, the universe manifests its creative intention.

"In the beginning: The energy, propeller and organizer of the many, prepares the planets where the future 'children of God' will be called to live and develop.

"In the middle: Incarnation permits the Word to divinize human nature, which He assumes, thus linking, once again, Creation with the Creator.

"In the end: the *pleroma* appears, formed by the totality of those who the Eucharistic divinization – generated by the incarnate Word in the middle of the universalized Supper – will consummate as children of the Father. ...

"Then the Son himself will submit to the One to Whom everything was submitted, so that God may be all in all."[84]

§ 61 The energy that Teilhard places in the beginning of Creation would be a tendency toward the spirit and toward Christ,

---

[82] Henri de Lubac, *Catholicisme – Les Aspects Sociaux du Dogme* (Paris: Cerf, 1968), p. 112.

[83] J.M. Mortier, *Avec Teilhard de Chardin, Vues Ardentes* (Paris: Seuil, 1967), p. 61.

[84] *Ibid.*, p. 21.

as it becomes clear in the document below. With this, Teilhard draws nearer to Ratzinger. Also, the immanence of the universal Christ in Creation becomes manifest:

"In the beginning of the sensible world there was the many. This many as a united block was already raised toward the spirit, attracted by the universal Christ who was engendered in it."[85]

§ 62

Von Balthasar sees in the immanence of Creation the source of love and the relationship among beings, which would intermix with one another. He affirms:

"The meaning of Creation remains indecipherable as long as the eternal image is veiled. If the heart were not to beat at the bosom of the threefold eternal life, this life would be nothing but implacable destiny, this time would be nothing but sadness and all love would be ephemeral. It is because life proceeds from this eternal source that it begins to flow in us also; it speaks the Word to us; it becomes itself word and language and transmits to us, as a brilliant mark of divine Love, the mission to announce the Father to the world.

"And it is thanks to the same source that, finally, the curse of solitude is destroyed. Because every face-to-face encounter is now a participation in the divine face-to-face encounter and, henceforth, all individual beings – men, women, animals, vegetables, minerals – far from being excluded from universal life, far from being locked in an obscure dungeon from which, impelled by nostalgia, they would uselessly try to escape, they all are intermixed, one with another and, as messengers of God, form the object of a sovereign re-creation that makes of them only one body, whose head reposes on the bosom of the Father."[86]

We consider that the overview of Item 1 is confirmed by these declarations of important conciliar theologians. We need only summarize the doctrinal content of the various affirmations.

*

---

[85] *Ibid.*, p. 62.

[86] H.U. von Balthasar, *Le Coeur du Monde* (Paris: Desclée de Brouwer, 1956), pp. 30-31.

D. Synthesis of the Progressivist Doctrine on Creation

§ 63 From what has been presented thus far, especially the affirmations of Fr. Joseph Ratzinger (Letter B), we can draw these points:

§ 64 • Creation would not be a past reality, but a present one. It would coincide with the evolution of the cosmos. Each new reality that appears in the universe and history would be a divine creation and, since it is a product of man's work, the latter would be a co-creator.

§ 65 • However, since everything is changing at every moment, it necessarily follows that the being is not stable, but an evolving reality. It also follows that God no longer provides for and sustains the being of His creatures, but is constantly creating an evolving being.

§ 66 • Now, since by evolution an ascension is taking place in the evolving being, it follows that evolution is the action of God in the universe, That is, evolution is divine *per se*.

§ 67 • The model of the universe in its beginning, the Alpha Point, is the *Logos*. It is this model that comes into act in each new mutation of evolution.

§ 68 • The end of the universe is also the Word, the Spirit of Christ or the *Pleroma*, the Omega Point. It is toward this point that the divine evolution of the universe tends.

§ 69 • Because evolution's beginning and end are both in God, its meaning or direction is good. That is, besides being essentially divine, it inexorably raises everything toward God.

§ 70 • By changing the very ontology of the being, evolution presents itself as a pan-ontological reality, that is, it is immanentist. Since, however, it pretends to be divine *per se*, in its beginning and end, the pan-ontological character of evolution is synonymous with its pantheistic character. In other words, the being of God would have a substantial communication with the evolving beings of the universe.

§ 71 • What is affirmed *in genere* (generically) about universal evolution is also affirmed *in specie* (in particular) about human history. It would be divine itself. There would be no difference between sacred and profane history; both would be the "history of salvation."

3. Victory of the Progressivist Current Consecrated at Vatican II

§ 72 John XXIII's pontificate, realized under the sign of *aggiornamento* and principally Vatican Council II, which took place under the sign of adaptation to the modern world, represented the consecration of the progressivist current.

In effect, in countless passages of the Council documents – although they often pay tribute to ambiguity [87] – we find a direct or indirect endorsement of Modern Philosophy, modern science, Historicism and Evolutionism.

Whoever has eyes to see – and the progressivists were the first to discern the texts that were more convenient for them – notes without difficulty the direct or indirect support of Vatican II for the progressivist conception of Creation.

The excerpts below include some that explicitly reveal the support of Vatican II for the various modern sciences, Historicism and evolution. In these cases we will have a cumulative demonstration.

A. Support for Modern Sciences

§ 73 The position of the Holy Church regarding the progress of science remained immutable throughout the centuries. She is not concerned about sciences except when, for some reason, they intervene in the fields of Faith and Morals. In these cases, she always takes a position in order to preserve the perennial deposit of her doctrine.

It was from this perspective that in the 17th century she very wisely condemned the philosophical and theological pretensions of Galileo Galilei,[88] and that today she condemns the

---

[87] Cf. Vol. I, *In the Murky Waters of Vatican II,* Chap. III *passim*.

[88] **a. *Status quaestionis*** – It became common in countless revolutionary milieus to criticize the Holy Inquisition and, by extension, the Catholic Church for the condemnation of Galileo. The progressivists endorse such critiques and repeat the catchphrase – the obscurant Church condemned science. They are quick to add that such condemnation would prove that the Magisterium of the Church is not infallible (cf. Charles Journet, *L'Église du Verbe Incarné*, Desclée de Brouwer, 1955, vol. 1, pp. 458-462).

Then, the progressivists assume another consequence: Galileo was condemned for applying scientific data to the exegesis of Holy Scripture. Since this condemnation was supposedly unjust, it would be valid to use scientific data either to alter the interpretation of Scripture, or even to demonstrate that it is wrong.

These arguments are sophistic, taking advantage of the confused boundaries between science, philosophy and theology that existed at the beginning of the 17th century. Such confusion can be verified not only in the texts of Galileo, but also in the sentence of his condemnation (1633). Galileo extrapolated scientific data and came to conclusions in the fields of philosophy and theology, supposing both to be in the realm of science. The judges of the Inquisition fell into a parallel confusion when they condemned the scientific theories of the scholar, thinking that they were condemning the unacceptable philosophical and theological extrapolations of Galileo.

That is, both sides based their conclusions on a fundamental imprecision of terms as we understand them today. That imprecision is what fed the myth that the Church condemned science. All the ensuing attacks against the Inquisition and the Catholic Church have been made without taking this basic confusion into consideration.

Such a confusion was pointed out by Fr. Mario Vigano, S.J., a scholar in History, who supports Enrico Berti, another Italian historian, when he deals with the relationship between science and religion. Vigano wrote: "Berti's point is that the problem of the relation between science and faith cannot be resolved by analyzing exclusively the two terms in question. The problem must be considered from a perspective that is neither that of faith nor of science, but rather that of philosophy. ... For Galileo and the theologians of his time, this problem did not exist because there was no distinction between science and philosophy" (Mario Vigano, "Galileo ieri e oggi," *La Civiltà Cattolica*, September 1984, p. 388).

It is indispensable, therefore, to know precisely what each party intended in that discussion. Let us analyze the historical data in order to set straight the confused situation.

b. The Church was not against science in the 17th century – There is no direct evidence that the Inquisition had the intention to attack science as such when it made the condemnation of Galileo. Several facts can be listed to support this position:

- The Inquisition had various advisers, several of them from the Roman College, *aka* the Academy of Lincei, one of the first Italian academies of science with many Jesuit scholars, which had a division on Mathematics specializing in scientific matters. This College had maintained cordial relations with Galileo for a considerable time, and warmly welcomed him during his visit to Rome in 1611.

- Important scientists such as Frs. Clavio, Scheiner and Grassi were members of the famed College.
- St. Robert Bellarmine acknowledged the seriousness of the Roman College by consulting its scholars several times on the scientific value of Galileo's theories.
- In response to one of St. Bellarmine's questions, Fr. Clavio affirmed that the proofs of Galileo "were more probabilities than established facts" (*ibid.*, p. 392).
- One of the arguments that failed to convince the scholars was his statement that the tides were moved by the moon, a theory based on considerations that were "merely qualitative and not quantitative," making it an "inadequate" argument (*ibid.*, p. 383).

The initial position of the Roman College favorable to Galileo, the seriousness of its scholars, the confidence St. Robert Bellarmine had in its opinion, and its specialized department of science do not present a picture of an institution opposed to the advancement of science, as presented by the revolutionary and progressivist myth.

Moreover, Pope Urban VIII was linked to Galileo by a personal friendship. Soon after he was raised to the Pontifical Throne, he highly praised Galileo's book *Il Saggiatore* and gave it an *imprimatur* (Ernest Lavisse & Alfred Rambaud, *Histoire Générale du 4eme Siécle à nos Jours,* Paris: Armand Collin, 1895, vol. 5, p. 485). In that work Galileo sustained a polemic with Fr. Grassi from the Roman College on the three comets that had appeared in 1417 (*ibid.*). Once again, these facts reinforce the idea that the Church was an impartial party in the scientific debate of that time.

c. Galileo's obsession with changing philosophy – In 1616 the Holy Inquisition issued its first condemnation of Galileo's hypothesis on heliocentrism, which added new data to Copernicus' theory (cf. *ibid.* p. 484). The advisors of the Inquisition did not base their judgment, however, on the scientific data Galileo presented; much less did they condemn Copernicus. They declared that the propositions presented were "foolish and absurd **regarding philosophy**" (M. Vigano, "Galileo Ieri e Oggi," p. 388).

In fact, Galileo went beyond the field of science, claiming that his discoveries meant "the funeral or, better said, the Last Judgment for pseudo-philosophy" (Agostino Favaro, *Opere di Galileo*, vol. 11, p. 296, *apud ibid.,* p. 387). That is, he was not just stating a hypothesis and offering scientific arguments; he imagined himself abolishing the Aristotelian-Thomistic philosophy in force at the time.

In a letter to the Grand Duchess Christina of Lorraine, Galileo obstinately insisted that he wanted to speak not as a mathematician, but rather in an absolute sense, as a philosopher. Otherwise, he asserted, science would be missing its principal aim (cf. "Lettera a Madama

Cristina di Lorena," *apud* A. Favaro, *Opere di Galileo*, vol. 5, p. 229-30, *apud* M.Vigano, "Galileo Ieri e Oggi," p. 388). He acknowledged, therefore, that what he was proposing went beyond the scientific realm and impinged directly upon that of philosophy.

Pope Urban VIII only broke his good relations with Galileo when he tried to ridicule the Aristotelian-Thomistic philosophy in dealing with the systems of Ptolemy and Copernicus. Only then, in 1633, did the Pope deliver him to be judged by the Holy Inquisition for the second time (E. Lavisse & A. Rambaud, *Histoire Générale*, vol. 5, p. 486).

He was judged and politely obliged to abjure his errors. Galileo himself acknowledged that he was treated indulgently by the Inquisition throughout the affair. The condemnation prescribed prison, but this sentence was not put into practice. He passed the year 1633 with the Archbishop of Sienna. Afterward, he was allowed to live in his own beautiful villa at Arcetri near Florence, where he soon recovered full liberty. He was never prevented from pursuing his studies and investigations in science (*ibid.*).

If Galileo had not left the field of science, therefore, and entered the realm of philosophy, most probably he would have continued to enjoy the favor of Pope Urban VIII and avoided problems in advancing his scientific discoveries. Fr. Mario Vigano confirms this: "If he would have realized that the object of science is restricted to mathematics and the laws of nature, he would have had no difficulty in following the counsels of Bellarmine and the Academy of Lincei, as well as the injunctions made by Urban VIII, in his writing of the *Dialogo*. If he would have taken this position, he would have avoided so many troubles" (M. Vigano, "Galileo Ieri e Oggi," p. 387).

The condemnation of the Holy Inquisition, therefore, should not be seen as a prohibition of the Church against science, but rather, against philosophy. If the condemnatory decree did not mention philosophy explicitly, this was because at that time the distinction between the two subject matters was not fully established. The intention of the condemnation, however, was quite clear.

d. Theological pretensions of Galileo – But Galileo did not limit himself to attacking Aristotelian-Thomistic philosophy. Leaving the terrain of science, he went further and entered the realm of theology as well. To harmonize his scientific discoveries with the Copernican theory, he proposed to modify the traditional interpretation of various texts of Scripture that mentioned the movements of the sun and earth. Further, he proposed that the Scripture contained errors.

Galileo was warned to avoid such interpretations by his fellow scientist Cesi, who wrote him and reported his conversation with Cardinal Maffeo Barberini. Through Cesi, the Cardinal counseled caution, advising Galileo not to delve beyond questions of a purely mathematical nature because "it is up to the theologians to explain Scripture." After transmitting this wise counsel, Cesi himself warned Galileo that he was endangering matters of Faith by defending such novelties (A. Favaro, *Opere di Galileo*, vol. 12, p. 146, *apud* M. Vigano, "Galileo Ieri e Oggi," p. 381).

Cardinal Dini, an eminent theologian consulted by Galileo, told him: "Despite the fact that the theory of Copernicus is 'plausible,' it has not yet been proven. ... He merely presented his theory as a mathematical hypothesis. At any rate, it is prudent not to throw yourself into theological quarrels regarding the denial of the texts of Scripture" (A. Favaro, *Opere di Galileo*, vol. 2, p. 155, *apud* E. Vacandard, entry *Galilée*, *Dictionaire de Theologie Catholique*, vol. 6, col. 1061).

Galileo had a friend, the Carmelite Fr. Paolo Antonio Foscarini, who defended analogous positions. In 1615, St. Robert Bellarmine wrote a letter to this priest, and indirectly to Galileo, in which he offered his possible support for the scientific theories in the case they were adequately demonstrated. At the same time, however, he expressed his concern about the theological consequences included in the question.

He wrote: "I say to you that it seems to me that Your Reverence and Galileo would act prudently to content yourselves with speaking *ex suppositione* [hypothetically] and not in an absolute manner, as I have always believed Copernicus spoke. For if you say that you *suppose* the earth moves and the sun stands still, then, all the appearances are saved better than with eccentricities and reversals. This does not present any danger and is proper for mathematicians. But, to want to affirm that the sun *really* is fixed in the center of the universe and only revolves around itself ... is taking a very dangerous risk, not only of irritating all the philosophers and scholastic theologians, but also of injuring our holy Faith and accusing Holy Scripture of being false. ... But, I tell you that if there were a true demonstration that the sun was the center of the universe ... that the sun did not travel around the earth, but the earth around the sun, then, it would still be necessary to proceed with great prudence in explaining the passages of Scripture that appear contrary. And we would have to say that we did not understand them, rather than declare wrong what has been established" (*ibid.*, col. 1062).

One can see that Galileo, even though warned by a Pope, a Saint, two Cardinals and various eminent scholars, persisted in assuming the role of reforming exegesis. With this extremely arrogant attitude, he in effect provoked the condemnation of his theological pretensions.

Instead of a serious scholar and meticulous scientist, Galileo presented himself as a rebel theologian applying the method of the free-examination that Luther had fabricated some 50 years before. Actually, he well deserved the condemnation he received.

e. A just condemnation recognized by many – The Holy Inquisition, therefore, acted correctly in condemning Galileo. That action was consistent with its mission of guarding the integrity of the Catholic Faith. It was justly defending the Catholic Theology and Philosophy attacked by Galileo Galilei.

In a speech delivered in Parma, Italy on March 15, 1990, even then-Cardinal Joseph Ratzinger endorsed the opinion of philosopher Paul Feyerabend against Galileo. Ratzinger stated: "At the time of Galileo the Church remained much more faithful to reason than Galileo himself. The process against Galileo was reasonable and just" (Joseph Ratzinger, *Corriere della Sera*, March 30, 1990; *30 Dias*, January 1993, p. 34).

Italian author and journalist Vittorio Messori was also critical of Galileo: "Galileo was not condemned for the things he said, but for *the way* he said them. He made statements with a sectarian intolerance, like a 'missionary' of a new gospel. ... Since he did not have objective evidence for what he said, the things he said in his private letters to those men [of the Roman College] made him suspect of dogmatism supporting the new religion of science. Anyone who would not immediately accept the entire Copernican system was 'an imbecile with his head in the clouds,' someone 'almost unworthy of being called a man,' 'a stain upon mankind,' 'a child who never grew up,' and so on. In the end, the certainty of being infallible seemed to belong more to him than to the religious authority" (Vittorio Messori, *Avvenire*, October 19, 1989).

Prof. Nicola Cabibbo, ex-president of the Italian Institute of Nuclear Physics, summarized the case: "Galileo was not condemned for his scientific theses, but because he wanted to formulate theology" (Nicola Cabibbo, *30 Dias*, January 1993, p. 33).

Therefore, there is no basis to say that the Inquisition and the Church erred when they condemned Galileo. There is even less basis to say that such a condemnation demonstrates that the Church is not infallible. Also, the hasty conclusion that the Church should open her doors to a scientific interpretation of Scripture is not correct.

Science lacks the competence to interpret Sacred Scripture; if it were otherwise, we would end by denying all the revealed mysteries, which are far beyond the capacity of physical and experimental sciences to explain. To introduce scientific criticism into questions of Faith would be to reduce them to human stature, which is tantamount to denying them.

f. The conciliar Church endorsed the revolutionary myth regarding Galileo – Notwithstanding this conclusion, the Pastoral Constitution *Gaudium et spes* of Vatican Council II "deplored" the condemnation issued by the Inquisition against Galileo, consequently giving a powerful support to the revolutionary myth. The following paragraph is considered a reference to Galileo's condemnation: "Indeed whoever labors to penetrate the secrets of nature with a humble and steady mind is being led by the hand of God, the Conserver of all things, Who made them what they are. Consequently, we **cannot but deplore certain attitudes – which are sometimes found, also, among Christians**

– **deriving from a shortsighted view of the legitimate autonomy of science; they have occasioned conflict and controversy and have misled many into opposing faith and science**" (GS 36b).

In one of the few footnotes of the 16 conciliar documents – a footnote to the excerpt quoted above – *Gaudium et spes* recommends to the reader the then recently published work *Vita e Opera di Galileo Galilei* (Life and Works of Galileo) by Pio Paschini (Città del Vaticano: Pontificia Accademia delle Scienze, 1964, 2 vols). The Bishops used this to mean that the quoted text should be understood as referring to Galileo.

John Paul II took the same path of reinforcing the revolutionary myth about Galileo when he criticized the attitude of the Church regarding Galileo on several occasions.

First, he issued a vague criticism on November 10, 1979, in the speech to the Pontifical Academy of Sciences in which he established the commission to study Galileo's case. Addressing the international scientific community, he stated: "I desire that theologians, scientists and historians, animated by a spirit of open collaboration, examine the case of Galileo more deeply and, in loyal recognition of errors from any party, extinguish those suspicions that impede a fruitful concord between science and Faith, between the Church and the world" (John Paul II, *apud La Repubblica*, September 23, 1989; *Corriere della Sera,* March 30, 1990).

Second, on September 22, 1989, when visiting the city of Pisa, he issued an indirect acerbic disapproval of the past condemnation of the Church: "Galileo, an example for all, and also for the Church" (*ibid.*).

Third, during that same visit, he put aside the indirect allusions and directly and harshly condemned the behavior of the Church. He said: "**Galileo Galilei, whose scientific work was in its beginning improvidently attacked**, is now recognized by all as an essential step in the methodology of research and, in general, on the road toward knowledge of the world of nature" (John Paul II, *Insegnamenti di Giovanni Paolo II*, vol. 12-2, 1989, Libreria Editrice Vaticana, 1991, p. 585).

This statement, considered "definitive" by the Vatican spokesman (Navarro-Valls, press conference, *Corriere della Sera*, March 30, 1990), raised the enthusiastic applause of revolutionaries and progressivists, and the chagrin of those charged with the impartial study. In fact, Cardinal Paul Poupard, head of the commission of studies on the condemnation of Galileo, admitted: "I do not know if the commission still exists ... I believe that the task is over" (Paul Poupard, *Corriere della Sera,* March 30, 1990).

g. The swan song of the myth – Despite the haste of John Paul II, who "definitively" judged on the topic before the scientific study was completed, Cardinal Poupard presented the final results of the research on October 31, 1992, in a meeting presided over by the Pope.

Under such powerful papal pressure, it is not surprising that Poupard tried as much as possible to tailor the commission's conclusions to fit the previous partial judgment by JPII. The Cardinal stressed the "relative character" of the condemnation of Galileo and touched superficially on the essential points of the issue.

He affirmed: "The philosophical and theological qualifications, abusively attributed to the new theories regarding the centrality of the sun and the mobility of earth, were the consequence of a *period of transition* in the realm of the knowledge of astronomy and an *exegetical confusion* regarding cosmology" (Paul Poupard, *L'Osservatore Romano*, November 2-3, 1992, p. 4, n. 5).

He concluded that those who condemned Galileo had committed a "subjective error of judgment." He ended his statement with words that revealed he was working under pressure: "We need to recognize these errors as Your Holiness asked" (*ibid.*).

Actually, this judgment is incomplete: It is partially right and partially wrong. It has been generally admitted in scholarly milieus that both parties in the controversy had gone beyond the realm of science. For Poupard to say that the Catholic party had been imprecise ("abusive") seems a banality just to please JPII. We do not note in his words, however, an impartial concern to explain the intention of both sides in order to clarify who was guilty and who was innocent. Above all, Poupard's conclusion failed to address the core of the problem.

In a certain way the issue at the heart of the problem was dealt with by John Paul II. At the same plenary meeting of the Pontifical Academy of Science (October 31, 1992), he read a speech in response to Poupard in which he admitted he was no longer able to sustain the "definitive" judgment he had pronounced in Pisa in 1989. He was obliged to recognize that there was a general confusion regarding science and philosophy in the 17th century. He said: "**Like the majority of his adversaries, Galileo made no distinction between the scientific approach to natural phenomena and a reflection on nature of the philosophical order, which that approach generally calls for**" (John Paul II, *L'Osservatore Romano*, November 1, 1992, p. 6, n. 5).

Although his speech was entirely favorable to Galileo and against the past decision of the Church, John Paul II had to acknowledge this fundamental error of Galileo. Doing this, in our opinion, he shattered the very myth of which he had been the chief supporter. Actually, if one admits that Galileo as well as the members of the Inquisition were confusing the terms science and philosophy, any serious student of History can understand that Galileo went beyond his competence by pretending to decide what should or should not be accepted in philosophy – as well as in theology. To conclude that he deserved correction and condemnation is not a long step to take.

What obliged John Paul II to make such a reversal on his former pronouncements? In our opinion, it is probable that serious scholars on

interference of genetic engineering in various phases of the process of human gestation.

So long as the sciences remain within the realm proper to them, without incursions into the ambit of Faith and Morals, the Church respects their autonomy. She often demonstrates her sympathy by offering science the contribution of her own scholars and scientists, never lacking in the ecclesiastic ranks.

§ 74 At variance with this just, serene and balanced position is the attitude of the progressivists. They use modern sciences as a battle horse to justify their fever to make adaptations and uphold their cult to man,[89] always seeking new motives to promote secularization and destroy the previous consistent position of the Church.[90]

§ 75 No matter how fluid, provisory or immoral a new scientific discovery may be, it is adopted by Progressivism in order to apply it to the Church. Thus, the discovery of the method of radiocarbon 14 dating to determine the antiquity of objects was hastily applied to the Shroud of Turin in order to affirm that the

---

the Galileo study commission closed the question. As we have seen in this note, it is almost impossible to deny the historic reality that Galileo was not condemned for his science. So, John Paul II faced a dilemma: Either his partiality in the case would be publicly exposed or he had to acknowledge the essence of the problem.

After that, the myth is potentially dead. It is still being spread by progressivists and other revolutionaries, but it has lost its credence in the scholarly sphere. Today, the weapons to extirpate the Galileo myth are available to any Catholic who wants to clarify the issue in his various circles.

The speech of JPII was planned to be a solemn glorification of Galileo by a Pope. It maintained all the appearances of doing exactly that, but, in reality, it killed the myth. It was the swan song of the myth.

Nonetheless, the media trumpeted a triumph for Galileo by emphasizing the progressivist criticisms of JPII and Poupard about the Inquisition. In this respect, Italian philosopher Emmanuelle Severino shrewdly remarked upon the contradictory position of the Church: "By making a *mea culpa* about Galileo, the Church attributes to science an absolute value at exactly the moment when science is recognizing that, in fact, it does not have truths that are absolute and indisputable" (Emanuele Severino, *30 Dias*, January 1993, p. 33).

It is a final irony that reveals another failure of the progressivists.

[89] Cf. Vol. V, *Animus Delendi II*, Part I, Chap. I, *passim*.

[90] Cf. *ibid*, Part I, *passim*.

sacred relic was a falsification.[91] Einstein's theory of relativity, today considered incomplete in the scientific milieu,[92] was used by progressivists as an imperative of science that demanded the Church to abolish the absolute character of the dogmas. The discovery of the contraceptive pill, scandalously immoral and also criminal, became the determinant factor progressivists used to modify the Church's moral teaching on the ends of marriage, downplaying procreation and raising up love as its first end.

§ 76 If they do so regarding recent theories and discoveries, they do not disregard others, certainly much less new, such as Darwin's Evolutionism, Marx' Communism and Freud's Psychoanalysis. Although these theories are more than a century old, they are considered modern; although they lack any basis in reality, they are considered scientific. In this sense, Marx, Freud and Nietzsche are called the "masters of suspicion,"[93] because they supposedly put to rest the "illusions and superstitions" that had nourished mankind until then. To wit the three suspicions are:

- The non-existence of God: Nietzsche declared Him dead;
- The non-existence of Morals: Freud tried to explain human behavior in the face of good and evil as a reflection of eroticism;
- The non-existence of metaphysical-moral values and su-

---

[91] A simple Internet search on the "flaws in radiocarbon 14 measurements" provides a plethora of results from serious sources showing that the method, although still useful, does not enjoy the infallibility it first pretended when it was discovered by Willard Libby in the 1940s. Examples of its mistakes are abundant: e.g. the shells of some freshwater clams caught in our days that were dated as having 1,600 years of age, or the sequoias of California, first dated to be many thousands of years old and now are known to be only several centuries old. Analogously, the measurements of the age of the Shroud of Turin are now admitted not to be conclusive as it was previously announced.

[92] Although the theory of relativity is not obsolete, it is considered incomplete. Einstein offered answers to complete Newton's theory of gravity. In turn, the quantum theory has rectified some points of the theory of relativity.

[93] It was the Protestant philosopher Paul Ricoeur who dubbed this triumvirate of the late 19th century and early 20th century thinkers as "the masters of suspicion." But this expression was soon accepted and assumed by progressivists, especially Congar, Chenu, de Lubac and their followers.

pernatural values: Marx taught that in History everything follows a predetermined course as a result of economic laws and material forces.

§ 77 Some add to these three a fourth "master of suspicion," Darwin, who, by supposing that one species is born from another through the process of Evolution, would have abolished the "myth" that God created each existent species. More importantly, He would not have created man directly in a single act, infusing in him a soul. Thus, Darwin, Marx, Nietzsche and Freud, expressions of the natural, sociological, philosophical and psychiatric sciences, are considered by the progressivists as the latest authorities of modernity to which the Church should adapt herself.

It is based on this progressivist background that the conciliar texts supporting the modern sciences must be read.

§ 78 Below, is the lamentation of *Gaudium et spes* on the condemnation of Galileo as it over-exalts scientific labor:[94]

"Indeed, whoever labors to penetrate the secrets of nature with a humble and steady mind is being led by the hand of God, the conserver of all things, who made them what they are. Consequently, **we cannot but deplore certain attitudes – which are sometimes found also among Christians – deriving from a shortsighted view of the legitimate autonomy of science; they have occasioned conflict and controversy and have misled many into opposing faith and science**" (GS n. 36b).

---

[94] We repeat here for the convenience of the Reader this text of *Gaudium et spes* already quoted in Note 88f.

That this n. 36 of the Pastoral Constitution is an indirect support of Galileo is explained by the footnote, which references and, thereby, recommends the book of Msgr. Pio Paschini titled *The Life and Work of Galileo Galilei* (*Vita e Opere di Galileo Galilei).*

In 1941 a decision was made by the Pontifical Academy of Sciences to commission a biography of Galileo in time for the 300th anniversary of his death in 1942. The work was entrusted to Msgr. Pio Paschini, professor of Church History in Rome at the Pontifical Lateran University. He duly completed this task (slightly late) within three years. The book was rejected, however – some said it was caused by the harshness of opinion Paschini demonstrated towards the Jesuits for their part in the affair – and only released some 20 years later, having been corrected for the "inappropriate" way it portrayed the Church (for more details, see Michele Maccarrone, *Mons. Paschini e la Roma Ecclesiastica*, in *Atti del Convegno di Studio su Pio Paschini nel Centenario della Nascita 1878-1978*, Udine: Tip. Vaticana, 1981, pp. 49-93). *Gaudium et spes* endorsed Paschini's book promoting Galileo.

Other excerpts of *Gaudium et spes* praising the sciences include:

- "Far from considering the conquests of man's talent and energy as opposed to God's power, as if man sets himself up as a rival to the Creator, **Christians ought to be convinced that the achievements of the human race are a sign of God's greatness and the fulfillment of His mysterious design**" (GS 34c).

- "**The circumstances of the life of modern man have been so profoundly changed** on the social and cultural levels that **we can speak of a new age of human history**. For this reason, **new roads are open for the development and further extension of culture. These roads have been prepared by the enormous growth of natural and human sciences – including social sciences – by technological progress and advances in developing and better organizing means of communication among men**. As a result, modern culture is marked by particular characteristics: **The so-called exact sciences greatly develop critical judgment. The more recent psychological studies more profoundly explain human behavior. Historical studies make it much easier to see things in their mutability and evolution**" (GS 54).

- "**Experts in other sciences**, notably biology, medicine, social science and psychology, **can greatly contribute to the welfare of marriage** and the family, along with the peace of mind of the people, **if by comparing their studies they labor to explain** more thoroughly **the various conditions favoring the honest regulation of births**" (GS 52d).

- "The faithful ought to live, therefore, in very close union with the other men of their time and strive to discern perfectly their ways of thinking and judging, as expressed in their culture. **Let the faithful integrate the knowledge of new sciences and doctrines and the understanding of the most recent discoveries with Christian customs and doctrine, so that their practice of religion and moral behavior may walk abreast among men in the same march of the knowledge of the sciences and of the relentless progress of technology**. In this way, they will succeed in evaluating and interpreting everything with an authentically Christian sense of values" (GS 62f).

*

B. Endorsement of Historicism

§ 79 We understand Historicism[95] as the movement established in certain ecclesiastic milieus from the 19th century onward, according to which it would be correct to dispute the narratives of Sacred Scriptures in matters unrelated to Faith and Morals. The partisans of this current affirm that certain conditioning factors would have influenced the sacred authors. These criteria would modify the traditional interpretation of the Divine Letters.

Thus, the historic knowledge of the sacred authors, the literary genres they employed, and the witnesses upon whom they based their narratives would have been imprecise and subjective. The consequence is that the advances of the historical, archeological and natural sciences, as well as the critiques based on them, can shed new light on biblical exegesis and not only modify the interpretation of the Scriptures, but give new meaning to many of their difficult passages.

§ 80 Although the principal target of Historicism is to attack the traditional interpretation of the Old Testament, as a secondary goal it also raises objections against the preaching of the Gospel. Indeed, under the pretext of inculturation and the pastoral care of those to whom they preach, the progressivists adapt the homiletic so radically to present day thinking and customs that evangelization itself – the spread of the truths of the Gospel – becomes falsified.[96]

Thus, the historicist obsession with adaptation changes the meaning of the Divine Letters both in their origin – the sacred texts – and in their end – evangelization.

§ 81 As a consequence, the very truths of Faith and Morals are conditioned: they also should be "re-read" under the light of History and the modern sciences. In brief, the critical spirit, free examination and relativism are installed in the study of Sacred Scriptures.

§ 82 Pius XII thus defines Historicism:

"The term 'Historicism' indicates a philosophical system that, in the whole spiritual reality, the knowledge of truth, morals

---

[95] In Chap. IV §§ 82-125 of this Volume we will analyze progressivist Historicism in more detail.

[96] A typical example of this false inculturation is the assimilation of fetishes and voodoo rituals into the liturgy, as we have seen in Brazil, cf. Vol. VII, *Destructio Dei*, Chap. I, Note 4.

and the law, recognizes nothing except mutation and evolution. Consequently, it rejects everything that is permanent, eternally valid and absolute. Such a system is certainly irreconcilable with the Catholic conception of the world."[97]

Firm opposition to this current can be found in the writings of various Popes.[98]

---

[97] Pius XII, Speech to the 10th International Congress of Historical Sciences, September 7, 1955, in *Discorsi e Radionessaggi di Sua Santità Pio XII*, Tipografia Poliglotta Vaticana, 1955-1956, vol. 17, p. 212.

[98] For instance:

a. Pius IX, in union with Vatican Council I, teach in regard to the authenticity of the Sacred Books: "These books of the Old and New Testament, in their entirety and in their parts ... must be accepted as sacred and canonical. The Holy Church holds them as such not because they were written only by human labor and, then, approved by the authority or because they contain a revelation exempt of error, but because they were written under the inspiration of the Holy Spirit and have God as Author, and were as such confided to the same Church" *(De Revelatione*, session III, chap, II, n. 1787).

b. Leo XIII in the Encyclical *Providentissimus Deus* of November 18, 1893, continuing the doctrine of the Councils Vatican I and Trent, affirms: "It was the doctrine of St. Irenaeus and the other Fathers that was adopted by Vatican Council [I] which – in renewing the decree of the Council of Trent about the interpretation of the written divine word – declared that in things of Faith and Morals belonging to the building up of Christian doctrine, one must consider the exact meaning of Holy Scripture that has been held and is held by our Holy Mother Church, to whom belongs the power to judge the true meaning and interpretation of the Sacred Books. Therefore, it is not licit for anyone to interpret the Scripture contrary to such interpretation or against the unanimous consensus of the Fathers (cf. *De Revelatione*, session III, chap. II; cf. Council of Trent, session IV, Decree on the editing and use of the Sacred Books) (*Providentissimus Deus* n. 46).

c. Further on, Leo XIII continues: "Wherefore, the Catholic commentator must consider it a most important and sacred duty to explain the established meaning of the Scriptural passages that have received an authentic interpretation either from the sacred writers themselves, guided by the inspiration of the Holy Spirit, as in many texts of the New Testament, or from the Church assisted by the same Holy Spirit, whether by means of her solemn judgment or by her ordinary and universal authority (Council Vatican I, session III, chap. III, *De Fide*). He must be convinced that this interpretation is the only one that can be approved according to sound hermeneutic laws" (*ibid*, n. 14?).

d. In accordance with this teaching, Benedict XV in the Encyclical

§ 83

Notwithstanding this papal opposition, Historicism continued to exist for the reasons pointed out in Item 1, and found powerful stimulus in excerpts of Vatican II's documents.

Among others, the following texts are noteworthy:

- "In determining the intention of the sacred writers, attention must be paid, *inter alia*, to 'literary forms.' For **truth is set forth and expressed differently in the various types of historical writings, prophetic and poetic texts, and other forms of literary expression. Hence, the exegete must look for what meaning the sacred writer, in a determined situation and given the circumstances of his time and culture, intended to express and actually did express by using a contemporary literary form. To correctly understand what the sacred author wanted to affirm in his work, due attention must be paid to both the customary and characteristic styles of perception, speech and narrative that prevailed at the time of the sacred writer, and to the conventions that people of his time followed in their everyday dealings with one another**" (*Dei Verbum* 12b).
- "**These books [of the Old Testament], even though they contain some things that are imperfect and provisional,** nevertheless show us true divine pedagogy" (*Dei Verbum* 15).

Spiritus Paraclitus of September 15, 1920, states: "St. Jerome's teaching on this point serves to confirm and illustrate what our predecessor of happy memory, Leo XIII, solemnly declared to be the ancient and traditional belief of the Church on the absolute immunity of Scripture from error: 'So impossible is it that divine inspiration can be exposed to the danger of error that, on the contrary, it not only of its very nature precludes the prescience of the least error, but as necessarily excludes it and forbids it, since God, the Supreme Truth, necessarily cannot be the Author of any error, even the least.'

"After quoting the definitions of the Councils of Florence and Trent, confirmed by those of Vatican I, Leo XIII adds: 'Consequently it is not possible to suggest that because the Holy Spirit used men as His instruments for writing, and that, therefore, while no error is attributable to the primary Author, it may well be due to the inspired writers themselves. For, by supernatural power, the Holy Spirit so stirred them and moved them to write, and assisted them as they wrote, that their minds could rightly conceive only those things which He himself bade them to write; only such things could they faithfully commit to writing and aptly express with unerring truth. Otherwise, God would not be the Author of the entirety of Sacred Scripture'" (n. 17; cf. nn. 16-28).

e. In the same sense, see. Pius XII, *Divino Afflante Spiritu*, nn.1, 2-4; *Humani generis*, nn. 37-38.

• "A change in mentality and in human structures frequently calls accepted values into question, especially among the youth … The institutions, laws and modes of thinking and acting as handed down from previous generations do not always seem to be well adapted to the contemporary state of affairs. … Finally, **these new conditions influence religion itself.** On the one hand, **a more critical ability purifies it of a magical conception of the world and of the superstitions still prevailing and demands an increasingly personal and explicit adhesion to the faith**" (*Gaudium et spes* 7).

• "Just as it is in the world's interest to acknowledge the Church as a social reality of history and its leaven, so also the **Church** herself **does not ignore how much she has received from** history and **the evolution of mankind**."

"**She profits** from the experience of past ages, **from the progress of the sciences and from the treasures hidden in the various forms of human culture, by which the nature of man himself is more fully manifested and new avenues to truth are opened**. For, from the beginning of her history, she has learned to express the message of Christ through the concepts and languages of the different peoples, and has tried to clarify it with the wisdom of the philosophers.

"**Her purpose has been to adapt the Gospel, insofar as possible, to the understanding of all men and the requirement of the learned. Indeed, this kind of accommodation in preaching of the revealed word must remain the law of all evangelization. In this way the ability to express the message of Christ in its own way and promote a living exchange between the Church and the diverse cultures of peoples must be encouraged in every country**.

"To promote such exchange, especially in our times when things change so rapidly and patterns of thought differ, **the Church requires the special help of those, believers and non-believers alike, who live in the world, are versed in its different systems and disciplines and grasp their innermost mentality.** With the help of the Holy Spirit, **it is the task of the whole People of God, especially pastors and theologians, to hear, distinguish and interpret the many voices of our times, and to judge them** in the light of the divine Word, **so that the revealed Word may always be** more deeply penetrated, better understood and **more suitably presented**" (*Gaudium et spes* 44).

C. Adaptation to Modern Philosophy

§ 84 The "philosophical problem," that is, the adaptation of Catholic thinking to Modern Philosophy, played an important role in changing the traditional conception of Creation – as we have seen in the overview presented in Item 1. As Vatican II endorsed Modern Philosophy, it indirectly rubber-stamped the victory of the progressivist conception of Creation. The following texts of *Gaudium et spes* express this quite well:

- "**When man works in the various disciplines of philosophy, history,** mathematics **and natural science** and when he cultivates the arts, **he can contribute greatly to raise the human family to a higher understanding of truth, goodness and beauty and to an evaluation of the universe** … As a consequence, the human spirit, freed from bondage to material things, can be more easily drawn to the worship and contemplation of the Creator …

"There is no doubt that today's progress in science and technology can lead to a certain phenomenalism or agnosticism. This happens when the scientific methods of investigation used … are unjustifiably considered the supreme norm for seeking the whole truth. … **These unfortunate results, however, are not necessarily due to modern culture, nor should they tempt us to overlook its positive values** (GS 57).

- "Although the Church has contributed much to the development of culture, experience shows that, for circumstantial reasons, it has sometimes been difficult to harmonize culture with Christian thought.

"These difficulties do not necessarily harm the life of faith, but rather can stimulate the mind to a deeper and more accurate understanding of the faith. In fact, **recent studies and findings of science, history and philosophy raise new questions that have an important bearing on life, and demand new theological investigations.** Furthermore, **theologians are now being invited**, within the methods and requirements proper to theology, **to seek continually for more suitable ways** – while safeguarding the same meaning and the same understanding– **to present doctrine to the men of their time;** for the deposit of Faith and the truths are one thing, and the manner of expressing them is quite another. **In pastoral care, sufficient use must be made not only of the theological principles, but also of the findings of the secular sciences, especially of psychology and sociology**" (GS 62).

D. Right of Citizenship Granted to Evolutionism

§ 85 As far as we could see in our research, the Council does not support Evolutionism as such. Perhaps this is due to the great controversy raised by the ensemble of the work of Teilhard de Chardin and the reaction it caused immediately before Vatican II was convened.

In the sessions of the Council, according to the report of Fr. Chenu, not even the progressivists considered it prudent to name the controversial French Jesuit. When they wanted to refer to him or to Evolutionism, they used a code: They cited chapter 8 of the Epistle to the Romans.[99] So, if even the progressivists took these precautions, it is understandable that Evolutionism does not appear in the official documents of Vatican II.

Nevertheless, the word evolution appears countless times in those documents.

§ 86 It is known that in documents of the Magisterium, principally in documents of Councils, each word is weighed, measured and counted before being used. Further, after Evolutionism entered the picture, ecclesiastical documents habitually use the word evolution only in reference to this theory. Now then, by frequently employing the word evolution when referring to different topics, Vatican II seems to implicitly disregard the previous precautions taken by the Magisterium on this subject. Vatican II, therefore, appears to give the right of citizenship to the word evolution and to Evolutionism as a theory.

§ 87 This is confirmed by the fact that in the conciliar documents sometimes the word evolution is used in a meaning quite close to the evolutionary concept.[100] Furthermore, there are other

---

99 Fr. Chenu gave this response to a question about Teilhard's influence at the Council:

Question: [In the Council] was the role of Teilhard in this matter of evolution perceptible?

Answer: Certainly. Teilhard was not quoted, obviously, even when his thoughts were implied in the interventions of his adversaries as well as of his friends. Instead, they would refer to the passages of St. Paul on the recapitulation of all Creation, including matter, by Christ and in Christ. Thus, chapter 8 of the Epistle to the Romans was quoted quite often" (*Jacques Duquesne Interroge le Père Chenu*, p. 186).

100 As we will see later in Chap. III §§ 21-30, the evolutionary theory assumed by the Council is not directly that of Darwin. It is the "Christified" version of it found in the thinking of Fr. Pierre Teilhard the Chardin.

passages in which the evolutionary concept is present without the use of the word evolution. The ensemble of these various uses of evolution – the word used without the concept, the word used together with the concept, and the concept used without the word – seems to convey the intent of freeing the evolutionary theory of any restraint.

We will present some examples of these different uses of evolution in the Constitution *Gaudium et spes*.[101]

a. The word evolution used without the concept

• "The understanding of the relationship between socialization and the autonomy and development of the person will vary according to the different regions and the evolution of peoples [*populorum evolutionem*]" (GS 75c).

• "While it [the Sacred Synod] presents teaching already accepted in the Church, the program will have to be pursued further and amplified since it often deals with matters which are in a state of continual evolution [*incessanti evolutioni*]" (GS 91b).

• "In our times, profound transformations are apparent also in the structures and institutions of peoples. They are the result of their cultural, economic and social evolution [*evolutionem*]" (GS 73a).

b. The word evolution used in close meaning to the Teilhardian concept

• "**The Church**, moreover, **recognizes everything good that is found in today's social dynamism, especially an evolution toward unity** [*praesertim evolutionem versus unitatem*], **the march of healthy socialization and of civil and economic cooperation** (GS 42c).

• "Just as it is in the world's interest to acknowledge the Church as a social reality of history and its leaven, so also **the Church** herself **does not ignore how much she has received from history and the evolution of mankind** [*quantum ex humani generis historia et evolutione acceperit*]" (GS 44a).

---

[101] We warn our Reader that the English translation of the conciliar documents often uses other words to translate evolution. Thus, we will take as point of reference for our study the Latin text, which is the official and definitive version of those documents, and will correct the English translation in this lack of objectivity. The original Latin words will be placed between brackets.

• "Since **the Church** has a visible social structure as a sign of her unity in Christ, she **can be and in fact is being enriched by the evolution of human social life** [*evolutione vitae socialis humanae*]" (GS 44c).

• "**The Spirit of God**, Who with admirable providence directs the unfolding of time and renews the face of the earth, **is present in this evolution** [102][*huic evolutioni adest*]. The ferment of the Gospel too has aroused and continues to arouse in the hearts of men an unquenchable thirst for human dignity" (GS 26d).

• "**In the face of the modern evolution** [*hodierna mundi evolutione*], **more and more persons are asking** the most basic **questions** or are recognizing them with keener insight: **What is man? What is the meaning of suffering, evil, death**, which continue to exist despite so much progress?" (GS 10a).

• "**Historical studies make it much easier to see things in their mutable and evolutionary aspects** [*sub specie suae mutabilitatis atque evolutionis*]" (GS 54).

• "**Among the salient features of the modern world is the growing development of interpersonal relationships. To their evolution** [*ad quam evoluendam]* **modern technical advances highly contribute**. Nevertheless genuine fraternal dialogue is advanced not so much by this technological progress as by the deeper level of communion between persons, which demands a mutual respect for the full spiritual dignity of men and persons. **Christian revelation contributes greatly to foster this *communio* between persons**" (GS 23).

c. The evolutionary concept without the use of the word evolution

• "Therefore, **this Sacred Council, proclaiming the high vocation of man and affirming that some divine seed exists in him, offers to mankind the sincere collaboration of the Church for the establishment of a fraternity of all men that corresponds to this vocation**" (GS 3b).

• "**Today mankind is in a new phase of its history, in which profound and rapid changes are spreading gradually around the whole world**. They are the products of man's intelligence and creative activity, but **these changes recoil upon man himself, upon his judgments and desires, both individual and collective, upon his way of thinking and acting with respect**

---

[102] Evolution of the social order toward the "good of persons."

to things and to people. Hence we can already speak of a true social and cultural transformation which has repercussions on the religious life itself" (GS 4b).

• "[**The Word of God Incarnate**] **teaches us that the fundamental law of human perfection, and consequently of the world's transformation, is the new commandment of love**. … The gifts of the Spirit are manifold: while He calls some to give a clear witness to the desire for a heavenly home and to maintain a vivid awareness of it before the human family, He calls others to dedicate themselves to the earthly service of men and in this way to prepare the way for the Kingdom of Heaven. Yet, **the Spirit frees all men** so that, by renouncing love of self and bringing all earthly resources into the service of human life, **they can devote themselves to that future day when mankind itself will become an offering agreeable to God**" (GS 38).

• "**We know neither the moment of the consummation of the earth and of man, nor the way the universe will be transformed**. The form of this world, distorted by sin, is passing away, but **we are taught that God is preparing a new dwelling place and a new earth** where righteousness dwells … Then, with death conquered, the sons of God will be raised up in Christ, and what was sown in weakness and corruption will be invested with incorruptibility. Charity and its works will remain, and all of Creation, which God made for man, will be set free from the bondage of vanity.

"We have been warned that it profits a man nothing if he gain the whole world and loses himself. **Far from diminishing our concerns, the expectation of a new earth should stimulate us to perfect this earth, for it is here that the body of a new human family grows, a body which even now gives a foreshadowing of the new age**. Hence, while we must be careful to distinguish **earthly progress** clearly from the growth of the Kingdom of God, such progress **is of vital concern to the Kingdom of God,** insofar as it can contribute to the better ordering of human society.

"**After we have spread on earth** all the good fruits of our nature and our work – the values of **human dignity, fraternal communion and freedom** – in the Spirit of the Lord and according to His command, **we will find them once again**, but cleansed of any stain, illuminated and transfigured, **when Christ hands over to the Father 'a kingdom eternal and universal**'" (GS 39).

§ 88 As far as we can see, the ensemble of documents presented in this Item 3 expresses well how Vatican II, by means of mostly ambiguous texts, favored the progressivist conception of Creation. Its support of modern sciences and, in particular, Evolutionism, Historicism and Modern Philosophy accelerated the disappearance of Scholastic Philosophy, the traditional interpretation of Sacred Scriptures and the creationist doctrine on man and the world.

If we want to go to the nucleus of the progressivist doctrine on Creation, it is the evolutionary theory, and its central point is its pretended scientific character. The Church should adapt her doctrine to Evolutionism because, the progressivist claims, its theory is fully demonstrated by modern science.

Let us see if this affirmation resists analysis.

* * *

CHAPTER II

THE FALSE SCIENTIFIC CHARACTER OF EVOLUTIONISM

§ 1 The Catholic doctrine found in the perennial teaching of the Magisterium on the origin of the universe, life and man is that the world – including all life and man – was created by God.

§ 2 The material universe as it came from the hands of God in its due state of perfection is not eternal.[1] It is, therefore, subject to the decay that everything that is not in the state of glory experiences. This can be said also of the vegetable and animal species that were created by God to populate the earth. There was, therefore, a first law of deterioration installed in natural creation before the creation of man.[2]

§ 3 In what concerns man, the king of the universe, the Church teaches that he was created in a state of natural perfection, but he sinned. Sin introduced into the state of integral nature [*natura integra*] a germ of disaggregation and decay by which man became subject in his body to sickness, pain and death; in his soul his intelligence became subject to error, his will became inclined toward evil, and his sensibility became disordered. This is what constitutes the state of fallen nature [*natura lapsa*].[3]

---

[1] It is possible to understand the word eternal as applied to the world in two meanings: Regarding the past, it can be understood as **from the beginning indefinitely** or ***ab aeterno*;** in this meaning, the universe is not eternal (cf. DR, 391, 501-503, 2317), but created simultaneously to time (cf. DR 428, 1784, 2123). Regarding the future, it can be understood as **forever indefinitely** or **perpetual;** in this meaning the universe will end along with time and *ipso facto* will not be eternal.

Thus, the word eternal can only be applied to the universe in an analogical sense since the world is indissolubly linked to time. Properly speaking, what is eternal has no beginning and no end, that is, God. For those spiritual creatures who have a beginning but no end, *aevum* is proper; for those creatures that have a beginning and an end – material creatures – time is proper (cf. St. Thomas Aquinas, I *Sententiarum*, d. 19, q. 2, 1, 2, c).

[2] "Interminability, which excludes any imperfection, is not communicable to any creature, given that no creature can be perfect *per se*" (St. Thomas Aquinas, I *Sententiarum*, d. 8, q. 22).

[3] Cf. Vol. X, *Peccatum – Redemptio*, Chap. I. 2.3.

Since man is the synthesis of Creation, his sin had, as a consequence, repercussions throughout the whole universe.[4] Thus, the law of degradation that governed human nature after original sin extended to the creatures of the animal, vegetal and mineral natures.

§ 4 Therefore, the law of degradation that came from human sin was added to the law of deterioration proper to material creation.

§ 5 Exempt from the deleterious influence of human sin are only the angelic creatures who, before the creation of man, had their own trial. Exempt from sin, yes, but for precision's sake, let us add that they were not indifferent to it. After the sin of man, which was incited by the Devil, the bad angels continue to strive to take souls to Hell as well as to make life perish in man, animals and plants in an attempt to establish in the world – if permitted – a defective and chaotic kingdom.[5]

---

[4] St. Paul teaches this about the solidarity of the elements of the universe: "For the expectation of the creature waited for the revelation of the sons of God" (Rom 8:19). Cornelius a Lapide observes that – according to St. John Chrysostom, Teodoretus, Teophilatus, St. Ambrose, Soto, Adam, Pereira and Toledo – we should understand creature or created world as referring to the heavens and the elements and all things that were created which await their renewal in the resurrection of man (cf. *Commentaria super Epistolam Pauli*).

Commenting on the same verse, a Lapide adds the opinion of St. Augustine, St. Anselm, St. Gregory, Andreas Maius, Catarinus and Cajetano, which affirms that we must understand creature as the microcosm of man, which in some way contains parts of all creatures (cf. *ibid.*). This also reveals the unity of all the elements of the universe.

Incidentally, this principle appears in the next verse of St. Paul: "For the creature was made subject to vanity, not by its own choice, but by the will of the one who made it subject, in hope that the creature itself also shall be liberated from its bondage to corruption and brought into the freedom and glory of the children of God. For we know that the whole creation groans and travails in pain together right up to the present time" (Rom 8:20-22).

In the same sense, see John Paul II, "Messagio per la Celebrazione della Giornata Mondiale della Pace." January 1, 1990, n. 5. (*L'Osservatore Romano*, January, 2-3, 1990. p. 5).

[5] St. Thomas teaches:"It is generally found both in human affairs and in natural things that every particular power is governed and ruled by the universal power; as, for example, the bailiff's power is governed by the power of the king. Among the angels also, as explained above (55, 3; 108, 1), the superior angels who preside over the inferior possess a more universal knowledge. Now, it is manifest that the power of any individual body is more particular than the power of

§ 6 To what degree does God permit devils to subvert the created order? As we register the problem, our intelligences register also our limitations: Here we enter into the mysteries of the angelic life and the Divine Wisdom that rules it.

Nonetheless, we note the presence of a constant law acting throughout History that allows us to glimpse something of the Divine Economy regarding the action of the angels and the devils. Insofar as the ensemble of men respond to the teaching of the Holy Church and divine grace, we believe the influence of the good angels increases and nature, in itself and by the action of the angels, becomes more propitious to man. On the other hand, insofar as men are unfaithful to Church teaching, the action of the good angels decreases and the diabolical action increases, making the material universe hostile to man.

§ 7 In brief, three factors act in the universe in different ways to propitiate its decay:

- The law of deterioration proper to all created matter;
- The law of degradation originating from sin;
- The deleterious action of the devils.

This is Catholic doctrine on created matter.

§ 8 The evolutionary conception is opposed to this doctrine.

It alleges that the teaching of the Church on Creation is nothing but a childish myth unworthy of modern man's high degree of learning and maturity. The development of the positive and experimental sciences would have relegated the description of Genesis to the ambit of superstition. The light of reason, freed from obscurantist prejudices of the past, would prove that the future must imperatively tread the path of evolution.

§ 9 Since this is the terrain chosen by the adversaries to attack Catholic doctrine on Creation, let us descend into it and use the weapons preferred by them. Let us see what the critiques of reason and of experimental science say about the evolutionary theory and, then, verify where in fact we find myth and superstition.

*

---

any spiritual substance; for every corporeal form is a form individualized by matter, and determined to the 'here and now'; whereas immaterial forms are absolute and intelligible. Therefore, as the inferior angels who have the less universal forms are ruled by the superior, so are all corporeal things ruled by the angels. This is not only laid down by the holy Doctors, but also by all philosophers who admit the existence of incorporeal substances" (*Summa Theologiae*, I, q. 110, a. 1).

§ 10 Since the Author of this work is not an expert in positive and experimental sciences, how is it possible for him to enter such a specialized field without temerity and pretend to defend Catholic doctrine on this topic?

The answer is not difficult.

§ 11 For someone who has a general idea of the doctrine of Evolutionism and the movement that supports it, it is a simple matter to note that already in the 1930s Darwinism was suffering a credibility crisis in scientific circles. Neo-Darwinism, which came to succor Darwinism, provided only a weak and ephemeral support to Evolutionism and has likewise been discredited.

Taking advantage of the inconsistencies in Evolutionism's "scientific" foundations, a disputation between creationists and evolutionists started in the United States in the 1980s, a debate that continues to this day. Creationists fight to demonstrate the bogus scientific base for Evolutionism and to keep it from being taught exclusively in primary and secondary schools. With this goal, they publish books with testimonies from famous scientists showing the state of infirmity in which Evolutionism presently finds itself.

So, for anyone who wants to know scholarly and highly credible scientific arguments demonstrating the false scientific foundation for Evolutionism, nothing is more opportune than to seek out the authors from the 1930s who contested it, as well as the much larger group who entered the polemic in the United States from 1980 to this day.

§ 12 Among those authors we have chosen two who published interview-books on these two critical phases of Evolutionism. These authors reproduce statements by scientific authorities from various currents. Thus, we came into possession of a vast mine of material of the highest scientific quality on this topic, which gave us conditions to present our Reader with an overview.

We have made a systematization of the works we used – by A.N. Field and Luther D. Sunderland – which tries to be as clear as possible for those who are unfamiliar with the topic.[6]

---

[6] The first book, *The Evolution Hoax Exposed* (Rockfort, Il: TAN, 1971, 104 pp.) by A.N. Field, was published for the first time in 1941. Centered principally on the controversy of the 1920s and 1930s, it presents interesting statements regarding Darwinism and Evolutionism in general.

The second book, *Darwin's Enigma – Fossils and Other Problems* (San Diego, CA: Master Book Publishers, 1984, 179 pp.) by Luther

1. Relationships of Evolutionism with other movements

§ 13

When we review how the evolutionary theory was born in Charles Darwin's mind – especially in his book *On the Origin of Species* [7] – we find a series of influences and contributions from different sources including:

- Some thinkers who preceded him or were his contemporaries defended similar theories;
- Some writers who generically defended beforehand the ensemble of the evolutionary theory;
- Other authors in specific branches of science who launched the central ideas of evolution, which were assumed by the English naturalist;
- Some theories that had an indisputable influence on Darwin's thought;
- And, finally, other factors that had a possible influence on him.

§ 14a

Three criteria, therefore, are intermingled in the genesis of the evolutionary theory: the time when the other theories were published, Darwin's total or partial dependence on this or that thinker, and the credibility of such dependence.

Let us apply these criteria to the origin, development and end toward which Darwinism tends.

D. Sunderland, portrays the present day embarrassment of Evolutionism in scientific milieus. Along with the lack of scientific credibility of Darwinism, it brings to light important statements that disqualify Neo-Darwinism.

Both authors had the good sense to not base their books exclusively upon statements of anti-evolutionist scientists. As we will see, there are numerous quotations from known proponents of Evolutionism, who acknowledge that their theory does not enjoy scientific foundation. They only admit it as a philosophical theory or a scientific hypothesis that must still be demonstrated.

The presence of evolutionist and anti-evolutionist scientists in both works confers an impartiality and seriousness to the studies and strengthens their demonstrative character and polemical efficacy.

[7] The complete name of Darwin's major work is: *On the Origin of Species by Means of Natural Selection or the Preservation of Favoured Races in the Struggle for Life*. It was first published on November 24, 1859.

A. Going Back in Time: from Charles Darwin to the Enlightenment

§ 14b The first datum that catches our attention when we consider the origins of Evolutionism is that Charles Darwin's grandfather, Erasmus Darwin (1731-1802), had already defended very similar concepts. Indeed, Erasmus, a well-known physician in England in his time, published the book *Zoonomy* (1794), in which he explained his ideas.[8] Among other questions, he asked these two central ones concerning Evolutionism: "Did all living creatures, including man, descend from a single common ancestor? And, if so, how could one species be transformed into another?"[9]

Erasmus' input did not limit itself to these questions. His studies encompassed almost all the important topics of modern Evolutionism such as overpopulation, competition and natural selection. He even proposed that the principal force of natural evolution would be the adaptation of species to the environment, including the inheritance of acquired characteristics.[10]

Erasmus' ideas were so widely discussed that already in his time they took the name of Darwinism. His grandson, however, did not seem to like being reminded of this precedent. According to Gertrude Himmelfarb in her biography *Darwin and the Darwinian Revolution*, "Darwin relegated his grandfather Erasmus to a footnote in his *Historical Sketch* as having anticipated the views and erroneous grounds of opinion of Lamarck."[11]

On this point, Sunderland comments: "It does seem rather inexplicable that Darwin failed to give his grandfather any recognition for his contribution to the theory of evolution, which he presented in *The Origin* as though it were an original idea."[12]

§ 15 It is significant that Erasmus Darwin became acquainted with Rousseau during the period when the latter was living in exile in England at Lichfield under the patronage of David Hume and corresponded with him thereafter.[13] Would it be possible to

---

[8] Cf. A.N. Field, *The Evolution Hoax Exposed*, p. 83.

[9] *Apud* L.D. Sunderland, *Darwin's Enigma*, p. 14.

[10] Cf. *ibid.*

[11] Gertrude Himmelfarb, *Darwin and the Darwinian Revolution* (New York: W.W. Norton & Co, 1968), p. 172, *apud* L.D. Sunderland, *Darwin's Enigma*, p. 14.

[12] L.D. Sunderland, *Darwin's Enigma*, p. 14.

[13] Cf. A.N. Field, *The Evolution Hoax Exposed*, pp. 83-84.

find an affinity between the ideas of Rousseau and Hume and the theses of the sprouting Evolutionism? To answer this question, a study would be needed, which we are not able to undertake at this moment. Nonetheless, we suggest here the possibility of a connection among the three thinkers.

§ 16

Jean Baptiste de Lamarck (1744-1829), a French botanist and zoologist who is commonly considered one of the pioneers of the evolutionary theory, defended the idea of evolution through the inheritance of acquired characteristics.[14] Lamarck, however, seemed to be merely drawing out the ideas of the Count of Buffon (1725-1773), whose children he tutored for several years.[15]

§ 17

Buffon, considered by many to be the father of modern Evolutionism, proposed a general theory of evolution and a long time scale for the history of the earth.[16] Field notes, "The Count of Buffon was a prominent figure among the French philosophers and men of letters inveighing against established religion and providing the ideas that were put into practical application in the French Revolution."[17]

What influence did Buffon and Lamarck have on Charles Darwin? It is difficult to demonstrate their effect with precision since, in the English naturalist's work, there is no mention of them; as we have seen, Darwin did not like to acknowledge precursors.

§ 18

Sunderland observes: "In *What Darwin Really Said*, historian Farrington recognized Darwin's lust for fame and, thus, his failure to acknowledge the previous contributions by others: 'No reader, however, could guess from the opening page of *The Origin* that descent with modification had a long history before Darwin took up his pen.'

"He [Farrington] showed how Darwin pretended to have just stumbled upon the idea while on the *Beagle* and on his return home. … Darwin wrote: 'After five years' work I allowed myself to speculate on the subject.' Not a word about his grandfather Erasmus, Lamarck or any of the others, like Matthew, who had written about the subject in 1831, … Farrington notes: 'The subject was already in the air, and Darwin does not say so.'"[18]

---

[14] Cf. *ibid.,* p. 15; L.D. Sunderland, *Darwin's Enigma*, p. 14.

[15] Cf. A.N. Field, *The Evolution Hoax Exposed*, pp. 15, 83.

[16] Cf. *ibid.*, p. 15.

[17] *Ibid.*, p. 83.

[18] L.D. Sunderland, *Darwin's Enigma*, p. 15.

§ 19 The only influence Darwin explicitly admits is that of Thomas Malthus (1766-1834). In fact, in *On the Origin of Species* Darwin remarks briefly on Malthus' concept of the struggle for existence: "It is the doctrine of Malthus applied with manifold force to the whole animal and vegetable kingdoms."[19]

§ 20 In his turn, in his *Essay on the Principle of Population,* Malthus acknowledges that his notion of the struggle for existence derived from Benjamin Franklin's book *Miscellany.*[20] Franklin was deeply involved in the French Enlightenment and exercised great influence in the circles that prepared both the American and the French Revolutions.

§ 21 Thus, the sources behind the thinking of the evolutionist Charles Darwin include Rousseau, Buffon and Franklin, who were partisans of the Enlightenment. It is not an exaggeration to affirm, therefore, that Evolutionism is a remote son of the Enlightenment.

B. Evolutionism, Marxism & Freudianism

§ 22 The affinities between Darwin and Marx are acknowledged by various socialists. Among them, the most expressive is Friedrich Engels, a close collaborator of Karl Marx. Field points out this connection:

"Engels, in his celebrated oration over the grave of Marx, declared Marx and Darwin to be twin discoverers of the law of evolution, saying: 'Just as Darwin discovered the law of evolution of organic nature, so Marx discovered the evolutionary law of human history – the simple fact that the production of the material necessities of life and the corresponding stage of economic evolution of a people or period provides a foundation upon which the national institutions, legal systems, art and even the religious ideals of the people in question have been built, and upon which, therefore, their explanations must be based.'"[21]

§ 23 Engels is not the only one to note such affinities. Enrico Ferri, an Italian socialist leader, asserted in his *Socialism and Modern Science* that Marxist Socialism "is nothing but a vital and logical corollary in part of Darwinian evolution, in part of Spencerian evolution."[22]

---

[19] *Apud* A.N. Field, *The Evolution Hoax Exposed*, p. 48.

[20] Cf. *ibid.*, p. 45.

[21] *Ibid.*, p. 73.

[22] *Ibid.*

§ 24 In his *Socialism in Theory and Practice,* American socialist Morris Hillquit said: "Karl Marx alone consistently introduced the spirit of Darwinism into the study of social phenomena by substituting the … doctrine of class struggle in the more modern stages of social development for the … doctrine of the struggle for existence in its lower stages."[23]

§ 25 Besides the unsuspicious testimony of Engels and other socialists, it is known that Marx had a special admiration for Darwin. It is often said that the author of *Das Kapital* wanted to dedicate his book to Darwin, but the English naturalist declined the homage.[24]

§ 26 As Darwin's theory was starting to lose credibility in the West, Marxist Theodosius Dobzhansky moved from Russia to the United States in 1927, carrying in his baggage the most important principles of the movement that soon would be known as Neo-Darwinism.[25]

§ 27 The exponents of Neo-Darwinism include the American scientists Stephen Jay Gould (1941-2002) and Niles Eldredge (1943-), co-proposers of the theory of punctuated equilibria. This theory replaced the already-defeated conception of a gradual evolution defended by Darwin. In an article published in the magazine *Paleobiology*, both authors admit their philosophical affinities with Marxism:

"Alternative concepts of change have respectable pedigrees in philosophy. Hegel's dialectical laws, translated to a material context, have become the official 'State philosophy' of many Socialist Nations. These laws of change are explicitly punctuational, as befits a theory of revolutionary transformation in human society."[26]

§ 28 We see, therefore, that from its origin to this day, Darwinism and Marxism have marched together hand in hand.

*

---

[23] *Ibid.*

[24] Cf. L.D. Sunderland, *Darwin's Enigma*, pp. 110; A. N. Field, *The Evolution Hoax Exposed*, p. 72.

[25] Cf. L.D. Sunderland, *Darwin's Enigma*, p. 110.

[26] *Ibid.*, p. 108; cf. pp. 108-110.

§ 29 There are also expressive affinities between Darwinism and Freudian Psychoanalysis. It was in the supposed evolution of man from the ape that Freud based part of his conception of liberating the animal cravings of the libido.

On this subject Field comments: "Among the varied offspring of the Darwinian doctrine of man's animal descent are the numerous 'scientific' doctrines of free-love. Mr. [Dan] Gilbert deals at length with these in his useful *Evolution: the Root of All Isms*. He points out, for example, that the late Prof. Freud in his *General Introduction to Psychoanalysis*, of which teaching he was the founder, asserts that 'man's animal nature is ineradicable,' and he makes this justification for 'giving full rein to one's sexuality.'

"Freud affirms this to be quite in order as evolution shows that man is 'an animal accustomed to the freedom of the jungle' and 'unadapted' to the restrictions of Christian Civilization. This is the entire burden of the psychoanalytic gospel.

§ 30 "A popular American university textbook, *An Outline of Psychoanalysis*,[27] edited by J.S. van Teslaar, states: 'Psychoanalysis represents but an extension of the theory of evolution, an application of the principle of evolution …'

"Dr. Samuel D. Schamalhausen, probably America's most popular and persistent champion of the so-called new morality of 'sex expression' and 'sex experimentation' with unlimited license, bases the arguments throughout his work on animal behavior and man's supposed descent. 'The sexual revolution is the terminal phase of the scientific revolution,' he says in his *Sex and Civilization*."[28]

We can conclude, therefore, that the pretended animal ancestry of man from apes defended by Evolutionism is one of the foundations of Freudianism.

§ 31 There are, then, important links of "scientific" Evolutionism: In its origin it is linked to the Enlightenment; in its development, to Marxism; in its end, to Freudianism.

---

[27] Freud has a book with the same name, *An Outline of Psychoanalysis*. The mentioned textbook is not a summary of Freud's work, but rather a collection of articles of Freud, Putnam, Jones, Pfister, Hinkle, Jung and others.

[28] A.N. Field, *The Evolution Hoax Exposed*, p. 75.

2. General Notion of Evolutionism

§ 32

Evolutionism pretends to replace the teaching that life *in genere* and man *in specie* were created by God. According to the evolutionary visualization, life would have appeared in the universe by spontaneous generation. From that first single celled organism with its own life – the protozoa – a process of ascent would have started whereby the less perfect species would have gradually produced more perfect species. This process gave birth to plants, mollusks, crustaceans, fish, reptiles, birds and animals of all the existent species; then, at a certain moment, the evolutionary process engendered man from the ape.

Each species would transcend itself to generate another more perfect through the "mechanism" of natural selection. Thus, the weaker specimens of each species would perish in the struggle for existence. Such a process of natural selection would cause only the stronger of the species to survive and have offspring. So, progressing from good to better, the species would refine themselves in a gradual process of perfection.

§ 33

To what end would this evolution tend? Is man the end of the process? Or should he also give origin to some nobler form of life? In this case, what would it be? Would it be a new type of man or an angel? It seems indispensable, for the sake of consistency, to have a postulation for the end of the process. We are unaware, however, of any explanation Darwin offered about this end.[29]

In summary, Evolutionism does not think of a Being Who created life. It postulates the existence of life as a fruit of spontaneous generation. Then, it tries to present a selective mechanism through which the species would transcend themselves, each giving rise to another more perfect one. It does not postulate an end toward which this process would march.

---

29 Positivism is a school of thought that relies on positive facts and denies causes (cf. §§ 61-72, Note 60); Darwin is generally included in this school (cf. F. Klimke, *História de la Filosofia*, Barcelona: Labor, 1947, pp. 652-653). Strictly speaking, therefore, Darwin could omit an origin or an end to his evolutionary process. We are not looking here, however, at the lack of internal coherence of Darwinism. We emphasize, rather, the metaphysical need for any process to have a beginning, a development and an end.

3. Terminology

§ 34

To allow our Reader to better follow the explanation on the topic of evolution, we offer here the meaning of a few key words, which obey a specific convention in use in the scientific milieu.

Philo = species; from it come other words such as ***philogenesis,*** the evolutionary development and diversification of a species, or ***philogenetic tree,*** a branching diagram showing the inferred evolutionary relationships among various biological species. Such terms are used to refer to all living beings descending from a common ancestor or protozoa.

Variation = a change that occurs within the same species but does not lead to another species.

Mutation = a change of one species to a higher one in the process of evolutionary ascent.

4. Foundations of Evolutionism

§ 35

The "scientific" foundations presented for the evolutionary theory are threefold: *first*, there are laws that supposedly govern natural history; *second*, there are proofs that pretend to justify these laws; *third*, there are subsidiary theories that emerged to support evolution as a science.

In this Item 4 we will limit ourselves to presenting the laws, proofs and theories in their general character. In Item 5 we will give their specific characteristics and refute them.

A. The Principal 'Laws' of Evolutionism

§ 36

Evolutionism pretends to be a science in the realm of Natural History. In this field, when one observes from experience phenomena that occur constantly, one says that there is a law. *Servata proportione*, in physics there is Newton's law of gravity and Gay-Lussac's law of free expansion of gases, among many others.

The principal "scientific" laws enunciated by Evolutionism are:

§ 37

- The law of spontaneous generation, which would be an experimental constant that would justify the spontaneous origin of life;

§ 38

- The law of the common ancestor or of transmutation, which would be the scientific verification that all species come from the same protozoa;

§ 39 • The law of natural selection, which would be the constant observed at all times and places establishing that species would self-destruct in the fight for existence, leaving only the better types to live;

§ 40 • The law of gradualism, which would be the scientific verification that each species ascends toward another through a slow and gradual process.

B. Principal proofs

Since Evolutionism is established on the mentioned "laws," let us look at the "proofs" upon which these "laws" are based.

§ 41 • For the *law of sponaneous generation*, it is very difficult to verify scientifically the origin of life in the universe. Such a difficulty is twofold: *first*, to know how life appeared; *second*, to know how the first living being in the evolutionary chain was formed.

In order to "resolve" the first difficulty, Evolutionism postulated that life is formed by chemical reactions of inorganic matter and, therefore, in the beginning life would have been formed in the same way, which would be the answer to the second difficulty.

However, no matter how many studies and research projects science undertakes, to this day it has not managed to create life either by a chemical reaction or any other means.

Therefore, the assertion that life is formed by chemical reactions has no experimental verification in its favor. If there is no proof, it is impossible to establish a law that expresses a constant in multiple experiments. Thus, the law of spontaneous generation is not a law, and the affirmation that life is formed by chemical reactions is gratuitous.

§ 42 • For the *law of the common ancestor*, the evolutionary "proof" would be the fossil record.

Due to the immense number of fossils that have been unearthed, the paleontological discoveries would reveal the process of gradualism working in evolution. The fossil records would demonstrate the existence of common traits among the various animal and vegetable species (homology), which would prove that all originate from the same ancestor.

We see, therefore, that the proof of the common ancestor relies on the proofs for gradualism and homology. We will deal with this further on in this Chapter.[30]

---

[30] Cf. § 103.

§ 43

- The *law of natural selection* presupposes the "evidence" that the species transcend themselves and generate other more perfect ones. Now then, such "evidence" simply does not exist. As we will see, [31] a considerable number of scientists – which is constantly increasing – decisively affirm that species do not undergo such mutations. They do suffer minor variations in adaptations to climate and environment, but these changes do not tend toward the perfection of the species, but rather, as time passes these variations either become stable or cause the species to deteriorate.

Since the "evidence" upon which the law of natural selection is established is nonexistent, this law becomes completely void.

§ 44

- It is Darwin's *law of gradualism* that boasts a larger number of "scientific proofs." Four type of proofs are habitually presented: fossil remains, such as the skeletons of primates, which would prove that man is a descendent of an ape passing through intermediary stages; embryology, which would prove that a human embryo passed through the different phases of evolution; homology, which would show that different species have similar organs, which, in turn, would prove that some are gradually mutating into others.

Since it is toward the demonstration of this law of gradualism that the largest number of evolutionary efforts concur as well as the largest number of denials, we will deal with it in Item 5 and limit ourselves here to a summary description of it.

First, however, since we are describing the "proofs" of the evolutionary theory, let us look briefly at two theories subsidiary to Darwinism that deny two of its principal laws: the law of spontaneous generation and the law of gradualism.

C. Subsidiary Theories of Evolutionism

§ 45

Realizing the impossibility of demonstrating the origin of life by spontaneous generation, Dr. Francis Crick, a biologist who was awarded the Nobel Prize for Physiology in 1962, defended the theory of panspermia, according to which life would have been transported to Earth by an inter-planetary aircraft from outside the solar system.[32]

§ 46

Realizing the lack of foundation for the Darwinian law of gradualism to support present day Evolutionism, in the 1970s Dr. Stephen Jay Gould and Dr. Niles Eldredge spread the theory

---

[31] Cf. §§ 104-122.

[32] Cf. L.D. Sunderland, *Darwin's Enigma*, pp. 54-55.

of punctuated equilibria, according to which the evolution of a species would not be gradual, but would occur by sudden leaps.[33]

It seems to us very significant that, in the evolutionary milieus themselves, the scientists realized that they must reject these two laws of Evolutionism.

Having presented the basics of Evolutionism in its general lines, let us now enter into a systematic refutation of it based upon the affirmations of renowned scientists.

5. Evolutionism's Lack of Credibility as Science

§ 47 The average man, who follows the ideas of the time, keeps up with the scientific reports spread by the media, reads articles and books on Evolutionism and is updated on the latest news on the topic, is led to form the conviction that Evolutionism is one of the greatest discoveries of modern science.

Surprisingly, in this point the average man, the media and the organs of dissemination are singularly ill informed.

At the beginning of the 20th century, science briefly assumed the Darwinian hypothesis. However, as time went by, the various "proofs" and "laws" of Evolutionism were discredited by new discoveries. Today, therefore, the theory of evolution is nothing but a philosophical theory. In the realm of experimental science, it is just a hypothesis and one that is sharply contested.

Let us turn now to the opinion of the scientists.

A. Notion of Science

§ 48 Before presenting the notion of science that is generally accepted by modern scientists, we should consider that today's science is a tributary of Positivism and Empiricism. To help the Reader understand the importance of these restrictions, we find it opportune to present the Scholastic conception of science as a term of comparison.

a. Scholastic Notion of Science

Definition

§ 49 Regarding the definition of science, St. Thomas Aquinas distinguishes two fundamental aspects. *In itself*, science is the collection of abstract notions, ordered to the understanding.[34]

---

[33] Cf. *ibid.*, pp. 98-100.

[34] Cf. St. Thomas, *Contra Gentiles*, 1, chap. 56; *III Sententiarum*, d. 14, 3, q. 4, c; *De Veritate*, q. 10, 2; q. 20, 2; q. 24, 4, 8m.

Relative to man, it is the intellectual assimilation of the thing understood through a concept – called an intelligible concept – which is similar to the thing that was understood.[35]

§ 50 Aristotle adopts a definition of science in function of the way of understanding that is based upon the knowledge of things through their causes. He says: "We judge to possess in an absolute way the knowledge of something … when we know the cause through which the thing is, we know that this cause is that of the thing and, further, that the thing cannot be other than what it is."[36]

§ 51 Commenting on Aristotle's definition of science, St. Thomas notes that the Greek philosopher at times considers science in a broad sense, that is, as a certainty of knowledge; at other times in its proper sense, that is, presented in function of the intellect. Thus, science is concerned with conclusions; the intellect, with principles.[37]

§ 52 Therefore, there are two essential elements in science: the conclusions reached by the consideration of determined things and the principles to which the intellect reduces such conclusions. Without both elements, there is no science in its proper sense. St. Thomas states that if science cannot be reduced to principles known in a natural way, we cannot say univocally that it is science.[38] In another place, he says that a science that does not deal with principles but only with conclusions is an inferior science.[39]

Types of sciences – natural & supernatural

§ 53 Considering the origin of human science, St. Thomas distinguishes that which is given directly by God – infused science – from that which is acquired.[40] In acquired science, he

---

[35] Cf. St. Thomas, *Summa Theologiae*, I, q. 14, a. 2; *De Potentia*, q. 7, 5, c.

[36] Aristotle, *Seconds anal,* I, 2, 71, b, *apud* Paul Foulquié, *Dictionnaire de la Langue Philosophique* (Paris: Presses Universitaires de France, 1969), entry Science, n. 27.

[37] Cf. St. Thomas, *Super Libros Posteriorum*, lect. 7, lect 44.

[38] Cf. St. Thomas, *III Sententiarum*, d. 33, q. 1, a. 2; q, 4, c.

[39] Cf. *De Veritate*, q. 14, 9, 3m.

[40] Cf. *Summa Theologiae*, I, q. 1, a. 1; q. 94, a. 3; III, q. 9, a. 4.

distinguishes that which proceeds from the data of Revelation – theological or supernatural science – from that which is proper to the light of human reason – natural science.[41]

Next, we will consider only acquired natural science.

Types of science regarding the way of knowing

§ 54

St. Thomas distinguishes acquired natural science in function of the way of knowing it. Such a differentiation is strictly coherent with the definition he gives, which covers all the sciences, as we will see.

The Angelical Doctor says that the sciences are differentiated according to the various ways of knowing.[42] He teaches, further, that knowledge of the universals and the particulars does not differentiate science in reference to the thing known, but in reference to the way of knowing.[43] In other places, he affirms that the types of things known are differentiated according to the different ways of defining them, either abstractly or materially.[44]

§ 55

Applying this criterion, he categorizes the sciences as speculative (ordered toward understanding) and practical (ordered toward action). He explains that the practical sciences are different from the thing known by the way of knowing it and by the end.[45] Regarding the way of knowing, St. Thomas teaches that the speculative sciences proceed by the resolutive or abstract way and the practical by the compositional or figurative way.[46] Regarding the end, he observes that the end of the speculative sciences is the knowledge of their subject; the end of the practical sciences, however, is their construction and operation.[47]

He adds that when a science is not ordered to its operation it is speculative; when it is ordered to its operation it is only practical; however, when it is speculative because of its way of proceeding and its end, then it is both speculative and practical.[48]

---

41 *Ibid.*, I, q. 1, a.1.

42 Cf. *ibid.*, I, q. 1, a. 1; I.II, q. 57, a. 2, c; *III Sententiarum*, d. 14, a. 3, q. 4; d. 33, q. 1, a. 1, q..1c.

43 Cf. *De Veritate*, q. 4, 12, 1.

44 Cf. *Super Libros Metaphysicorum*, 6, lect. 1; *De Anima*, lect. 2; *Super Libros Posteriorum*, lect. 41.

45 Cf. *Summa Theologiae*, I, q. 14. a. 16; *De Veritate*, q. 3, a. 3.

46 Cf. *Super Libros Ethicorum*, lect. 3.

47 Cf. *Super Libros Posteriorum*, lect. 41.

48 Cf. *Summa Theologiae*, I, q. 14, a. 16; *De Veritate*, q. 2, 8; q. 3, 3.

§ 56 St. Thomas considers three divisions of the speculative sciences in ascending order: natural science – that is, physics,[49] which studies only that being which is the object of science; mathematics, which studies only the reason of the being;[50] and metaphysics, which studies both things simultaneously.[51] He affirms that science is principally intellectual, because intellectual matter is what can more often be understood, either by reason of causality, universality or immateriality. All of this pertains especially to metaphysics.[52]

§ 57 The principal practical sciences that St. Thomas points out are economics, politics and ethics (or "monastic").[53] He asserts that the more an operative science considers the particular, the more perfect it is.[54]

To fully grasp the Thomist concept of science and compare it to the modern one, it seems indispensable to also present the Thomist concept of art.

---

[49] Cf. *ibid.* II.II, q. 48.

[50] We see that this conception of mathematics is much broader than that of the present day. St. Thomas considers mathematics as a part of philosophy. Modern mathematics does not consider the reason of the being, but only or principally the quantitative and numerical relationships of what exists and, increasingly often, of what exists experimentally in the fields of physics and chemistry. Hence the definition presented by P. Foulquié: Mathematics is "that which belongs to the domain of science, having quantity as its proper object" (*Dictionnaire de la Langue Philosophique*, entry *Mathématique*, adj. A). He also offers another meaning: Mathematics "regarding the object: is a group of deductive sciences that has as its object number, extension and order" (*ibid.*, entry *Mathématiques*, noun, A).
The present day tendency of mathematics clearly reflects the observation of Auguste Comte (1798-1857): "Today … mathematical science is much less important for its knowledge that directly pertains to it – although this knowledge is real and very important – than for being the most powerful instrument the human mind can employ in the research of the laws of natural phenomena" (*Cours de Philosophie Positive*, I. 36, *apud* P. Foulquié, *Dictionnaire de la Langue Philosophique, ibid.*, n. 10).

[51] Cf. St. Thomas Aquinas, *De Trinitate*, 17, c; *Super Libros Metaphysicorum*, 6, lect. 1.

[52] Cf. *Super Libros Metaphysicorum*, prol.

[53] Cf. *Summa Theologiae*, II.II, q. 47, a. 11.

[54] Cf. *ibid.*, I, q. 22, a. 3.

Types of art

§ 58

According to Scholasticism, art is the right understanding of feasible works and the corresponding execution of that work.[55]

The arts that are ordered to the works of the mind are called the liberal arts. Those that are ordered to the physical works are called the mechanical or servile arts.[56]

Following this classification, the medieval universities studied the seven liberal arts – grammar, rhetoric, dialectics or logic, arithmetic, music, geometry and astronomy – which prepared students for the liberal professions. The servile or mechanical arts prepared persons for the various labors and guilds.[57]

Every application of right reason to something that can be done or made belongs to art. Therefore, art is in some way speculative.[58] Thus, the liberal arts are speculative and are called art in that they have something similar to an operation.[59]

Difference between science & art

§ 59

Since there is a speculative character in both the sciences and the arts and the study of the way of operating, we can ask: What differentiates one from the other?

The differentiation exists in the consideration of the end toward which they are ordered. Science, both the speculative and the practical, is turned toward knowing. Art, both the liberal and the mechanical, is turned toward doing.

Evidently there are fields in which science and art fall upon the same object. Thus, politics as a practical science is the knowledge of public affairs that derives from the analysis of the particulars; while politics as art is the application of such knowledge to model public affairs to a determined end.

---

[55] "The good of these things to be made," Aquinas explains, "depends on the goodness of the work done; for a craftsman as such is commendable not for the will with which he does a work, but for the quality of the work. Art, therefore, properly speaking is an operative habit" (*Ibid.*, I.II, q. 57. a. 3; II.II, q. 47, a. 5).

[56] Cf. *ibid.*, I.II, q. 57, a. 3.

[57] The medieval classification of the mechanical arts included weaving, armament, commerce, agriculture, hunting, medicine and theater. Cf. P. Foulquié, *Dictionnaire de la Langue Philosophique*, entry *Art*, B.

[58] Cf. St. Thomas Aquinas, *Summa Theologiae*, II.II, q. 47, a. 2. 3.

[59] Cf. *ibid.*, I.II, q. 57. a. 3; II.II, q, 47, a. 2.

§ 60

With this explanation, we discover the richness of Scholastic thinking on science. It presents a broad panorama, encompassing all the fields of human knowledge. It is established in the most rigorous logic, which proceeds from very simple universal principles. Also notable is the background unity that harmonizes the whole and the hierarchy that orders all the sciences among themselves.

In all the sciences, there is the same quest for universal principles; in all of them, there is a gradual ascension: economics rises to politics, which ascends to morals. In the speculative sciences, physics and the sciences it encompasses rise to mathematics, which ascends to metaphysics. Each of them, as well as the ensemble, rise to the supernatural science. How extraordinarily architectonic and beautiful the Scholastic conception of science is! The same could be said about art.

b. The modern notion of science

§ 61

When we consider the notion of science that generally has been adopted from the Enlightenment onward, we see that it suffered a radical change from the Scholastic conception. In effect, modern science is preponderantly turned toward knowledge derived from experience and considers the quest for universal principles, causes and ends as useless metaphysical conjectures, lacking a positive character and, therefore, any link to science.

Given that experience is almost the only procedure admitted by modern science, the highest degree of abstraction it can attain is in its "laws." A law, according to this conception, is the empirical common denominator observed in countless verifiable experiences.

Thus, we can affirm in a general way that modern or positive science is limited to experiences and the laws common to them.

§ 62

This conception of science is principally a tributary of Positivism.[60] To give the Reader an overview of this current of

---

[60] Although there are many notions of modern science – for example, that of Kant, who defines science "in general as being any doctrine that forms a system, that is, an ensemble of knowledge ordered according to principles" (*Met. Anfangsgründe der Naturwiss,* Preface §§ 2, 3, *apud* André Lalande, *Vocabulaire Technique et Critique de la Philosophie*, Paris: Presses Universitaires de France, 1956, 7th ed., *verb. Science, critique*) – in the practical order and in the evolution of the concepts of modern thinking, contemporary man "views science

thought, we transcribe below some observations and commentaries by scholars on the topic.

§ 63 Regarding the doctrines that are tributaries of Positivism, André Lalande observes:

"Positivism, by extension, is a name given to the doctrine of Auguste Comte or teaching similar to it, at times even remotely so. They all share the belief that only the knowledge of facts is significant, that only the experimental sciences can provide certainty about anything, that human thinking – in philosophy and in science – cannot escape verbalism or error unless it is constantly in contact with experience and renounces every principle *a priori*, and, finally, that the domain of 'things in themselves' [that is, metaphysics] is inaccessible and thinking can only discover relationships and laws. Such is the teaching of J.S. Mill, de Littré, Spencer, Renan, and even Taine, which gradually moved away from Positivism."[61]

§ 64 Regarding the origin of this conception, Lalande quotes the observation of the 19th century French philosopher Marcellin Berthelot:

"What we call Positivism ... is an ensemble of ideas or intellectual tendencies associated more with Condorcet than Auguste Comte because they borrowed – as Comte admitted – much of Condorcet's thinking: the doctrine that attributes to the constitution and progress of positive science a preponderant importance for the progress of all knowledge, no matter what it may be, even philosophical."[62]

---

as nothing but a system of entries, which permits one to classify and predict phenomena" (*ibid., in fine*).

Thus, although modern science assumes different concepts of science, some conferring to it this or that metaphysical basis, by its own dynamism it tends toward the hegemony of the positivist concept, that is, the denial of metaphysics and the undeviating exaltation of the experimental, factual and phenomenological.

We do not deny that modern science may have important connections with the English Empiricism of Bacon, Locke, Berkeley and Hume (cf. F. Kimkle, *História de la Filosofia*, pp. 395-406). However, given that Positivism proceeds from Empiricism (cf. *ibid*, p. 639) and has a much larger audience than the English system, we judge it more accurate to say that modern science is principally a tributary of Positivism.

[61] A. Lalande, *Vocabulaire Technique et Critique de la Philosophie,* entry *Positivisme*, B.

[62] *Apud ibid.*, Obs. 2.

§ 65 The anti-metaphysical character of Positivism is admitted by Comte himself:

"The fundamental character of the positivist philosophy is anti-metaphysical because it considers all phenomena as subject to invariable natural laws, whose discovery and reduction to the least possible number is the objective of all our efforts. The search for what is called causes, either first or last, is considered absolutely unattainable and meaningless."[63]

Comte further affirms that Positivism "formally professes to absolutely ignore the inner nature of anything."[64]

§ 66 French philosopher Émile Littré also observes: "Anything beyond positive knowledge – be it material, such as the measurement of limitless space, or intellectual, such as the linking of endless causes – cannot be known by the human mind."[65]

§ 67 Berthelot confirms Positivism's denial of the metaphysical: "Positive science chases after neither the primary cause nor the end of things; rather, it progresses by verifying facts and linking them by immediate relationships. It is the linking of these relationships that constitutes positive science."[66]

§ 68 On this anti-metaphysical path, we find French naturalist Lamarck, the precursor not only of Darwin but also of Comte. Lamarck used to say that "for man there are really no positive truths upon which he may solidly rely except those facts that he can observe and the consequences he draws from them."[67]

§ 69 Besides the anti-metaphysical character of Positivism and the modern sciences, of which the former is the main foundation, we can point out the profound relativism that they breed.

Auguste Comte himself declares that the significance of Positivism "naturally points to the always relative character of the new intellectual system, since modern reason cannot remove

---

[63] A. Comte, *Philosophie Positiviste*, I. 16, *apud* P. Foulquié, *Dictionnaire de la Langue Philosophique*, entry *Positif*. 19.

[64] A. Comte, *Cours de Philosophie Positiviste*, 2nd lesson, in *Oeuvres Choisies*, pub. by H. Gouhier, p. 121, *apud ibid*.

[65] Emile Littré, *Auguste Comte et la Philosophie Positiviste*, p. 519, *apud ibid*., 12.

[66] M. Berthelot, *Lettre à Renan*, in Renan, *Dialogues et Fragments Philosophiques*, p. 195, *apud ibid*., 13.

[67] Jean-Baptiste Lamarck, *Philosophie Zoologique*, XXV, *apud ibid*., 4.

itself from the critical spirit of the past unless it renounces every absolute principle. When the Western world understands this last connection … then, the *positive* will become inseparable from the *relative* everywhere, just as today it is from the organic, the precise, the secure, the useful and the real."[68]

§ 70 Regarding its application to the modern sciences, the relativism of Positivism is evident. The modern sciences themselves postulate that their theories are relative.

British philosopher John Stuart Mill confirms this postulation:

"We have no knowledge of anything but phenomena; and our knowledge of phenomena is relative, not absolute. We know neither the essence, nor the real mode of production of any fact, but only its relations to other facts in the way of succession or of similitude. ... The laws of phenomena are all we know respecting them. Their essential nature and their ultimate causes, either efficient or final, are unknown and inscrutable to us. "[69]

§ 71 It is curious to consider that modern science, which pretends to do away with metaphysics and replace it with "solid" positive knowledge, nonetheless declares that everything is unstable and relative when it establishes the foundation to justify its theses.

§ 72 As far as we can see, these are the principal characteristics of modern science: an exclusive reliance on the experimental, the abolition of metaphysics, and the denial of the absolute.

*

§ 73 Important consequences follow these points.

First, to deny metaphysics is to eliminate the very object of man's intellective potency in order to consider, as the positivist sciences do, only the object of his sensitive potency. It would be like someone who obstinately denies the value of light to the point of perforating his own eyes so that he might be guided only by touch. Thus, the denial of metaphysics confers to modern science its materialist character.

---

[68] A. Comte, *Le Système de Politique Positive*, I, p. 57-58, *apud ibid*. 3.

[69] John Stuart Mill, *Auguste Comte and Positivism* (London: N Trübner & Co., 1865), p. 6

§ 74 In parallel, if modern science abolishes metaphysics, how can it seriously pretend to be a philosophy? Is it possible to have a philosophy without metaphysics? Hence, the criticism of 19th century French philosopher Antoine Cournot is valid when he affirms that "the very designation 'positive philosophy' is a contradiction in terms."[70]

§ 75 *Second*, by denying the Absolute, modern science attacks metaphysics, which lives from the quest and love for the absolute and the desire to integrate with it. It also attacks Religion because the Absolute is, in the final analysis, the philosophical designation for God. Thus, the denial of the Absolute confers to modern science its atheistic character.[71]

§ 76 *Third*, by denying metaphysics and God, modern science lacks the criteria it needs for its own unity, order and harmony. In other words, modern science is established upon the principles of disunion, contradiction and chaos. Thus, the ensemble of modern science is not, and in principle cannot be, reducible to a great uniform and coherent body.

*

---

[70] Antoine Augustine Cournot, *Considérations* ... II, p. 91, *apud* P. Foulquié, *Dictionnaire de la Langue Philosophique*, entry *Positif*, 25.

[71] Someone could object that the Positivism of Auguste Comte is not atheistic, since he later founded a religion that adores a "great Being" (cf. F. Kimkle, *História de la Filosofia*, p. 643).

To this, we answer:

a. In fact, the positivist religion, termed the "Religion of Humanity" by Comte, rejects Theism in its proper sense; it cannot be called atheistic since it also rejects Atheism (cf. ibid.);

b. However, this religion, although adopted by Freemasonry (cf. ibid., note 1), had very little cultural significance;

c. The following were the principal cultural sequels of Positivism, in our opinion: a general disposition of their co-religionists to consider the natural and human universe as closed on itself, and an inherent aversion toward what is sacred and religious, considered crutches for sentimental and weak spirits. On the contrary, the "strong spirit" of the positivist – in his more characteristic expressions – is opposed to God, or at least indifferent to Him.

It is in this broad sense that we say Positivism and modern science are atheistic.

§ 77 Notwithstanding modern science's fundamental disorder, which generates countless partial, disputable and relative classifications, we can distinguish two large groups that rely on the verification of sensory experience: the natural sciences and the so-called human sciences.

Included in the natural sciences are those that empirically analyze inorganic and organic nature, including human nature, e.g., physics, chemistry, geology and biology.

In the human sciences man's behavior is analyzed; this group includes, among other subjects, anthropology, human biology, psychology and sociology. Lalande explains: "This expression [human sciences] puts an emphasis above all on the exterior characteristics observed in the way men behave, individually and collectively."[72]

Relations between modern science & technology

§ 78 Just as Scholasticism distinguishes between science and art – the first turned toward knowledge, the second toward making – so also today there is a difference between science and technology. It is, in fact, to technology that modern progress owes its rapid advances.

§ 79 The use of mechanical energy by steam, internal combustion and jet engines produced, successively, the Industrial Revolution, the mechanization of agriculture and easier and faster means of transportation.

§ 80 The use of electrical energy by systems of generators and condensers, on the one hand, further accelerated industrial and agricultural development by offering a cheaper energy. On the other hand, the addition of electromagnetic waves in the use of electicity gave birth to the telegraph, telephone and telex, which together with the radio, cinema and television, engendered Informatics, which reached its apex with the arrival of the computer.

Because of the large quantity of data computers can accumulate and classify and the constantly increasing speed of the delivery of this information, they were adopted *en masse* as focal points of modern organization. They added new acceleration to the industrial, agricultural and inter-communication processes, generating what is called the Cybernetic Revolution or Informatics.

---

[72] A. Lalande, *Vocabulaire Technique et Critique de la Philosophie*, entry *Science, Sciences humaines*.

§ 81 The pacific use of atomic energy in nuclear power plants, providing a cheaper and cleaner energy source, was brought to fruition with caution, replacing in various countries the more expensive sources of electrical energy.

§ 82 The use of the optical or photonic energy, which uses light sources to perform electronic functions, is also being developed. Perhaps we will see a Photonic Revolution, which will be to the Cybernetic Revolution what the latter was to the Industrial Revolution.

§ 83 To what degree can these various technologies be termed sciences? We would say that they are sciences to the degree they give man new elements of knowledge. However, since human observation is increasingly dependent on mechanical, electronic and optical instruments and on the data furnished by televisions and computers – as in the case of the exploration of the macro-cosmos by telescopes and the micro-cosmos by microscopes – the question arises: What role is still played by positive experience and empirical observation, which was established as the foundation of modern science?

§ 84 We would respond that modern technology is so overwhelming that it is in fact replacing the modern science that generated it.

There is irony in the fact that modern science, which wanted to banish metaphysics from the horizon of knowledge, now seems to be on the verge of being banished itself by technology, that is, by the mere doing.

§ 85 Thus, we would be reaching the end of a long process of successive revolts from the Enlightenment to our day: Initially philosophy rose up against the Faith, declaring itself autonomous in the name of the light of human reason; next, science became independent of metaphysics in the name of the positive certainties of sensory experience; now, technology tends to dethrone science in the name of efficiency of operation.

§ 86 These notions are useful to objectively situate modern science in its proper perspective, taking into account its pretensions, limitations and fragilities.

c. The present day notion of science

§ 87 Currently, the most accepted definition of science is that of Prof. Karl Popper (1902-1994), a German professor and philosopher of science who worked primarily in England. Popper won many awards and honors in his field, gaining widespread prestige. Nobel prize-winner Peter Medawar called Popper "incomparably the greatest philosopher of science who has ever lived."[73]

Sunderland describes Popper's positivist notion of science:

"Popper strongly supports the idea that a theory in science must be testable and for the tests to be valid they must be capable of falsifying the theory if it is not correct. It follows that a true scientific theory, in order to be tested, must be about a process that can be repeated and observed either directly or indirectly.

"One-time-only historical events may be true, but they are not part of science for there is no way of repeating them, observing them and subjecting them to testing. Also, for a theory to be testable, it must be possible for those conducting the tests to use it to make predictions about the outcome of the tests. If a theory is not suitable for use by scientists to make specific predictions, it is not a scientific theory."[74]

Having established this notion of science as the prevailing opinion of our days, let us see what several of today's greatest scientists say about Evolutionism.

B. Scientists Say Evolutionism Is Not a Scientific Theory

§ 88

In his book *Evolution,* Dr. Colin Patterson, famous paleontologist and editor of the British Natural History Museum journal, writes:

"If we accept Popper's distinction between science and non-science, we must ask first whether the theory of evolution by natural selection is scientific or pseudo-scientific (metaphysical) ... Taking the first part of the theory, that evolution has occurred, it says that the history of life is a single process of species-splitting and progression. This process must be unique and unrepeatable, like the history of England. This part of the theory is, therefore, about unique events, and unique events are, by definition, not part of science, for they are unrepeatable and so not subject to test."[75]

---

[73] Beverly Halstead, "Popper: Good Philosophy, Bad Science?," *New Scientist*, July 17, 1980, v. 87, n. 1210, pp. 215-217, *apud* L.D. Sunderland, *Darwin's Enigma*, p. 26.

[74] L.D. Sunderland, *Darwin's Enigma*, p. 26.

[75] Colin Patterson, *Evolution* (London: British Museum of Natural His-

§ 89 During an interview with Dr. Patterson in London, Sunderland presented him with this statement by L.T. More: "The more one studies paleontology, the more certain one becomes that evolution is based on faith alone, exactly the same sort of faith which is necessary to have when one encounters the great mysteries of religion."[76]

Then, Sunderland asked Patterson his opinion about the quote. Patterson answered, "I agree."[77]

§ 90 Karl Popper himself, although a partisan of Evolutionism and a confessed anti-theist, writes in his autobiography *Unended Quest*:

"I have come to the conclusion that Darwinism is not a testable scientific theory, but a metaphysical research programme – a possible framework for testable scientific theories."[78]

§ 91 Evolutionist Dr. Leonard Harrison Mattews, Scientific Director of London's Zoological Society, affirms that evolution is a faith, not a proved scientific theory, in the introduction to the 1971 edition of Darwin's *On the Origin of Species*:

"The fact of evolution is the backbone of biology, and biology is, thus, in the peculiar position of being a science founded on an unproved theory – is it, then, science or faith? To believe in the theory of evolution is, thus, exactly parallel to belief in special creation – both are concepts which believers know to be true, but neither, up to the present, has been capable of proof."[79]

§ 92 Interviewed by Sunderland, Dr. Niles Eldredge, one of the exponents of Neo-Darwinism, considers Evolutionism to be nothing but a body of axioms:

"We have a body of axioms – the creationist has one and the evolutionist has another – for which I can't think of a crucial

---

tory, 1978), pp. 145-146, *apud* L.D. Sunderland, *Darwin's Enigma*, pp. 26-27.

[76] R.L. Wysong, *The Creation-Evolution Controversy* (Midland, MI: Onquiry Press, 1976), p. 31, *apud ibid.*, p. 27.

[77] L.D. Sunderland, *Darwin's Enigma*, p. 27.

[78] Karl Popper, *Unended Quest* (Glasgow: Fontana Books, 1976), *apud ibid.*, p. 28.

[79] L. Harrison Mattews, *Introduction to The Origin of Species by Charles Darwin* (London: G.M. Deut and Sons, 1971), pp. X-XI, *apud ibid.*, pp. 30-31.

test." Further on, he repeats: "I can't think of any experiments which I might set up that would reject one theory in favor of the other."[80]

§ 93 These are general statements of some of the 20th century's greatest scientists about the character of Evolutionism, which they affirm to be not scientific, but rather philosophical or religious.

Besides these declarations, there are many others that are more specific. Let us go on to look at them next.

C. The 'Laws' and 'Proofs' of Evolutionism Are Not Scientific

About the "laws" and the "proofs" of Evolutionism, the following is what leading scientists say.

a. The law of spontaneous generation

§ 94 Concern about how the first living cell appeared, which would have given origin to the process of evolution, has been present since Darwin. Most of the quests were made in the area of chemistry. It was anticipated that determined chemical reactions of elements found on our planet, when realized in an atmosphere of gases that supposedly reproduced Earth's atmosphere in its primordial times, would generate a living cell.

For this purpose, the well known Miller-Urey experiment (1952) was conducted: An artificial atmosphere composed of methane, ammonia, water, steam and oxygen was submitted to an electrical charge. Under certain conditions, this process generated some amino acids.

Despite the fact that amino acids *per se* are not alive – they are only part of living cells – this experiment was lauded as an "indisputable" step forward for the discovery of life. For more than 30 years, it was acclaimed by the scientific establishment and described in textbooks at all levels as being a confirmation of Evolutionism.[81]

§ 95 Based on the Miller-Urey research, Sidney Fox, an American scientist and Professor of Microbiology at the University of Florida, made another experiment. He heated three types

---

[80] L.D. Sunderland, *Darwin's Enigma*, p. 31.

[81] Cf. *ibid.*, p. 53.

of amino acids to a high temperature, a procedure that generated various globules, which he called the world's first proto-cell.[82] Again, despite the fact that those globules *per se* are not alive – they are elements that integrate the living cell – this experiment raised new acclamations and euphoria. The day when life would be created in a laboratory could not be far away…

§ 96 However, the Miller-Urey experiment, which first generated this excitement, was carried out in a "reducing atmosphere" with no free oxygen. This is because that "reducing atmosphere" could not support the presence of free oxygen since it is highly destructive to the other components of the experiment, thus preventing the formation of amino acids.[83]

Now then, further comparative studies on the atmosphere of planets have revealed that there was a certain quantity of free oxygen present in the primitive atmosphere of the Earth.[84] Further, highly credited archeological research demonstrated that carbon dioxide and layers of oxidized iron were found in the older rocks of our planet,[85] which necessarily presupposes the presence of free oxygen in the Earth's primitive atmosphere.

These new discoveries effectively invalidated the Miller-Urey experiment and marked the end of the hope to make life appear in a "reducing atmosphere."[86]

§ 97 Sunderland offers more data on this topic:

"Nobel Prize winner and co-discoverer of DNA,[87] Francis Crick, recognized the problem of getting life to form spontaneously on Earth if oxygen were present. When he wrote the book *Life Itself* in 1981, evidence for oxygen in the earliest Pre-Cambrian rocks was just beginning to be discussed. He wrote:

"'If it turns out that the early atmosphere was not 'reducing' but containing a fair amount of oxygen, then the picture is more complicated. … If this were really true, it would support

---

82 *Ibid.*, pp. 53-54.

83 *Ibid*, p. 54.

84 *Ibid*.

85 *Ibid*.

86 Cf. *ibid*.

87 DNA = Deoxyribon Nucleic Acid is a molecule that contains all the genetic data in humans and almost all other organisms. It has a quite complicated structure and is the principal element of the chromosomes of living cells.

the idea of Directed Panspermia,[88] because planets elsewhere in the universe may have had a more reducing atmosphere and, thus, have on them a more favorable pre-biotic soup.[89]“[90]

§ 98 Sunderland continues his analysis: “Professor Carl Sagan agrees with this, for in a lengthy discussion following the author’s lecture at Cornell University on April 24, 1984, he said: ‘If there were free oxygen in the early atmosphere of the Earth before the development of green plants, we would have a serious contradiction.’”[91]

§ 99 In commenting on the great improbability of the spontaneous generation of a reproducing system, Dr. Crick wrote:

“What is so frustrating for our present purpose is that it seems almost impossible to give any numerical value to the probability of what seems a rather unlikely sequence of events. ... An honest man, armed with all the knowledge available to us now, could only state that in some sense the origin of life appears at the moment to be almost a miracle.”[92]

§ 100 Commenting on the notion of a reducing atmosphere, the magazine *New Scientist* noted:

“It used to be widely thought and widely taught that the original ‘primitive’ atmosphere of the early Earth was a ‘reducing’ atmosphere. ... The reasoning behind this assumption developed primarily from the belief that such an atmosphere would be ideal, and might be essential, for the development of the complex non-living molecules that preceded life. ... This picture captured the popular imagination and the story of life emerging in the seas or pools of a planet swathed in an atmosphere of methane and ammonia soon became part of the scientific folklore that every schoolchild knows.

“But now, this particular house of cards seems to have been demolished and a new scientific edifice is arising in its place.”[93]

---

[88] Cf. L.D. Sunderland, *Darwin’s Enigma*, pp. 88-89, 155-156.

[89] Pre-biotic soup would be an emulsion of solid, liquid and gas elements that would have conditions to generate life.

[90] Francis Crick, *Life Itself* (New York: Simon and Schuster, 1981), p. 87, *apud* L.D. Sunderland, *Darwin’s Enigma*, p. 54.

[91] L.D. Sunderland, *Darwin’s Enigma*, p. 54.

[92] F. Crick, *Life Itself*, p. 88, *apud ibid.*, pp. 54, 55.

[93] *New Scientist,* May, 13, 1982, *apud ibid.*, pp. 55-56.

§ 101 Another testimony comes from Sir Fred Hoyle, well-known English mathematician and astronomer who conceived the steady-state theory of nucleogenesis (formation of the universe). This theory holds both that the universe is expanding and that matter is being continuously created.

He published a book in 1981 titled *Evolution from Space*, in which he corrected himself regarding the origin of life. He and co-author Chandra Wickramasinghe affirmed that, although both were atheists, they had come to the conclusion that the high degree of order and specificity in the universe demanded a pre-existing intelligence similar to that of God.[94] They wrote:

"When we see … that the probability of life originating at random is so utterly minuscule as to make it absurd, it becomes sensible to think that the favorable properties of physics, on which life depends, are in every respect deliberate. … It is, therefore, almost inevitable that our own measure of intelligence must reflect higher intelligences … even to the limit of God."[95]

According to Sunderland, they came to this conclusion because of their analysis of the statistical improbability of a single cell originating in the primitive atmosphere in the supposed 4.6 billion years of Earth's history. According to their calculations, the probability of life originating by random processes was one chance in $10^{40,000}$ that is 1 in 10 to the 40,000th power, an inconceivable number.[96]

Hoyle addressed the same topic in *Nature* magazine on November 12, 1981:

"The chance that higher life forms might have emerged in this way is comparable with a chance that a tornado sweeping through a junk yard might assemble a Boeing 747 from the material therein."[97]

Many other similar testimonies of highly qualified scientists could also be cited.[98]

---

[94] Cf. L.D. Sunderland, *Darwin's Enigma*, p. 57.

[95] Fred Hoyle & Chandra Wickramasinghe, *Evolution from Space* (London: J.M. Dent and Co., 1981), pp. 141, 144, *apud* L.D. Sunderland, *Darwin's Enigma*, p. 58.

[96] Cf. L.D. Sunderland, *Darwin's Enigma*, p. 58.

[97] "Hoyle on Evolution," in *Nature*, November 12, 1981, p. 105, *apud* L.D. Sunderland, *Darwin's Enigma*, pp. 58-59.

[98] Cf. L.D. Sunderland, *Darwin's Enigma*, pp. 23, 61-62, 132, 135-136,

§ 102 Based on this overview, we can conclude that, regarding the "law" of spontaneous generation:

- The verified experiments did not produce life; they only produced amino acids and globules without life; therefore, they are not solid proofs;

- The supposition that such experiments would be applicable to the Earth's primitive atmosphere was shown to be false since more recent discoveries have revealed that there was free oxygen on our planet, which was not present in the "reducing atmosphere," the basis for the mentioned experiment; therefore, this supposition is without foundation;

- In the face of more recent discoveries, the "law" of spontaneous generation came to be considered so radically improbable that many scientists admitted that there are only two ways to explain life: Either to admit the existence of God, who created life, or to imagine that life was brought to Earth by some extra-terrestrial craft that came from another planet outside of our solar system; therefore, the "law" of spontaneous generation was abandoned;

- From this we see that these "proofs" were not correct, the hypotheses had no foundation, and the theory of spontaneous generation was abandoned; therefore, it is absurd to speak of spontaneous generation as a scientific law.

b. The law of the common ancestor

§ 103 If Evolutionism had been able to prove the law of spontaneous generation, it would have been possible to study the potentialities contained in that single living cell generated in a laboratory and test whether they could have been the source of all earthly forms of life.

The analysis of such potentialities would have furnished an important confirmation or denial of the law of the common ancestor imagined by Darwin. However, since the "law' of spontaneous generation was not proved and, judging by the testimo-

---

139-140, 149; A.N. Field, *The Evolution Hoax Exposed*, pp. 15, 82, etc; see also more recent books such as Andrew J. Petter & Laurie R. Godfrey, *Scientists Confront Creationism: Intelligent Design and Beyond* (NY: W. W. Norton & Company, Inc., 2007), John F. Ashton, *In Six Days: Why Fifty Scientists Choose to Believe in Creation* (Green Forest, AR: Master Books, 2001), Stephen C. Meyer, *Darwin's Doubt* (NY: Harper Collins, 2013).

nies we transcribed in Letter a, it seems impossible that it ever will be, we lack the elements necessary to study the law of the common ancestor from the origins.

Studying the common ancestor for Evolutionism remains contingent, therefore, on studying the supposed mechanism that would make less perfect species transmutate into more perfect species. This study generated the so-called law of gradualism, which is a fundamental piece of all evolutionary theories that we will analyze further on in Letter d.

c. The law of natural selection

§ 104 The idea of natural selection is one of the pillars upon which Darwin pretended to base his evolutionary theory. According to this concept, within each species a fight for life is established that would purify it and make it able to mutate into a more perfect species. It is essential, therefore, to know what the scientists say about the possibility of these changes in order to know whether this "law" can be taken seriously.

§ 105 Paleobiologist Steven Stanley, professor at Johns Hopkins University, is a well known proponent of the theory of punctuated equilibria, a theory in biology which proposes that, once formed, most species exhibit little net evolutionary changes for most of their geological history, but rather maintain an extended stability or state of *stasis*.

He wrote an article published in the June 1982 edition of *Johns Hopkins Magazine* titled "The New Evolution," in which he essentially denies natural selection:

"Having carefully scrutinized data from the fossil record during the past decade … I have demonstrated a biological stability for species of animals and plants that I think would have shocked Darwin. Certainly it has jolted many modern evolutionists."[99]

Stanley gives examples of various species that remained stable for millions of years.[100] Analyzing the supposed changes proposed by Darwin that would take place by the law of natural selection, the same author comments:

---

[99] Steve Stanley, "The New Evolution," *Johns Hopkins Magazine*, June 1982, *apud* L.D. Sunderland, *Darwin's Enigma*, p. 103.

[100] He lists species such as miniscule Foraminifera, mollusks, beetles, mammals, mosses and higher plants. Cf. *ibid.*

"We see nothing of these slow changes taking place, until the hand of time has marked the long lapse of ages."[101]

§ 106 Sunderland, who himself is an authority on fossil evidence, confirms the research of Stanley, affirming:

"Large volumes of fossil data now available from all over the world (not available in Darwin's time) permit us to make these generalizations:

"Once established, an average species of animal or plant will not change enough to be regarded as a new species, even after surviving for something like a hundred thousand or a million or 10 million generations. ... Something tends to prevent the wholesale restructuring of a species once it has become well established on earth."[102]

§ 107 In a 1966 symposium at the Wistar Institute in Philadelphia, in the paper titled "Inadequacies of the New-Darwinian Evolution as a Scientific Theory," known mathematician Murray Eden, calculating the possibilities of mutation in the simplest bacteria, showed that it would be impossible for even a single ordered pair of genes to be produced by DNA mutations in the bacteria *E. coli* in five billion years.

Eden calculated that "to have any reasonable chance of getting such a result, you would need a population of that organism weighing 100 trillion tons, enough to cover the entire Earth to a thickness of nearly one inch. ... This relates to the possibility of getting just one ordered pair of genes, but hundreds of genes are present in this bacterium."[103]

Applying his conclusions to the law of natural selection, the mathematician states:

"Concepts such as natural selection by the survival of the fittest are tautologous;[104] that is, they simply restate the fact that only properties of organisms which survive to produce offspring ... will appear in succeeding generations."[105]

---

[101] S. Stanley, *The New Evolution*," *apud ibid*.

[102] L.D. Sunderland, *Darwin's Enigma*, p. 104.

[103] Murray Eden, "Inadequacies of the New Darwinian Evolution as a Scientific Theory," *apud ibid*., p. 130.

[104] Tautology = a way of arguing where the presupposition of the argument is the same as the intended conclusion.

[105] M. Eden, "Inadequacies of the New Darwinian Evolution," *apud* L.D. Sunderland, *Darwin's Enigma*, p. 130.

§ 108 At the same Philadelphia Meeting, biologist George Wald refuted the thesis of Gaylord Simpson, who defended that all changes in proteins originated from adaptations. Wald presented his estimates on the necessary time for a mutation to occur in a human population:

"If you make a rough estimate … it looks as if something of the order of 10 million years is needed to establish a mutation. That is, each of these single amino acid changes appears relatively frequently in individuals as pathology; but to establish one such change as a regular characteristic in a species seems to take something of the order of 10 million years."[106]

§ 109 Let us turn now to testimonies of earlier scientists presented by Field in his 1941 work *The Evolution Hoax Exposed.*

Joseph LeConte, a respected 20th century geologist and president of the Geological Society of America, stated:

"The evidence of Geology today is that species seem to come into existence suddenly and in full perfection, remain substantially unchanged during the terms of their existence, and pass away in full perfection. Other species take their place, apparently by substitution, not by transmutation."[107]

§ 110 Other scientists, although admitting the essential stability of the species, consider that they can deteriorate and at times even become extinct for this reason.

As Prof. William Bateson said to the Congress of the American Association for the Advancement of Science in Toronto in 1921:

"When students of other sciences ask us what is now currently believed about the origin of the species, we have no clear answer to give. … The conclusion in which we were brought up, that species are a product of the summation of variations, ignored the chief attribute of species, that the product of their crosses is frequently sterile in great or less degree. Very early in the debate, Huxley[108] pointed out this grave defect in the evi-

---

[106] Moorehead and Kaplan, "Mathematical Challenges to the Neo-Darwinian Interpretation of Evolution," in *The Wistar Symposium Monograph*, n. 5 (Philadelphia: Wistar Institute Press, 1967), p. 19, *apud ibid.*, p. 131.

[107] *Cf.* W. Bell Dawson, *The Bible Confirmed by Science*, p. 75, *apud* A.N. Field, *The Evolution Hoax Exposed,* p. 25. Field quotes other statements of scientists confirming this opinion on pp. 29, 49, 78-79.

[108] Thomas Huxley was one of the principal disseminators of Evolutionism. He died in 1895, outliving Darwin by 13 years. Four years before his death, Huxley acknowledged that Evolutionism still needed

dence, but before breeding researches had been made on a large scale, no one felt the objection to be serious. Extended work might be trusted to supply the deficiency. It has not done so, and the significance of the negative evidence can no longer be denied."[109]

§ 111 In his book *A Study in Human Evolution* published at Oxford in 1922, Prof. A.M. Carr-Saunders observed:

"The course of evolution has generally been downwards. The majority of species have degenerated and become extinct or, what is perhaps worse, have gradually lost many of their functions. The ancestors of oysters and barnacles had heads. Snakes lost their limbs and penguins their power of flight. Man may just as easily lose his intelligence."[110]

§ 112 Baron Raglan, president of the anthropological division of the British Association of the Sciences, made this observation in his 1939 work, *How Came Civilization?*: "No savage society, when left to itself, has ever made the slightest progress."[111]

He observes, rather, declines in civilizations, such as the Polynesians, whose language and customs probably originated from the same race that inhabits the Pacific Islands from Hawaii to Easter Island and across New Zealand. He notes that archeological evidence shows their ancestors must have had large seagoing vessels and erected buildings of large stone. In the time since they have been known to the Europeans, however, they have only small canoes that can travel the coastline and are completely ignorant of the art of building in stone.[112]

§ 113 American anthropologist Roland B. Dixon confirms this decay visible in the anthropological evidence: "The Polynesians in their eastward drift into the Pacific lost textiles, pottery and metal-working and gave up the use of the bow."[113]

---

to be scientifically demonstrated (cf. A.N. Field, *The Evolution Hoax Exposed*, p. 14).

[109] William Bateson, in *Nature*, n. 29, 1922, *apud ibid.*, pp. 14-15.

[110] A. Carr-Saunders, *Evolution*, p. 125, *apud ibid.*, p. 100.

[111] Geoffrey Somerset, Baron of Raglan, *How Came Civilization?* 1939, pp. 56-57, *apud ibid.*, p. 86.

[112] Cf. A.N. Field, *The Evolution Hoax Exposed*, p. 86.

[113] Roland B. Dixon, *The Building of Cultures*, p. 280, *apud ibid.*, p. 86.

§ 114 Baron Raglan devotes a chapter in his work to instances of the deterioration of culture among different savage races, and he affirms that savage races are capable of being civilized by missionary effort but are incapable of civilizing themselves.[114]

§ 115 These are credible statements that uphold precisely the opposite of what is affirmed in Darwin's "law" of natural selection.

§ 116 Perhaps the most expressive proof of the unscientific aspect of this "law" comes from Darwin himself. While publicly he defended his "law," privately he admitted its lack of any foundation. In a letter to Dr. George Bentham dated May 22, 1863 – let us keep in mind that his book on the origins of the species came to light in 1859 – Darwin confessed:

"In fact, belief in natural selection must at present be grounded entirely in general considerations. … When we descend to details, we can prove that no one species has changed (i.e., we cannot prove that a single species has changed); nor can we prove that the supposed changes are beneficial, which is the groundwork of the theory. Nor can we explain why some species have changed and others have not."[115]

§ 117 Taking into consideration the proofs presented in this Letter c,[116] we see that past and contemporary scholars and scientists consistently deny that the "law" of natural selection has any scientific character. They consider its arguments to be tautological and lacking any scientific proof.

§ 118 Norman Macbeth wrote a critique of Darwinism titled *Darwin Retried: An Appeal to Reason*, reviewed and approved by renowned philosopher of science Karl Popper. Regarding natural selection, Macbeth states:

"I argued it [the law of natural selection] was a tautology in my book because it seemed to go round in a circle. It was, in effect, defining survival as due fitness and fitness as due

---

[114] Cf. *ibid.*, pp. 86-87.

[115] Charles Darwin, *Life and Letters*, iiii, 25, *apud ibid*, p. 14.

[116] In summary, these proofs are:
- The enormous improbability that there are mutations, even of the simplest order, in bacteria;
- The same high improbability that there have been mutations in man;
- Such mutations are not verifiable in the fossil record;
- Rather, there is evidence that in many species there is degradation and not evolution;
- Darwin's confession that his "law" did not come from scientific verification.

survival. I also found people like Waddington [known English evolutionist] saying it was a tautology at the Darwinian centennial in 1959 in Chicago. Nevertheless, he said it was a wonderful idea that explained everything.

§ 119 "Prof. Ronald H. Brady goes a little more deeply into it in his long articles in *Systematic Zoology* and the *Biological Journal of the Linnean Society*. ... I will not attempt to summarize Brady's view, but I think it destroys the idea of natural selection and this is certainly the opinion of many people at the American Museum of Natural History. It shoots to pieces the whole basis for the synthetic theory."[117]

§ 120 Hungarian-British author Arthur Koestler, dealing with the non-scientific nature of Darwinism, affirmed that the educational system does not adequately inform the public about the flaw in the "law" of natural selection:

"In the meantime, the educated public continues to believe that Darwin has provided all the relevant answers by the magic formula of random mutations plus natural selection – quite unaware of the fact that random mutations turned out to be irrelevant and natural selection a tautology."[118]

§ 121 Gregory Pesely is another scientist who maintains that natural selection is a tautology:

"One of the most frequent objections against the theory of natural selection is that it is a sophisticated tautology. Most evolutionary biologists seem unconcerned about the charge and only make a token effort to explain the tautology away. The remainder, such as Professors Waddington and Simpson, will simply concede the fact. For them, natural selection is a tautology which states a heretofore unrecognized relation: The fittest – defined as those who will leave the most offspring – will leave the most offspring."[119]

---

[117] Norman Macbeth, *Darwin Retried: An Appeal to Reason* (Boston: Gambit, 1971), *apud* L.D. Sunderland, *Darwin's Enigma*, pp. 34-35.

[118] Arthur Koestler, *Janus: A Summing up* (New York: Vintage Books, 1978), p. 185, *apud ibid.*, p. 32.

[119] Gregory Alan Pesely, "The Epistemological Status of Nature Selection," in *Laval Théologique et Philosophique*, vol. 38, February 1982, p. 74, *apud ibid.*, p. 36. Other declarations of scientists against the "law" of natural selection can be found in L.D. Sunderland's *Darwin's Enigma*, pp. 60, 102-103, 117, 127, 130, 132, 136, 145-146, and in A.N. Field, *The Evolution Hoax Exposed*, p. 49.

§ 122 Thus, we clearly see that the "law" of natural selection has no scientific foundation. Those who continue to believe in it do so as an act of faith, not as a consequence of scientific verification.[120]

d. The law of gradualism

§ 123 Gradualism would be another law of Evolutionism establishing its supposedly indisputable foundation as a fruit of scientific verification in four different fields:

- In Paleontology, the fossil record would make gradualism evident;
- In Anthropology, the study of the skeletons of supposed primates would reveal a chain of increasingly more evolved beings, starting from the ape and ending with man;
- In Embryology, experiments would demonstrate that the fetus passes through various phases of the evolution of life in the universe;
- In Homology, the existence of analogous organs in various beings would prove that one being is transmutating into another.

Let us analyze these different fields in which Evolutionism has found "proofs" for its theory and deduced its "laws."

d.a. Gradualism in the fossil record

§ 124 Charles Darwin gave the highest importance to the fossil record. Although in his time the record still presented gaps, he expected that with future discoveries intermediary elements would be found that would justify the gradual transmutation of one species into another. In *The Origin of Species*, he affirmed:

"The geological record is extremely imperfect and this fact will to a large extent explain why we do not find intermediary varieties, connecting together all the extinct and existing forms of life by the finest graduated steps. He who rejects these views on the nature of the geological record will rightly reject my whole theory."[121]

This excerpt translates well the importance Darwin gave to the fossil record. It further shows that he left to future discov-

---

[120] Cf. L.D. Sunderland, *Darwin's Enigma*, p. 36.

[121] Charles Darwin, *The Origin of the Species* (London: John Murray, 1902), pp. 341-342, *apud* L.D. Sunderland, *Darwin's Enigma*, p. 9.

eries the onus of demonstrating his thesis. It clearly shows that the "law" of gradualism in the fossils was not conceived as a scientific law born from experience, but as a simple hypothesis to be proved in the future.

§ 125 In his book on evolution published in 1984, Sunderland, recognized as an expert in fossils,[122] wrote about the paleontological discoveries to date:

"Now, after over 120 years of the most extensive and painstaking geological exploration of every continent and ocean bottom, the picture is infinitely more vivid and complete than it was in 1859. Formations have been discovered containing hundreds of billions of fossils, and our museums now are filled with over 250,000 different species. The availability of this profusion of hard scientific data should permit objective investigation to determine if Darwin was on the right track.

"What is the picture that the fossils have given us? Do they reveal a continuous progression connecting all organisms to a common ancestor? With every geological formation explored and every fossil classified it has become apparent that these, the only direct scientific evidences relating to the history of life, still do not provide any evidence for which Darwin so fervently longed. The gaps between major groups of organisms have been growing even wider and more undeniable. They can no longer be ignored or rationalized away with appeals to the imperfection of the fossil record."[123]

§ 126 Sunderland asked Dr. Colin Patterson, a paleontologist at Britain's Natural History Museum who defends Darwin's gradualism, why he did not include any photograph of a fossil in transition between species in his book *Evolution*. Patterson responded in a letter from which we reproduce some excerpts:

"I fully agree with your comment on the lack of direct illustration of evolutionary transitions in my book. If I knew of any, fossil or living, I would certainly have included it. You suggest that an artist should be used to visualize such transformation, but where would he get the information from? I could not, honestly, provide it, and if I were to leave it to artistic license, would that not mislead the reader? …

---

[122] Testimonies of several scholars can be read in his book on pp. 1-2, 5-6.

[123] L.D. Sunderland, *Darwin's Enigma*, p. 9.

"There is not one such fossil for which one could make a watertight argument. ... It is easy enough to make up stories of how one form gave rise to another, and to find reasons why the stages should be favored by natural selection. But such stories are not part of science, for there is no way of putting them to the test."[124]

Later, in an interview with Sunderland, Patterson confirmed this lack of fossil evidence:

"If you ask, 'What is the evidence for continuity?' you would have to say, 'There isn't any in the fossils of animals and man. The connection between them is in the mind.'"[125]

§ 127 Dr. Donald Fisher, paleontologist at the New York State Natural History Museum, also affirms definitively: "There are intermediaries within families and even within orders, but not between *phyla* [species]."[126]

§ 128 Dr. Niles Eldredge, a scientist at the American Museum of Natural History, calls the evidence for gradualism inaccurate. In an interview with the *Los Angeles Times*, he affirms:

"But no one has found any such in-between creatures. This was long chalked up to 'gaps' in the fossil records, gaps that proponents of gradualism confidently expected to fill in someday when rock strata of the proper antiquity were eventually located. But all of the fossil evidence to date has failed to turn up any such missing links, and there is a growing conviction among many scientists that these transitional forms never existed. And if this is so, then the gradualist view of evolution is an inaccurate portrayal of how life developed."[127]

§ 129 Dr. Stephen Jay Gould also rejects the hypothesis of a gradual change in the fossil record. He states:

"The fossil record is full of gaps and discontinuities, but they are all attributed to the notorious imperfection of the fossil record. The fossil record is imperfect, but I think that is not an adequate explanation ... One thing it does show that cannot be attributed to its imperfection is that most species don't change. ... They may get a little bigger or bumpier but they remain the

---

[124] Colin Patterson, letter to L.D. Sunderland, *apud ibid.*, p. 89.

[125] Colin Patterson, Interview granted to L.D. Sunderland, *apud ibid.*, p. 90.

[126] *Apud ibid.*, p. 91.

[127] George Alexander, "Alternative Theory of Evolution Considered," *Los Angeles Times*, November 19, 1978, *apud ibid.*, p. 99.

same species and that's not due to imperfection and gaps, but *stasis*. And yet this remarkable *stasis* has generally been ignored as no data. If they don't change, it's not evolution, so you don't talk about it."[128]

§ 130 In an article entitled "Conflicts between Darwinism and Paleontology," Dr. David M. Raup, a University of Chicago paleontologist, stated that the 250,000 species of plants and animals recorded and deposited in museums throughout the world did not support the gradual unfolding hoped for by Darwin.[129]

§ 131 We conclude, therefore, that there is no scientific foundation for Darwin's gradualism based upon the fossil record.

d.b. Gradualism & the primates

§ 132 Given that the fossil record encompasses those related to man, it follows that, once it is proved that there are no intermediary elements among the existent species, such evidence is also absent between the ape and man. This is the indispensable corollary of what was demonstrated above.

§ 133 However, since it is toward the supposed evolution of the ape to man that the revolutionary propaganda is primarily turned, and since this is the main "scientific" foundation to challenge the words of Genesis, let us delve more deeply into this theory.

Let us analyze the "proofs" upon which the "law" of gradualism applied to the ape-to-man hypothesis is based.

§ 134 The revolutionary saga presents this chain of primates between the ape and man by order of discovery:

- Neanderthal man – 1850;
- Java man or *Pithecanthropus erectus* – 1891-1913;
- Piltdown man or *Eoanthropus* – 1912-1933;
- Peking man or *Sinanthropus* – 1921-1929;
- Some evolutionists add the *Australopithecus* – 1924.

---

[128] Stephen Jay Gould, "Is a New and General Theory of Evolution Emerging? " Conference at Hobart and William Smith College, February 14, 1980, *apud ibid.,* p. 106.

[129] Cf. *Field Museum of Natural History Bulletin*, January 1979, vol. 50, n. 1, pp. 22-29, *apud ibid.*, p. 10.

§ 135 The criteria to classify these supposed anthropoids are principally two: the volume of the skull and the more or less erect position of the body. According to these criteria, the hypothetical evolution from the ape to man obeys this hierarchy:

- *Australopithecus*: skull capacity = 500 cm^3;
- *Pithecanthropus or* Java man: skull capacity = 900 to 950 cm^3;
- *Eoanthropus or* Piltdown man: skull capacity = 1,000 cm^3;
- *Sinanthropus pekinensis or* Peking man: skull capacity = 900 to 1,200 cm^3;
- *Homo Neanderthalensis or* Neanderthal man: skull capacity = 1,500 to 1,700 cm^3;
- *Cro-magnon* or *Homo Sapiens*: skull capacity = 1,500 or more.[130]

Obviously, to prove that there was an evolution from one species to the other, we must suppose that each species is previous to the next.

Let us analyze each of these groups bestowed with such expressive names and apparently forming such a harmonic hierarchy.

§ 136 * ***Australopithecus*** – These fossils come from an extinct genus of apes that walked erect. British evolutionist scientist Houghton Brodrick considers the thesis that members of the *Australopithecus* family are direct ancestors of man extravagant.[131*] Another scholar, I. Desmond Clark, also opposes this same thesis based on arguments of morphology and pre-historic archeology.[132*] [133]

§ 137 * ***Pithecanthropus* or Java man** – Dutch military physician Dr. Eugène Dubois travelled to the island of Java with the deliberate intent to find the lost link between the ape and man.

---

[130] Cf. Atanásio Aubertin, “A Revolução, a Filogênese Humana e o Pe. Teilhard de Chardin (I),” *Catolicismo*, Campos, May 1963; cf. A.N. Field, *The Evolution Hoax Exposed*, pp. 33-35. We note that these measurements vary from author to author, which is understandable, given the extreme fluidity of the “scientific” data of these discoveries.

[131*] Cf. *El Hombre Pré-Histórico*, Fondo de Cultura Economica, 1955.

[132*] Cf. *IDC – Scientific American*, vol. 199, n.1, 1958.

[133] Cf. A. Aubertin, “A Revolução, a Filogênese Humana e o Pe. Teilhard de Chardin (III),” *Catolicismo*, September 1963.

In September 1891, Dubois discovered a molar on the bank of the Solo River. One month later, he discovered a skullcap about a yard from the tooth. In August of the following year he discovered a femur (thighbone) about 17 yards from the skullcap, and a second tooth some five yards from the femur. Putting this all together, he considered his specimen was a transition from ape to human and named it *Pithecanthropus erectus* (upright ape-man).

§ 138 Studies made by the Smithsonian Institution and published in 1913 revealed that the skullcap had been eroded by water, signifying that it had been washed up onto the river bank; the other bones, however, were not eroded, but were natural fossils on that site.[134]

§ 139 In the report on his discoveries that he made in 1896 to the Berlin Anthropological Society, Dr. Dubois revealed that, along with those bones, he had found fossil remains of an elephant and a small deer and, further on, the remains of a buffalo, antelope, ox, pig, rhinoceros and hyena. In his book *Antiquity of Man,* Sir Arthur Keith states that he and Dr. Dubois removed from that site the fossils of 27 different species of mammals between the years 1891 and 1894. A two-year German expedition (1907-1908) led by Mrs. Lenore M. Selenka unearthed an enormous quantity of miscellaneous fossils at that same site.[135]

§ 140 Notwithstanding the presence in the same dig of a large quantity of fossils coming from a variety of animals, with the four reported elements – a skullcap, two teeth and a femur – Dr. Dubois composed the famous *Pithecanthropus* or Java man, which became a principal piece of "demonstration" for the evolution of man from the ape. The evolutionary propaganda did not spare eulogies for the new "scientific" discovery, soon adopted by the media and introduced into school curricula. With this, the "demonstration" of the hypothesis of Darwin took flight…

§ 141 Nonetheless, after the *Pithecanthropus* had become generally accepted as "science," Dubois himself confessed that, after a long anthropological study of the bones of the *Pithecanthropus* and other material in his possession from the same site that had not been previously publicized, he had come to the conclusion that "we are involved here with a gigantic ape."[136]

---

[134] Cf. A.N. Field, *The Evolution Hoax Exposed*, pp. 33-34.

[135] Cf. *ibid.*

[136] *Apud ibid.*, p. 36.

§ 142 Regarding Dubois' new conclusion, Field offers us this decisive information:

"In making this announcement in its February 26, 1938 issue, *Nature* flatly refused to yield up Java man as evolution's prize exhibit. Dr. Dubois's new conclusions about his fossils, it said, had been received 'with respect, but not with general acceptance and, in the light of the new evidence, must be regarded as definitively disproved.'"[137]

§ 143 Thus, like the *Australopithecus,* the *Pithecanthropus* was a fraud,[138] being nothing more than a simple ape.

§ 144 * ***Eoanthropus* or Piltdown man** – In 1908 Charles Dawson, a British solicitor and amateur paleontologist, discovered in Sussex Downs nine fragments of skull bones and half of a chimpanzee-like jawbone. Later, Dr. Arthur Smith Woodward from the British Museum and Fr. Pierre Teilhard de Chardin, who had received some training in paleontology, joined the excavation.[139]

The bones were pieced together, filled with plaster to form a skull and presented to the scientific community at a sensational meeting of the Geological Society in London on December 18, 1912. The Piltdown man was born, thus, in an atmosphere of triumph; this translated later into a monument at the Piltdown site dedicated to Mr. Charles Dawson and the elevation of Smith Woodward to the presidency of the Geological Society; soon after the latter was knighted and received the title of Sir.[140]

§ 145 Despite these honors, a discussion soon opened in scientific milieus about the authenticity of the construction presented as the Piltdown man. Then, it came to light that, along with the

---

[137] *Apud ibid.*

[138] We leave aside the arguments that affirm the skullcap and femur found by Dubois were human and that only the molar belonged to an ape. If this were true, we would still be facing a fraud since Dubois would have presented a deceptive composition of human and ape bones as an intermediary hominoid. This is what some scholars maintain, as, for example, O. Fribaut and A. Dubois, "La Question de l'Homme Fossile" in *La Pensée Catholique*, n. 7, 1948, *apud* A. Aubertin, "A Revolução, a Filogênese Humana e o Pe. Teilhard de Chardin (I); A.N. Field, *The Evolution Hoax Exposed*, pp. 33-36.

[139] Cf. A.N. Field, *The Evolution Hoax Exposed,* p. 36.

[140] Cf. *ibid*, pp. 36, 37.

skullcap and jawbone, other fossils had been found at that site: the teeth of a mastodon, a hippopotamus and a beaver, as well as the femur of an elephant that had been chiseled for use as a tool.[141]

§ 146

Further investigations made it clear that the Piltdown man was a fraud. An article published in *The New York Times* on November 21, 1953, categorically stated: "Part of the skull of the Piltdown man, one of the most famous fossil skulls in the world, has been declared a hoax by authorities at the British Natural History Museum."[142]

Moreover, a group of British researchers, including names such as Sir W. Le Grou Clark, Oakeley, Weiner, Claringball, Hey and de Vries, demonstrated that everything in the discovery of the Piltdown man was fraudulent: The chimpanzee jaw was added to the human head and, then, both were immersed in iron sulfate to make it appear ancient. Although some scientists thought the head was older and the jaw more recent, carbon-14 dating[143*] revealed that the "pre-historic" skull of the supposed Piltdown man was only 600 years old and the jawbone somewhat younger.[144]

§ 147

* ***Sinanthropus Pekinensis* or Peking man** – Austrian paleontologist Otto Zdansky, searching in an excavation site in Chou K'ou-tien (Zhoukoudian) near Peking, discovered what appeared to be a fossilized human molar in 1922. In 1926 Swedish geologist Johann Gunnar Anderson returned to the site and announced the discovery of two more molars.

Another Swedish paleontologist, Anders Birger Bohlin, discovered another tooth in 1927 and published his analysis in *Nature* journal, identifying his find as belonging to a whole new species and genus and baptizing the hypothetical owner of the teeth with the name *Homo Pekinensis* or *Sinanthropus Pekinensis*. The excavations continued – financed by the Rockefeller Foundation – and in 1928 a lower jaw, several more teeth and some skull fragments were added to the ensemble.

In 1929, Fr. Teilhard de Chardin joined the excavation team and was present when the smooth dome of a second skull

---

[141] Cf. *ibid*, p. 37.

[142] Cf. *ibid*, note from the editor.

[143*] H. de Vries & H.P. Oakley, *Nature*, vol. 184, 1959, p. 224.

[144] Cf. A. Aubertin, "A Evolução das Espécies: Apriorismos e Confissões Gnósticas," *Catolicismo*, January, 1962.

was found. New discoveries were made, and by 1937 there were already five almost complete skulls, dozens of complete jaws and many isolated teeth fragments discovered at the site.[145]

§ 148 In the September 27, 1930, issue of *Nature* magazine, internationally known geologist George B. Barbour, who was involved with the discoveries of the Peking man, revealed that at that same dig, the fossils of 50 different types of mammals, as well as frogs, snakes, turtles and birds had been found.[146]

It is curious to note that the bases of all the skulls found had incisions on the occipital, which suggests that those individuals suffered a violent death. This discovery, in addition to various tools found at the same site, led French scientist Marcellin Boulez to opine that these skulls were hunting trophies brought to Chou K'ou-tien by men who lived long ago.[147]

§ 149 Many scientists were of the opinion that the Peking man was a composition similar to that of the Java man.[148]

The case was still being examined when the fossils were packed into large crates in 1941 during World War II and loaded onto a US Marine vessel bound for China. From there they were sent by ship to the American Museum of Natural History in New York, but the fossils vanished en route, leaving no trace.[149]

§ 150 We see, therefore, that the least we can say is that there is nothing scientifically proven about the Peking man.

§ 151 * **Neanderthal man** – When the first of the Neanderthal skulls was found in 1856 near the Neander Valley in Germany, the discovery was hailed as a proof in favor of Evolutionism. Anthropologist Marcellin Boulez spread the idea that the Neanderthal man, a supposed separate species and precursor to man, walked with bent knees, stooped over like gorillas.

Further, the skull's *foramen magnum* – the large hole where the head attaches to the spinal column – was different from the one found in modern human skulls, which led to ana-

---

[145] *Ibid.*

[146] A.N. Field, *The Evolution Hoax Exposed*, p. 38.

[147] Cf. A. Aubertin, "A Revolução, a Filogênese Humana e o Pe. Teilhard de Chardin (II)," *Catolicismo*, July 1963.

[148] Cf. A.N. Field, *The Evolution Hoax Exposed*, p. 37-38; A. Albertin, "A Revolução, a Filogênese Humana," *ibid.*

[149] Cf. A. Aubertin, "A Revolução, a Filogênese Humana," *ibid.*

tomical conclusions favoring the idea that the Neanderthal man was an intermediate species between the ape and man. Scientific and pseudo-scientific literature presented the poor Neanderthal as a hairy, stooped over ape-man with a protruding jaw and flat nose.

§ 152 Today, that image has fallen into complete discredit in scientific milieus. Skulls found later at that same site presented the *foramen magnum* in a position identical to modern human skulls, sweeping aside the fantasy that the Neanderthal was stooped like a gorilla.

§ 153 Further, it was demonstrated that the skull configuration of the Neanderthal is not very different from that of primitive inhabitants of Africa. Alan Houghton Brodrick, author of numerous works on man's supposed pre-history, notes that some time ago a skull was found in Norway with typical Neanderthal characteristics. He proposesd that some dysfunction of the pituitary gland produces Neanderthal skulls.[150]

§ 154 More recent scientific studies made on the multiple fossils revealed that the Neanderthal bones were found to have modern human DNA. Furthermore, serious study of the culture of the Neanderthals showed they had advanced stone tools, buried their dead and made works of art. [151] These discoveries put to rest the hypothesis that the Neanderthal man was a brute ape-man, an intermediary step in the evolutionary process from the ape to man.

§ 155 We see, therefore, that the Neanderthal man was a simple man and not a link in the evolutionary transition of the ape to man.

§ 156 Having analyzed these cases in the purported chain of apes leading to man, we conclude that the various fossil constructions commonly presented as demonstrative of evolutionary gradualism are either imaginary creations or frauds, lacking any serious scientific evidence or support.

§ 157 Consequently, present day scientists of the caliber of Dr. David Plebian, one of the great experts in the field of Paleoanthropology (the study of human fossils), affirm that not even one specimen exists that justifies evolutionary gradualism from the ape to man. Although an evolutionist himself, he has repeated

---

[150] *Ibid.*

[151] Jack Cuozzo, *Buried Alive: The Startling Truth about Neanderthal Man* (Green Forest, AR: 2008), pp. 94, 98, 250.

many times: “Our theories have clearly reflected our current ideologies instead of actual data. Too often they have reflected only what we expected of them.”[152]

d.c. Gradualism & embryology

§ 158 Embryology, *aka* the Biogenetic Law, constitutes another foundation of Evolutionism as presented to the public. In effect, Darwin and, after him, Ernst Haeckel imagined that the embryos of all animal species at the beginning of gestation are similar, indicating a common ancestor of all animals.

Haeckel believed that, over the course of time, evolution added new stages in the pre-natal life to produce new life forms. Thus, embryonic development was actually a record of evolutionary history. The single cell corresponded to amoeba-like ancestors, developing eventually into a sea squirt, a fish, and so on. Haeckel coined a name for the process – “the biogenetic law” – as well as a summary motto: “Ontogeny recapitulates phylogeny.” Thus, the law of gradualism would be proved by this scientific verification.

§ 159 Let us look at an overview presented by Sunderland on the topic, followed by the assessments of credited scientists.

“Although Darwin recognized that the fossil record did not give any support for the theory of evolution, he was most impressed by what he thought was the best evidence for a common ancestry of all life, namely, embryological development. He said that it was ‘second to none in importance.’ The hypothesis that, during embryological development, higher organisms like man relived their evolutionary history was popularized by Ernest Haeckel in Germany at about the time Darwinism was gaining acceptance.

“The concept, however, was originated in 1811 by Johann Meckler before scientists took the theory of evolution seriously. He thought that embryonic stages of development in higher forms of life paralleled the adult stages of lower forms. Fifteen years later Karl von Baer argued that it was the embryonic stages of lower forms rather than the adult stages that were paralleled by higher forms.

“Then, in 1864, Fritz Muller proposed that the higher forms added stages to the embryonic stages passed through by

[152] Cf. L.D. Sunderland, *Darwin’s Enigma*, p. 86; similar statements can be found on pp. 87-93; cf. A.N. Field, *The Evolution Hoax Exposed*, pp. 39-42, 89.

the lower forms in their development. Ernest Haeckel, in 1866, simply combined the ideas of others and popularized the theory which he called 'the fundamental biogenetic law.'

"Haeckel, demonstrating his considerable artistic skills, made wood carvings which indicate that the embryos of a fish, tortoise, hare, pig, monkey and man had similar appearances at various stages. He was one of Charles Darwin's staunchest supporters and claimed that his discoveries validated the theory that all life had come from a common ancestor."[153]

§ 160 Already by the turn of the [20th] century, scientists had discovered many cases that defied Haeckel's so-called law. Regarding evolutionary embryology, University of Chicago paleontologist Dr. David Raup affirms:

"The biogenetic law – embryologic recapitulation – I think, was debunked back in the 1920s by embryologists."[154]

§ 161 Two other scientists offer confirmation:

"Famous anthropologist Prof. Ashley Montagu, in a debate with Dr. Duane Gish on April 12, 1980, at Princeton University, verified Dr. Raup's claim that the 'law' had been debunked in the 1920s. First, Dr. Gish commented on the harmful effects of evolution theory on research:

"'Years and years of embryological research were essentially wasted because people, convinced of the theory of evolution and that embryos recapitulated their evolutionary ancestry, spent much of their time in embryological research trying to develop phylogenies based on data of embryology. As I mentioned earlier, embryologists have abandoned the theory of embryological recapitulation. They don't believe it. They know it is not true. …'

"In response, Dr. Montagu stated: 'The theory of recapitulation was destroyed in 1922 by Prof. Walter Garstang in a famous paper; since then no respectable biologist has ever used the theory of recapitulation …'

"Dr. Gish made a further comment: 'Unfortunately, as Dr. Montagu said, it is a thoroughly discredited theory, but it is still taught in most biology books and most universities and schools as evidence for evolution.'"[155]

---

[153] L.D. Sunderland, *Darwin's Enigma*, p. 118.

[154] *Apud ibid.*, p. 119.

[155] *Ibid.*, pp. 119-120.

§ 162 In the October 1979 issue of *Parent's Magazine*, which contains photos of the various stages of the human embryo, the author observes:

"Since the human embryo has been photographed at every stage of development, it is now known to be specifically human in every stage."[156]

Such a photographic verification has put to rest the pseudo-scientific suppositions of embryologic recapitulation.

§ 163 Sunderland synthesizes the "scientific" position of Haeckel, the greatest champion of the Biogenetic Law:

"Haeckel forged some of his drawings of embryos to make them appear in accord with his theory and used the same sketches to represent several different animals. He was even accused of altering drawings of embryos made by others. For his forgery, he was convicted by a German court. His forgeries were brought to the attention of the public in 1911 in a book called *Haeckel's Frauds and Forgeries*."[157]

§ 164 Since Haeckel's theory is not supported by any scientific evidence, it can only be accepted as an act of faith. The renowned British historian Charles Singer comments on this "religion" in his book *A History of Biology*:

"His [Haeckel's] faults are not hard to see. For a generation and more he purveyed to the semi-educated public a system of the crudest philosophy – if a mass of contradictions can be called by this name. He founded something that wore the habiliments of a religion, of which he was at once the high priest and the congregation."[158]

d.d. Gradualism & homology

§ 165 Homology – the similarity of organs among various living beings – is another discipline that served as "proof" for Evolutionism. Evolutionists suppose that the existence of homologue structures indicates that all beings proceed from a common ancestor. Parallel to this proposition is the notion of gradualism, since it is supposed that this or that living being, as it passes

---

[156] *Apud ibid.*, p. 122.

[157] *Ibid.*, p. 120.

[158] Charles Singer, *A History of Biology* (London: Abelard-Schuman, 1931), p. 487, *apud ibid.*, p. 121.

from an inferior stage to a superior one in the filo-genetic tree, would leave a print, common to the various phases of evolution.

§ 166 Sunderland comments on this theory: "Certainly, similarities in organisms can indicate closeness of relationship, but this is not a dependable guide, because there are many cases of close similarity that could not be due to inheritance from a recent common ancestor. If similarities show evolutionary relationship, then dissimilarities should conversely show lack of relationship."[159]

The author continues: "The following structures are very similar to those of humans: the octopus eye, pig heart, Pekingese dog's face, milk of the ass and the *pronto quadrates* muscle of the Japanese salamander. When the concentration of red blood cells is considered, man is more similar to frogs, fish and birds than to sheep. Do these homologies indicate close evolutionary relationships? Obviously not. There could hardly be two organisms further apart on the assumed evolutionary tree than the octopus and man."[160]

§ 167 Today's evolutionists themselves have left aside the imaginary proofs of homology. This is the case, for example of the preeminent British scientist Gavin de Beer, who, in his book *Homology, an Unsolved Problem* (1971), declares:

"It is now clear that the pride with which it was assumed that the inheritance of homologous structures from a common ancestor explained homology was misplaced; for such inheritance cannot be ascribed to identity of genes. The attempt to find homologous genes has been given up as hopeless…"[161]

§ 168 On the question of the genetic dissimilarity in the pretended proof of homology, Sunderland asks:

"Since evolution is supposed to be a change in the genes which changes the structures that they control, how could the structures remain virtually unchanged while the genes that control them changed completely? William Fix quoted Randall, who described the situation very clearly:

"'The older text-books on evolution make much of the idea of homology, pointing out the obvious resemblances between skeletons of the limbs of different animals. Thus the *pent*

---

[159] L.D. Sunderland, *Darwin's Enigma*, p. 122.

[160] *Ibid.*, p. 123.

[161] Gavin de Beer, *Homology, An Unsolved Problem* (Oxford: Oxford University Press, 1971), *apud ibid.*, pp. 123-124.

dactyl limb pattern is found in the arm of a man, the wing of a bird and the flipper of a whale, and this is held to indicate their common origin. Now, if these various structures were transmitted by the same gene-complex, varied from time to time by mutations and acted upon by environmental selections, the theory would make good sense. Unfortunately, this is not the case. Homologous organs are now known to be produced by totally different gene complexes in the different species. The concept of homology in terms of similar genes handed on from a common ancestor has broken down.'"[162]

§ 169 We see, thus, that also in the realm of homology no scientific proof was found in favor of the evolutionary theory.

§ 170 Throughout this Letter C we analyzed the "laws" and "proofs" presented by Evolutionism in favor of its theory. We verified that the scientific milieus do not consider it to be a theory with scientific credibility. This is affirmed not only by those who are against Evolutionism but also by those who are evolutionists themselves. The latter consider Evolutionism to be a philosophical or religious proposition, but not scientific.

D. Subsidiary Theories

§ 171 For our critique of Evolutionism to be complete, it is necessary to dedicate some space to its subsidiary theories. In effect, such theories, while admitting the failure of Darwinism, try to save Evolutionism by distancing it from the non-scientific conceptions of Darwin. This could lead to the supposition that these new theories enjoy great prestige in the scientific milieu and have overcome the insurmountable obstacles in Darwinism.

It is important, therefore, to update the picture of Evolutionism and to show that the subsidiary theories born from it also do not enjoy support in highly considered scientific circles.

a. Theory of punctuated equilibria

§ 172 The nucleus of the theory of punctuated equilibria is the affirmation that the evolutionary process develops by sudden jumps and not gradually, as Darwin imagined. This hypothesis

---

[162] William Fix, *The Bone Peddlers* (New York: Macmillan Publishing Company, 1984), p. 189, *apud ibid.*, p. 124.

has the advantage of avoiding the insuperable obstacle of the lack of any evidence in the fossil record, which clearly demonstrates that there was no gradualism.

§ 173 The notion of evolution by jumps had already been proposed by Hugh de Vries,[163] a pioneer in Genetics who in 1900 postulated that evolution occurred through large scale mutations vs. Darwinian gradualism. Later, in the 1930s, others, such as German paleontologist Otto Schindewolf, also defended sudden evolutionary change by macro-mutations.

§ 174 In the 1940s a famous American geneticist, Dr. Richard Goldschmidt, invented the hopeful monster theory, according to which the individuals in a particular species born with defects – the monsters – would be an expression that evolution would be on the brink of a transmutation through a jump into another higher and nobler species.

Goldschmidt's monster theory was widely criticized and even ridiculed when first publicized. It was quickly dismissed because at that time Simpson, Mayr and Dobzhansky were launching the well-publicized and promoted Neo-Darwinism.

§ 175 By the '50s and '60s, however, the creationist movement had demonstrated the lack of any evidence for the transition of one species to another in the fossils and in the living organisms. For this reason, Evolutionism needed another theory to save it from the checkmate it was facing. In 1972 American scientists Dr. Niles Eldredge and Dr. Stephen Jay Gould stepped into the picture and elaborated the theory of punctuated equilibria.

§ 176 In an article in *Discover* magazine of May 1981, Gould declared:

"In 1972 my colleague Niles Eldredge and I developed the theory of punctuated equilibria. We argued that two outstanding facts of the fossil record – geologically 'sudden' origin of new species and failure to change thereafter (*stasis*) – reflect the predictions of this new evolutionary theory, not the imperfections of the fossil record."[164]

---

[163] The data in these two paragraphs summarize Sunderland's presentation in his work *Darwin's Enigma,* pp. 97-99.

[164] Stephen J. Gould, "Evolution as Fact and Theory," *Discover*, May 1981, p. 36, *apud* L.D. Sunderland, *Darwin's Enigma*, pp. 98-99.

§ 177 Let us see what other scientists say about this theory, which Gould himself called the "return of the hopeful monster,"[165] the new-look of Evolutionism applauded by media organs as a scientific success.[166]

§ 178 Dr. Colin Patterson, paleontologist of the British Natural Science Museum and author of a general textbook on evolution, makes this assessment of the theory of punctuated equilibria:

"Well, it seems to me that they have accepted that the fossil record doesn't give them the support they would value, so they searched around to find another model and found one. .... When you haven't got the evidence, you make up a story that will fit the lack of evidence."[167]

§ 179 Dr. David Raup, curator and Dean of Science at the Field Museum of Natural History in Chicago and author of the book *Revolution and Evolution*, gave this opinion about the theories of the hopeful monsters and of punctuated equilibria:

"All the authors of the Neo-Darwinism theory, which they formulated back in the '30s and '40s, are losing their influence. They are getting old and dying. I predict that that whole concept will be thrown out in the next 10 years and a new theory will be devised to takes its place."[168]

§ 180 Dr. Norman Macbeth, who met with 160 other scientists in Chicago in 1980 to discuss macro-evolution, was asked if most of the participants supported some sort of punctuated equilibria, as *Newsweek* magazine had reported.

He responded: "The impression I got from two or three people who attended it was one of a spectacular bankruptcy. They had no theory whatsoever to explain macro-evolution. It is still in the condition it was in Goldschmidt's time, with Gould

---

[165] In the June-July 1977 issue of *Natural History*, Gould has an article titled "The Return of Hopeful Monsters" in which he revisits Goldschmidt's theory and attempts to dust it off.

[166] For example, *O Estado de S. Paulo* dedicated a full page of its November 26, 1989 issue to promote Dr. Gould, who was presented by the newspaper as "one of the most brilliant successors of English naturalist Charles Darwin." Gould went to Brazil for the launching of his book *The Panda's Thumb: More Reflections in Natural History.*

[167] *Apud* L.D. Sunderland, *Darwin's Enigma*, p. 100.

[168] *Apud ibid.*

and others now recognizing it. They have nothing to offer except the faint hope that in epigenesis[169] they may someday find something."[170]

§ 181 These opinions and others allow Sunderland to expose the scientific embarrassment of the defenders of punctuated equilibria:

"The theory of punctuated equilibria is causing much turmoil among evolutionists. They know that there is no actual mechanism that would explain rapid jumps from one species to another, and yet they also know the fossil record does not support gradualism. They are left on the horns of a dilemma."[171]

b. Theory of the panspermia

§ 182 The theory that life originated external to earth is the panspermia or "seeding" hypothesis. The term panspermia means "seeds everywhere."

§ 183 One version of the panspermia hypothesis maintains that suitable spores, chemicals and bacteria brought life from passing comets. In 1974 Fred Hoyle and Chandra Wickramasinghe argued that life on earth originated in a microbe invasion from outer space that began as a result of the impact of a comet. This view proved to be too outlandish for the scientific community and the hypothesis was discredited.[172]

§ 184 In 1981, Nobel Prize winner Dr. Francis Crick, who co-discovered DNA, proposed a theory of Directed Panspermia to account for the origin of life on earth. Crick speculated that billions of years ago there was already an advanced civilization in our galaxy. This extra-terrestrial civilization, he proposed, discovered potentially habitable zones that they seeded with life, sending bacteria by means of directed space probes.[173]

---

[169] Epigenesis is the biological theory according to which plants and animals develop from a structureless germ cell into a new creation through a sequence of steps in which cells differentiate and organs form. This occurs through the action of outside influences over the protoplasm.

[170] *Apud* L.D. Sunderland, *Darwin's Enigma*, p. 102.

[171] L.D. Sunderland, *Darwin's Enigma*, p. 104.

[172] David Lamb, *The Search for Extra-Terrestrial Intelligence: A Philosophical Inquiry* (NY: Routledge, 2001), pp. 81-82.

[173] *Ibid.*, pp. 83-84; we have already mentioned this in § 97 of this Chapter.

§ 185 As science journalist David Lamb points out, philosophically the panspermia hypothesis is a weak explanation, as it does not address the question of where life originated in the first place, but only moves it back.[174]

§ 186 It is quite obvious that scientifically this hypothesis lacks a basis since human knowledge – despite the inter-planetary flights that have been made – cannot make generalizations about an origin of life that lies outside our solar system. The theory can only be posed today as a speculation.

§ 187 For this reason, the theory of the panspermia was not well accepted in the scientific milieus. Sunderland points out that, in view of Dr. Crick's prestige in scientific milieus, "his acceptance of the panspermia theory has caused great consternation in the established scientific community."[175]

*

§ 188 As we close this Item 5, after having analyzed the modern notion of science, the "laws" and "proofs" of Evolutionism in its classical version of Darwinism as well as in its remodeled form of Neo-Darwinism, we can affirm with certainty that Evolutionism cannot pretend to be scientific. It cannot do so according to the definition of science presented by Popper; it also cannot do so in the general sense defended by Positivism; and, with all the more reason, it cannot be considered science in the Catholic sense, as taught by St. Thomas Aquinas.

§ 189 Nothing about Evolutionism has been scientifically proved. Conversely, the opposite of what it affirms was proved. For this reason, growing numbers of scientists today consider Evolutionism a baseless proposition. They deem Evolutionism would be better called a philosophy or a religion since, in their view, in these fields no scientific demonstration is needed to believe their tenets.

§ 190 French writer André Frossard ironically compares the two conceptions about the origin of life – Creationism and Evolutionism – and concludes that the latter is "an admirable fantasy, much superior to the naïveté of Sacred History, which has only one original miracle, while Scientificism [or Evolutionism] offers us a miracle every millisecond, starting from the origin of time."[176]

---

174 *Ibid.*, p. 82

175 L.D. Sunderland, *Darwin's Enigma*, p. 55.

176 *Apud* Gastone Lambertini, "Quelli Errori Consueti del Neo-Evoluzionism," *L'Osservatore Romano*, August 19, 1989, p. 3.

6. Progressivism, the Scientific Hoax of Evolutionism & Immanentism

§ 191 Given that Evolutionism lacks scientific proof, how does Progressivism accommodate it so readily? For the progressivists declared that, by an imperative of science, the Church must change her interpretation of Genesis. Now that it is demonstrated that Evolutionism is not scientific, will the progressivists return to the path of traditional doctrine?

§ 192 It is naive to think that Progressivism will embrace traditional exegesis and Thomism because Evolutionism is unscientific. The myth of Evolutionism is a tool that has served progressivists well; they used it as a battering ram to break down the gates of exegesis and dogma. When these gates have been totally destroyed, their aim will be achieved and they will have no more need for a battering ram. Progressivism will continue its advance in the conquest of the city – the Catholic Church – with or without Evolutionism.

§ 193 Undoubtedly, if the myth continues, the situation is better for the progressivists. It gives them the appearance of sincerity. Insofar as the myth disappears, however, they will invent other pretexts to continue their attack. They will never stop defending their evolutionary philosophy and theology.

§ 194 The most expressive defender of this theological and philosophical Evolutionism is Teilhard de Chardin, as we have seen in many places. Also Rahner,[177] von Balthasar, Ratzinger, Congar, Chenu, Schillebeeckx and many others,[178] defend evolution in the cosmos and in the essence of dogmatic truth.

§ 195 Once the progressivist theory of evolution is shown to have no basis in empirical science, as it pretends, it reveals itself to be nothing but a philosophical cosmo-vision and a religious belief of an immanentist nature, completely opposed to Thomist Philosophy and Catholic Doctrine. We see, then, that we are facing a confrontation of faith against Faith, of church against Church.

* * *

---

[177] Cf. Vol. VI, *Inveniet Fidem?,* Chap. III §§ 209-221.

[178] Cf. *ibid.*, Chap. IV §§ 35-93.

CHAPTER III

EVOLUTION, 'DOGMA' OF PROGRESSIVIST RELIGION, NEW FOUNDATION OF PHILOSOPHY & THEOLOGY

§ 1 Since they lack any scientific foundation, the progressivists adopt evolution as a "dogma." In our assessment, it is one of the central "dogmas" of the Conciliar Religion. From it very important consequences follow.

Progressivist theologians readily present evolution as the nucleus of their new religion and the vehicle to modify Catholic Philosophy and Theology.

1. The 'Sanctity' of Evolution

§ 2 Fr. Teilhard de Chardin hails evolution with a true religious fervor:

"Evolution is holy," he affirms.[1]

§ 3 In his "Hymn of the Universe," he makes a litany in honor of the sanctity of matter in its stages of evolution:

"Blessed be you, mighty matter, irresistible evolution, ever nascent reality; you who, by constantly shattering our mental limits, obliges us to go ever further in our pursuit of the truth.

"Blessed be you, universal matter, unlimited duration. Ether without frontiers, … you who, by overflowing and dissolving our narrow standards or measurement, reveals to us the dimensions of God.

"Blessed be you, impenetrable matter, you who one day, by dissociating yourself from us, will take us forcibly into the very heart of that which exists. …

"I bless you, matter, and I praise you, not as the pontiffs of science or the preachers of virtue depict you – reduced to a mass of brute forces or low appetites – but as you appear today, in your totality and your truth.

"I praise you, inexhaustible capacity of being and transformation wherein the chosen substance germinates and grows.

---

[1] J.M. Morthier, *Avec Teilhard de Chardin – Vue Ardentes* (Paris: Seuil, 1967), p. 22.

"I praise you, universal power which brings together and unites, through which the multitudinous monads are bound together and in which they all converge on the path of the Spirit.

"I praise you, harmonious summation of souls, the pure crystal from which the new Jerusalem is fashioned.

"I praise you, divine milieu, charged with creative power, ocean stirred by the Spirit, hard clay animated by the Incarnate Word. …

"If we are ever to reach you, matter, we must, having first established contact with the totality of all that moves here below, come little by little to feel that the particular forms of everything we have laid hold on are fading away in our hands, until finally we face the sole essence of all existences and all unions.

"If we are ever to possess you, after having taken you rapturously in our arms, we must go on to sublimate you through sorrow.

"You reign, O matter, in those serene heights where Saints thought to avoid you – but where your flesh is so transparent and agile as to be no longer distinguishable from spirit.

"Raise me up, O matter!, to those heights through struggle, separation and death; raise me up to that place where, at long last, it will be possible to chastely embrace the universe."[2]

This is a good example demonstrating how the progressivists consider evolution as something holy and divine.

2. The 'Dogmatic' Character of Evolution

§ 4

Besides conceiving evolution as divine and holy, its dogmatic aspect for the progressivists appears in the following affirmation by Teilhard:

"Like everything in a universe where time has installed itself … as a fourth dimension, **life is, and can only be, an element of an evolving nature and dimensions**. Physically and historically, life corresponds to specific function X, which defines the position of every living thing in space, duration and form. **This is the fundamental fact that requires an explanation, but the evidence of it is, from now on, above all verification and also beyond any further refutation by experience**.

---

[2] P. Teilhard de Chardin, *Le Coeur de la Matière* (Paris: Seuil, 1976), pp. 89-91.

"In this general perspective, we can say that **the question of 'transformism'** [the controversy over scientific evolution] no longer exists. It **has been definitively settled. From now on, to shake our conviction of the reality of a Biosphere, we would have to undermine the entire structure of the world and uproot the tree of life.**"[3]

§ 5 Again, he explains his unshakeable belief in evolution:

"**Evolutionism has ceased to be a hypothesis a long time ago** – insofar as it merely expresses that it is experimentally impossible for us to perceive any being (living or non-living) unless it is engaged in a time-space series – **and has become a dimensional condition that all hypotheses in physics and biology must henceforth satisfy**. Currently, biologists and paleontologists still argue about modalities – and principally about the mechanisms – of life's transformations, about the preponderance of Neo-Darwinian chance or the Neo-Lamarckian play of invention in the appearance of new characteristics.

"But, all the scholars are now in agreement about the general and fundamental fact of the existence of an organic evolution regarding life considered globally, as well as in each living being taken individually. This is so for the simple reason that they could not be scientists if they thought otherwise."[4]

§ 6 Further on, he expresses the same "dogmatic" conviction:

"**Is evolution a theory, a system, a hypothesis? … Absolutely not. It is much more than this; it is, from now on, a general condition that all theories, hypotheses and systems must obey and satisfy in order to be conceivable and true. A light that illuminates all facts,** a curvature that is followed by all traits, **behold this is what evolution is**. …

"**What makes and classifies a man as modern** (and, in this sense, countless of our contemporaries are still not modern) **is to have become capable of seeing, not only in space or time, but in duration … It is also to become incapable of seeing nothing, nothing in another way, departing from himself**."[5]

For Teilhard, therefore, evolution is something "dogmatic" that must be believed independent of demonstrations.

---

[3] P. Teilhard de Chardin, *O Fenômeno Humano* (Porto: Tavares Martins, 1970), p. 140.

[4] *Ibid.*

[5] *Ibid.*, pp. 234-235.

§ 7 Joseph Ratzinger seems to have the same opinion when he presents evolution as something "intrinsically believable":

"The fixed grafted limits of the essences disappear, the mobility of the real is stressed, **the doctrine of evolution becomes**, so to speak, **intrinsically believable** and achievable by man. ...

"**Today we witness the failure of everything that exists; we witness a reality that is not stability but evolution.**"[6]

§ 8 Karl Rahner also considers evolution as a "dogma":

"**Our departure point is the present day evolutionary image of the world, supposing it to be true rather than explaining it.**"[7]

These statements prove the importance Progressivism gives to the "dogma" of evolution.

3. The 'Dogma' of Evolution & the New Ontology

§ 9 The "dogma" of evolution is assumed by Rahner as the basis to enunciate a supposed change in the order of being itself, which he terms "active self-transcendence":

"If there is truly a future – which is not only a fact of experience, but a fundamental axiom of theology itself, otherwise the freedom, responsibility and accomplishments of man by his responsible actions would not make any sense – then, this future cannot be understood ... as a mere *altero*-future in which a reality becomes purely and simply another; rather, it must be understood as a *plus*-future ... as a realization of a greater plenitude of being.

"This '*plus,*' however, cannot be imagined as simply added to that which existed up to now, but must be, on one hand, what has been done by what existed and, on the other hand, its ontological increase. What future means ... must be understood as active self-transcendence, a self-surpassing, an active achieving of one's plenitude across emptiness."[8]

§ 10 This does not seem so different from what is defended by Ratzinger:

---

[6] Joseph Ratzinger, *Fé e Futuro* (Petrópolis: Vozes, 1971), p. 60.

[7] Karl Rahner, "La Cristologia Dentro de Una Concepción Evolutiva del Mundo," in V.A., *Escritos de Teologia* (Madrid: Taurus, 1964), vol. V, p. 183.

[8] *Ibid.*, pp. 188-189.

"What is the exact concept of the world when we understand it in an evolutionary way? What is certainly essential for this is that being and time appear closely linked. Being not only has time, but it is time. It is only *in fieri* [in evolution] and it develops itself until it achieves becoming itself. Accordingly, being is understood dynamically, as an essential and ordered movement: It is not always going around the same thing, but it is a movement that goes forward."[9]

§ 11

Given that the essence of each being would cease to be stable and immutable and would become mutable, the consequence is that such an essence would not be different from evolution, which would cause it to be continuously changing from one state to another. That is, there would be a constant migration of essences between the energy that drives evolution and all the beings in the universe. This would be, therefore, a Pan-Ontologism[10] departing from the concept that evolution is a latency immanent in all things.

We see, then, a radical change in the conception of being and, with this, a revolution in Ontology, in Metaphysics and in all of Scholastic Philosophy.

4. The 'Dogma' of Evolution & the New Theology

§ 12

If the consequences of admitting evolution are profound in Philosophy, its importance is no less substantial in Theology. In effect, we can ask: Given that the evolutionary theory is founded on a divine latency that would be present in all beings, to what degree can we consider that this latency is something different from God?

§ 13

Fr. Schoonenberg seems to indicate that there is no substantial difference between God and creatures when he affirms that "God does not act outside of all this, but expressly in it."

This is affirmed in the following context:

---

[9] J. Ratzinger, "Fé en la Creación y Teoria Evolutiva," in V.A., *Es Esto Dios?* (Barcelona: Herder. 1973), p. 239.

[10] Here we understand Pan-Ontologism as a migration that takes place between the essences of beings and the universal evolutionary energy. Obviously, this implies that all the essences can permeate one another. Such a mixture of essences comes close to the Ontologism condemned by the Church (cf. DR 1659-1665), although this condemnation is turned especially toward the Pantheistic and Gnosological consequences of Ontologism.

"Summarizing the whole question of the relationship between God and the world, we can say that it contains two principal themes: *first*, **we can fully agree with the discoveries of science regarding evolution from Creation to man**; *second*, **we can approve what the sciences see as the continuation of this process throughout human history**. From the religious point of view, **this implies that God does not act outside of all this, but expressly in it, inside the structures**. …

"Also, **revelation always takes place in the experience a man has of God** as the One who brings him salvation and in man's communication of this message to his neighbors. God reveals himself in the inter-human relationship."[11]

§ 14 Rahner is still more categorical when he affirms that "the world receives God in such a way that God himself becomes its deepest inner life." The context is this:

"This self-transcendence of the cosmos in man toward its own totality and foundation … is only fully and truly achieved … when the cosmos finds in the spiritual creature its goal and apex, beyond that which is established from its foundation, that is, the created, the immediate self-communication of its own foundation. **When this immediate self-communication to the spiritual creature takes place with that which we call grace** (considered in its historical course) … **God not only creates what is different from Him**, but gives himself to what is different. **The world receives God in such a way that God himself becomes its deepest inner life**."[12]

That is, the cosmos would become divine by means of the immediate self-communication of God.

§ 15 Holy Mother Church teaches us that grace is a created gift given by God to elevate man to the supernatural life.[13] Therefore, the communication between God and man is made **mediately** by grace.[14] An action of God that is **immediate** could

---

[11] J. Schoonenberg, no title, in V.A., *Cinco Problemas que Desafiam a Igreja Hoje* (São Paulo: Herder, 1970), pp. 73-74.

[12] K. Rahner, "La Cristologia Dentro de Una Concepción Evolutiva del Mundo," p. 196.

[13] Cf. St. Thomas Aquinas, *Summa Theologiae*, I.II, q. 114, a. 3, c; II.II, q. 19, a. 7, c; III, q. 2, a. 10, 1; q. 3, a. 4, 3; q. 62, a. 1, 2, c; *De Veritate*, q. 27, 7, c.

[14] Cf. Vol. VII, *Destructio Dei*, Chap. IV. §§ 33-43.

not be grace, but rather some essential communication of God to man. We have already studied that there are two divine actions of this type, which are creation and sustentation of being.[15]

Now then, if we admit that creation is always *in fieri* and that there is no longer being but only a coming-into-being, the two concepts of creation and sustentation are replaced by evolution. And the latter is stimulated by the immediate action of God. In the text above, therefore, a new concept of grace surfaces that seems to correspond to a mixing of the divine and human essences.[16] This is frontally opposed to Catholic doctrine.[17]

§ 16

It is to such a mixture of essences that Rahner refers when he introduces the notion of a divine experience that man would have of the ascending movement of the cosmos, which he calls grace:

"If the history of the cosmos is always at depth a history of the spirit, then its desire for realization and its foundation will be the immediate character of God's self-communication to the spiritual creature and, through it, to the cosmos in general. ... **We are those who**, by experiencing grace ... **experience** the occurrence of the promise of the proximity of the absolute mystery, which is the foundation for everything, and we have, for this reason, the legitimacy of **the courage of faith in the fulfillment of the cosmos' ascending history and**

---

[15] Cf. *ibid.*, §§ 26-32.

[16] Cf. Vol. VI, *Inveniet Fidem?*, Chap. III §§ 209-220, 225-227; Vol. X, *Peccatum – Redemptio*, Chap. VIII.2.B-E.

[17] The Church condemned various propositions of Eckart and Miguel de Molinos that sustain the human soul is transformed into God and identified with the divine essence (cf. John XXII, Constitution *In agro Dominico* of March 27, 1329, DR 510-513; Innocent XI, Apostolic Constitution *Coelestis Pastor* of November 20, 1687, DR 1225).

Vatican Council I solemnly declared: "If anyone shall say that the essence of God is one and the same with all things, let him be anathema" (Canons on the Catholic Faith, DR 1803).

The same Council affirmed: "If anyone shall say that the finite things, both corporal and spiritual, or at least the spiritual ones, have emanated from the divine substance, or that divine essence by a manifestation or evolution of itself becomes all things or, finally, that God is universal or indefinite being because, by determining himself, He constituted all things distinct in genre, species and individuals, let him be anathema" (*ibid.*, DR 1804).

the respective individual cosmic consciousness, which consists in the immediate experience of God in authentic and generous self-communication."[18]

We see, thus, that the "dogma" of evolution bears as a consequence a change in the concept of God[19] and all of theology.

§ 17 Fr. Carlo Molari, professor emeritus of Dogmatic Theology in the Lateran, Urbanian and Gregorian Universities in Rome, also refers to this radical change in theology based on evolution:

"Science completely changed the vision of the world the ancients had and upon which they projected their religious experiences.

"Let us consider a much simpler formula: Our Father who art in Heaven. Certainly many Christians for long centuries included in this expression a certain way of seeing the world, where God was established above the clouds, beyond the horizon of the celestial sphere.

"**We could examine the semantic changes experienced by the theological formulae related to the creation of the world, matter, evil and man's action in the world after the discovery of radioactivity and transformation of matter into energy**.

"**The theory of biological evolutionism is changing the concept of the creation of man and his relationship with the order of living beings, as well as all the 'protology,' the doctrine about the primitive state and original sin**, in the same way that the theory of Copernicus in the 16th century radically changed the meaning of various theological formulae regarding the action of God over the world.

"The development **of the human sciences changes the perspectives upon which theological notions such as grace, trial, sin, conversion, etc. were based**."[20]

---

[18] K. Rahner, "La Cristologia Dentro de Una Concepción Evolutiva del Mundo," p. 197.

[19] Cf. Vol. VII, *Destructio Dei, passim*; Vol. VIII, *Fumus Satanae, passim.*

[20] Carlo Molari, *La Problematica del Linguaggio Teologico* (Milan: Ancora, 1970), pp. 65-66.

The various fields of theology that Molari examines, principally under the prism of semantic changes, could be enlarged to encompass all of Dogmatic Theology, revealing a radical change in theological concepts.

§ 18 It is to this change that Rahner refers:

"**There is also an evolution** and history **of doctrine that cannot be explained as just acquiring new additional knowledge**, since it conceives old and 'permanent' truths in a new way …

"**In Catholic Theology there is a new Christological re-thinking that** is clearly necessary and **must work with modern concepts**."[21]

§ 19 A new religion springs up on the horizon as a consequence of a theology and philosophy changed by the "dogma" of evolution. Teilhard de Chardin foresees and hails this religion of evolution as he affirms:

"Even if we are not fully aware of it, the most pressing question set before mankind in the process of a planetary merging is the problem of spiritual activation. As our hands touch the atomic, we touch the primordial source of the energy of evolution. This decisive conquest could not be achieved unless, symmetrically, on the opposite pole, we find the means to cultivate, in equal proportions, the élan of evolution, in the bosom of the *Noosphere.* A new power calls for new longings. …

"**What does such a hope-filled faith in some coming consummation represent, in the more authentic and psychological sense of the word, except a 'religion'?**

"**A Religion of Evolution: behold, finally what man increasingly needs to survive and continue forward from the moment he becomes aware of his power and his duty to go beyond his self-realization as man.**"[22]

§ 20 Thus, the acceptation of the "dogma" of evolution leads Progressivism to re-think theological concepts and long for a new religion.

*

---

[21] K. Rahner, *Magistero e Teologia dopo il Concilio* (Brescia: Queriniana, 1967), p. 30.

[22] P. Teilhard de Chardin, *Le Christique* (Paris: Seuil, 1976), p. 111.

5. The 'Dogma' of Evolution, Vatican II & the New Ecclesiology

§ 21 Let us now consider how Vatican II, according to theologians who figured as *periti* at the Council, accepted evolution.

Dealing with changes in doctrine, Fr. Chenu reports how the word evolution was introduced into *Gaudium et spes* against the traditional teaching of the Church:

"This strategic move [whereby the Church no longer defines eternal laws but tries to understand the world in movement] certainly was not made to the detriment of the truth of Christ, given that Christ himself entered history and that history is the place where the reality of Christian economy is expressed. …

"**The word evolution itself, obstinately suspicious until then, entered three or four times**, despite the negative reactions, **into the redaction of critical points of *Gaudium et spes*, as reinforcement for the word 'history.'** …

"About 50 new words, which were not part of the vocabulary of the Church, entered the [texts of the] Council and are now in circulation. 'Evolution' is one of them. **I am pleased to quote this text by Paul VI, then Cardinal Montini**, who superbly comments: '**The order toward which Christianity tends is not static; it is an order in permanent evolution toward a better form, it is an equilibrium in movement**.'"[23]

Chenu continues: "**Relative was a terrible word** until that moment – as it was **until the Council**. **'Official' theology considered the formulae through which the faith expresses itself as immutable realities and rejected the word evolution, which the Council would introduce into its vocabulary**."[24]

In another work, he comments on *Gaudium et spes*:

"**Already in chapter II**, where the promotion of the common good of the human community was described, **the presence of the Spirit in the 'evolution' of the world was affirmed**: '**The Spirit of God** Who, with an admirable providence, directs the unfolding of time and renews the face of earth, **is present in this evolution**' (GS 26)."[25]

---

[23] *Jacques Duquesne Interroge le Père Chenu*, pp. 185-186.

[24] *Ibid.*, p. 47.

[25] M.D. Chenu, "Les Signes des Temps – Réflexion Théologique," in Y. Congar & M. Peuchmaurd, *L'Église dans le Monde de ce Temps* (Paris: Cerf, 1967), vol. 2, p. 212.

§ 22 Advocating the abolition of the traditional exegesis of the Sacred Letters, the same Chenu writes:

"For this Word [of God] is not an ensemble of old texts that experts, called exegetes, decode by means of learned research. **The Word of God speaks today in an always timely re-reading, assisted by the Spirit, Who is always present in the evolution of the world** (*Gaudium et spes*, 26). This is the link between fidelity and movement."[26]

§ 23 Schillebeeckx also attributes to Vatican II the acceptation of the word evolution:

"**The Council affirmed the salvific presence of God in the political, social and economic evolution of mankind in the secular world.** Regarding social development for the common good of all men, the Pastoral Constitution says: '**The Spirit of God … is present in this evolution**' (n. 26)."[27]

§ 24 Msgr. Gérard Philips, as final redactor of *Lumen gentium*, speaks with authority on the thinking behind that Constitution. He explains that the intention of that important document was to insert the Church into the evolution of the world moving toward unity:

"**The Council does not renounce its insertion into time; it does not speak abstractly, but turns, first, to the men of our century**, who live in a determined place not only in spiritual history, but in history simply. Nor does it disregard the future, but strives to formulate its message in terms that will be valid for future generations. …

"**Now then, the contemporary world is characterized above all by an accelerated evolution toward unity, be it in the economic-social terrain or that of technical progress and cultural exchange**. Despite the harsh conflicts that often raise up one people against another, man has never felt so much solidarity with others as he does today. Although the possibilities of material and spiritual exchanges may be multiplied to the infinite, they will never of themselves attain the goal of making all human hearts beat in unison. The total and universal unification of mankind cannot be realized except on a higher plane, that of

---

[26] M.D. Chenu, "O que Muda e o que Permanece," in V.A., *A Igreja e o Futuro* (Petrópolis: Vozes, 1973), p. 90.

[27] E. Schillebeeckx, no title, in V.A., *Cinco Problemas que Desafiam a Igreja Hoje*, p. 51.

the salvific grace of Christ. On the other hand, the fact remains that, **alongside the constant progress of unity in the temporal sphere, religious unification becomes more necessary and urgent**. …

"Although a unified temporal order on a world scale and the installation of the universal divine kingdom through Christ are two different realities, one would need to be blind to deny the interaction linking one to another. It suffices to think about the spread of ecumenism in the last years, also due to the Council, and one sees the importance of the pursuit of Christian confessions for unity, even from the perspective of the earthly well-being of mankind and of secular history."[28]

Thus, according to Philips, one of the primary intentions of *Lumen gentium* was to bring the Church to adapt herself to the longings of universal evolution for unity.

§ 25

When he describes what the Council understands by mystery,[29] Msgr. Philips again subtly brings in the notion of evolution, although he avoids the actual word. Commenting on n. 52 of *Lumen gentium*, he affirms:

"Here we are before the divine mystery revealed and continued in the Church. The term mystery can be considered the key word of the entire Constitution. It starts with it and ends with it. …

"An overly cerebral conception deprives the notion of mystery of the plenitude of its biblical meaning. St. Paul uses this rich notion to refer to the plan of salvation that the Father conceived from all eternity, which He revealed and realized in time in order to fulfill it and make it shine with its full light in the end times. In other words, **we can affirm that the mystery** is eternal and temporal, since it is nothing else but the will of salvation of the eternal God that comes to us in time. It does not reduce itself to a theoretical knowledge that increases our understanding; it **is a force that transforms us**. The mystery of the coming of Christ started when, conceived by the Holy Spirit, He was born from the womb of the Virgin.

---

[28] Gérard Philips, *La Chiesa e il Suo Mistero – Storia, Testo e Commento della Lumen Gentium* (Milan: Jaca Books, 1982), p. 73.

[29] Cf. *Lumen gentium* 1, 8.

"But, once the mystery begins to act, not outside time but in time (and in space), **the revelation of Christ continues,** thanks to the Church, **until the moment in the end times when it will disembogue in eternity**. …

"Mystery, [divine] missions, the history of salvation: all this is inscribed on a single line coming from the Father, through the Spirit, toward the Church. …

"**Mystery is not an individual communication, but an appeal that stimulates the formation of a community**. … It is in the Church that the communitarian spirit demonstrates its power beyond the separation that may exist between time and place."[30]

§ 26 Mystery would be, then, the divine "transforming force" present in men, manifested by the continued revelation of Christ, expressed in its best form in communitarian "revelations" and in the direction of the history of salvation. This notion of a "transforming force" would coincide with what we have studied in the previous Letters of this Chapter.

§ 27 If we admit this interpretation of Philips, evolution as synonymous with mystery would be the very nucleus of the Dogmatic Constitution *Lumen gentium*, which is the most important document of the Council.

§ 28 This interpretation is all the more credible when we consider that another key concept of Vatican II is that of Pilgrim Church – a Church in continuous change – which seems to presuppose also the notion of a universal evolution. Basing himself on the official documents of Vatican II, Bishop Boaventura Kloppenburg, a conciliar *perito* and member of the International Theological Commission, refers to a Church that is always in-the-making as a "universal sacrament of salvation":

"The Gospel concretely incarnated in a determined cultural, historic or geographic situation can produce excellent fruits of salvation and sanctification and constitute a flourishing and most Christian Particular Church (in the sense of the Decree *Orientalium Ecclesiarum* 2 – OE – or LG 13c). This concrete incarnation of the Gospel will have, then, its particular uses, its own ways of praying, thinking and expressing the content of the faith. …

[30] G. Philips, *La Chiesa e il Suo Mistero*, pp. 518-519.

"This is the necessary and indispensable pluralism in the one sole Church of Christ. But, for men of the Church, there is always the grave temptation to fix the Church in one concrete and successful form of incarnation; of making her perpetual in that style even after those previous circumstances have ceased to exist; or to try to repeat her in the exact same way in other situations. This would be a conservatism that leads to formalism, legalism, juridicism and a dangerous form of phariseeism and the ghetto.

"On the day the Church considers herself finished, complete, accomplished, always the same, immutable, permanent, definitively structured in her institutions and laws, she would stop being a leaven, light and salt; she would cease to be the universal sacrament of salvation, she would no longer fulfill her essential mission … and she would begin to be essentially unfaithful.

"**Always unfinished, always on the road, always tending to consummation, always placed in new situations, always in a world that passes and changes, the Church must always be *in fieri* [in evolution], always in continuous progress**. *Ecclesia in via peregrinans vocatur a Christo ad hanc perennem reformationem qua ipsa, qua humanum terrenumque institutum. perpetuo indiget* [The Pilgrim Church is called by Christ to this continued reform. As a human and earthly institution, she is always in need of it] (UR 6).[31]

§ 29 Cardinal Suenens, one of the four Moderators of the Council, refers to this constant evolution that should exist in the Church without using the precise word:

"The invitation, now, is to place Vatican II in the context of the future. For **the Church is a Church who is on the road, a pilgrim Church. She never has the right to become a fixed point, and her pauses are just preparations for new stages of the trip**.

"**Under some aspects, the Church is always 'transitory.'** John XXIII liked to say: 'They call me a Pope of transition.' And he added, 'It is true, but **the continuity of the Church is made of transition after transition**.'"[32]

---

[31] Boaventura Kloppenburg, *A Eclesiologia do Vaticano II* (Petrópolis: Vozes, 1971), p. 97.

[32] Leo Jozef Suenens, "Co-responsibility: Dominating Idea of the

§ 30 We see, therefeore, that the "dogma" of evolution, whether the word is used or not, is also present in the deepest conception of conciliar ecclesiology.

6. The 'Dogma' of Evolution & the New Religion

§ 31 The "Religion of Evolution" dreamed of by Teilhard de Chardin [33] does not seem to be so different from the Conciliar Church. In effect, if we compare the notion of "Church sacrament of the world" or "Pilgrim Church" of Vatican II with the Christianity longed for by Teilhard in the excerpt below, we see that they appear to be the same thing.

"The renewal of the cosmic conceptions that characterizes the 'modern spirit' has provoked a crisis of such severity in almost all of the old religions that, if they have not yet died from it, we can predict that they will never recover. Closely bound to untenable myths or steeped in a pessimistic and passive mysticism, it is impossible for them to adapt themselves to the precise immensities or the constructive demands of space-time. They are out of step both with our science and with our action.

"Now then, **under the shock that is rapidly causing its rivals to disappear, Christianity, which at first sight we could also judge to be shaken, on the contrary, is showing signs of a new impetus forward. For, precisely because of the new dimensions considered to be the universe, Christianity reveals itself both as inherently more vigorous in itself and as more necessary to the world than it has ever been before**.

"*More vigorous*. To live and develop Christian conceptions requires an atmosphere of grandeur and union. The bigger the world becomes, the more organic its interior connections will be, and the more the perspectives of the Incarnation will triumph. That is what believers, much to their surprise, are starting to discover. **Although frightened for a moment by evolution, the Christian now perceives that it offers him nothing but a magnificent means of feeling more at one with God and of delivering himself more to Him.**

"In a pluralist and stactic nature, the universal domination of Christ could, strictly speaking, still be regarded as an extrinsic and super-imposed power. In a spiritually converging

---

Council and its Pastoral Consequences," in V.A., *Theology of Renewal*, vol. 2, p. 9.

[33] Cf. § 19.

world, what urgency, what intensity does this Christic energy not reveal? **If the world is convergent and if Christ occupies its center, then the *Christogenesis* of St. Paul and St. John is nothing more and nothing less than the extension**, both awaited and unexpected, **of that *Noogenesis*, in which,** as regards our experience, **the *Cosmogenesis* reaches its apex**. Christ invests himself organically with the very majesty of His Creation. And thus it is not metaphorical to say that man becomes capable of experiencing and discovering his God in the whole length, breadth and depth of the world in movement. **We can say literally to God that we love Him**, not only with our whole body, our whole heart and our whole soul, but also **with the whole universe on its way to unification. That is a prayer that we can only say in space-time**.

"*More necessary*. To say of Christianity that, despite appearances to the contrary, it is acclimating itself and expanding in a world prodigiously enlarged by science, is to point to no more than half of the picture. In a certain way, **evolution infuses new blood into the perspectives and aspirations of the Christian**. In return, **is not the Christian faith destined, or even now ready, to save or even replace evolution?**

"I have tried to show that we can hope for no progress on earth without the primacy and triumph of the personal[34] at the apex of the spirit. Now, at the present moment and on the entire surface of the *Noosphere*, Christianity represents the only current of thought sufficiently audacious and progressive to practically and efficiently encompass the world in an embrace, at once complete yet capable of indefinite perfection, where faith and hope reach their fulfillment in charity. Only it, Christianity, absolutely only it in the world today, shows itself capable to reconcile, in a single vital act, the all and the person. Only it can lead us not only to serve, but to love the tremendous movement of the world which bears us along.

"What does this mean except that **Christianity fulfills all the conditions we are entitled to expect from a religion of the future, and that henceforth, through it, the principal axis of evolution truly passes**, as it affirms?"[35]

---

[34] The concept of person and personal, referred to here by Teilhard as a shield to protect the pantheist and immanentist character of his doctrine, was already analyzed in Vol. VII, *Destructio Dei*, Chap. IV §§ 188-320.

[35] P. Teilhard de Chardin, *O Fenômeno Humano*, pp. 328-330.

The background of the notion "Church sacrament of the world" would be nothing less than the new religion of evolution.[36]

§ 32 The documents presented in this Chapter are sufficient, in our opinion, to demonstrate that Evolutionism is understood by the progressivists as the central point of conciliar philosophy, theology and religion.

* * *

---

[36] Regarding these affirmations by Teilhard, we cannot restrain from pointing out, in passing, that the progressivists consider all the other religions to be on the brink of dying. From this comes – our comment – a new interpretation of their ecumenism and inter-religious dialogue. The common presentation is that it would tend to a union of all the religions in equal conditions, where each one gives up some of its beliefs and adopts something from the others. Instead, it would be a voluntary assistance that the religion of evolution – that is, the progressivist creed – would give to all the religions.

In this way Progressivism, in addition to its own apostasy from the Catholic Church, synthesizes the errors and evil of the false religions. In this, Progressivism is analogous to Modernism, "the synthesis of all heresies" (cf. *Pascendi*, n. 39). But it goes further and surpasses Modernism since it wants to preserve the false religions, which would die without its succor.

CHAPTER IV

PROGRESSIVIST CONCEPTION OF HISTORY

§ 1 When we described the genesis of the progressivist attacks against the Catholic conception of Creation,[1] we saw that they can be considered from three different points of view: the so-called philosophic, scientific and historic "problems." They are called problems in the sense that they are challenges that the modern times made against Catholic Philosophy, Exegesis and Dogmatic Theology, obliging them to change their structures in order to adapt to the modern thought.

We already addressed the philosophical "problem" when we analyzed the progressivist attack against the universal and abstract character of the truths of the Faith.[2] There we saw the immanentist origin of certain ideas that rule progressivist thought today and the influence they had at Vatican II.

In the last Chapter, we analyzed Evolutionism, which constitutes the nucleus of the scientific "problem." We concluded that there is nothing scientific about it; its background is philosophical-religious and its matrix is Immanentism.

§ 2 We should now analyze the historic "problem."

To do so, we will *first* provide the traditional Catholic thinking on the topic. *Second*, we will apply these criteria to make a brief analysis of some modern systems of the Philosophy of History. *Third*, we will scrutinize the progressivist conception of History, both its Philosophy and Theology of History. The three items of this Chapter will correspond to these three aims.

1. Catholic Thinking on Philosophy & Theology of History

Let us establish some initial sound criteria indispensable to evaluate the subject matter.

A. Reality & Myths on These Topics

§ 3 When we analyze some authors who deal with the Philosophy and Theology of History, we observe a sort of electricity or magnetism that surrounds these topics. It is implied that one who would possess the criteria to understand the Philosophy and

---

[1] Cf. Chap. I §§ 7-40.

[2] Cf. Vol. VI, *Inveniet Fidem?*, Chap. III.

Theology of History or, at least, make studies on these themes, would be gifted with an indefinable divine participation, which would elevate him above other men and topics.

Thus, we note a certain promotional charge that gives prestige to those who study the Philosophy and Theology of History and adopt a determined focus. Conversely, we notice a sanction against those who do not adopt that focus. The two themes are transformed, therefore, into "talismans," which either promote or discredit the ones who address them.

§ 4 We would say that two fundamental elements are present in this talismanic charge. The *first* is vanity: an over-valorization made by the persons addressing these topic. The *second*, much more profound, is the historicist and progressivist concept of a "divine revelation" that would take place throughout History by means of individual and communitarian experiences of the Divinity. This second element, much more than the first, is the cause of the talismanic charge that surrounds the themes of Philosophy and Theology of History.

§ 5 However, independent of mythifications and mystifications, the Philosophy and Theology of History are simply the application of the principles of this or that philosophy to History. Thus, there will be as many philosophies of History as there are philosophies: Thomistic, Aristotelian, Platonic, rationalist, idealist, existentialist, etc. Similarly, there will be many theologies of History: Catholic, Schismatic, Protestant, Jewish, Muslim, Buddhist, etc.

B. History Reflects a Single Objective Reality, which Tends to Be Completely Explained

§ 6 Given that "God is one, Christ is one, His Church is one and the Faith is one,"[3] it is necessary that there be only one true interpretation of History. For History is the sketching of the divine plan in time, fulfilled in this or that way by men either in their ensembles or individually.

§ 7 The complexity of the divine plan becomes more or less knowledgeable to us depending on the degree of mystery with which God wants to surround it. It also relies on the mutability of human psychology, which responds in different ways to the

---

[3] St. Cyprian, *De Catholicae Ecclesiae Unitate*, chap. IV, n. 23, in PL (Paris: J.P. Migne, 1844), vol. 4, 500-501.

plans of God. In principle, therefore, only at the Last Judgment will men know the historic reality with full objectivity and from the highest perspectives.

§ 8a

However, analyses of such plans have been made by Saints, Fathers and Doctors of the Church, at times by Popes and Councils in documents of the Magisterium, at other times by Catholic thinkers reflecting the *sensus fidelium* and, finally, also by holy or pious souls gifted by God with the gift of prophecy. [4]

With these various contributions – from authors who were assisted by special graces – the Catholic interpretation of History, although very difficult, becomes increasingly complete. Following this path, we may conjecture the harmonic marriage of the Theology of History with the exegesis of the *Apocalypse*, which, according to some authors, would reveal the general architecture of God's plans and the way they were executed.[5]

---

[4] Among the most preeminent in this last family of souls, we find the grand moral profile of St. Louis Grignion de Montfort, who prophesized the end of the present day revolutionary era of History and the implantation of a new era, the Reign of Mary.

[5] We transcribe the erudite synthesis by Msgr. José Balthasar Pereira in his *Comentários sobre o Novo Testamento – Apocalypse* (Bahia: Typografia de São Francisco, 1912). He describes the schools of thoughts in the interpretation of the *Apocalypse* following the most credited authors:

"Cornely reduces the systems of interpretation of the *Apocalypse* to three: One considers that it encompasses the entire History of the Church. ... The first system is adopted by La Chétardie, Holzhauser, Drach, Walter, etc. Those who follow it, however, develop it in different ways. According to some, the principal events of each age, above all those grave and sad ones, are announced in [chronological] order; according to others, the events proper to each age are described by letters, seals, trumpets, etc, but in such a way that the same things are repeated four or five times, at times considering one aspect, at other times another. Some believe that only the major events are predicted, but others consider that even the smallest details of those events are predicted" (vol. 3, p. 598).

Pereira stresses that Dessaily prefers the first system and he considers Holzhauser's interpretation of it is the best (cf. *ibid.*, p. 600). He comments:

"Drach also opines that the systems of interpretation of the Apocalypse can be reduced to three: ... The second, inaugurated in the 11th century by Joachim of Fiore and followed by many modern and contemporary authors, sees in the combats of the Apocalypse a history,

C. The Magisterium on the Philosophy & Theology of History

§ 8b Given that Catholic Philosophy and Theology are the basis for the interpretation of History, for this intellectual labor to be accepted by the Church as her own, it must be exempt from error. Over these matters, therefore, the Church must exercise a vigilant tutelage.

However, since it is very difficult to arrive at an interpretation that approximates an objective description of God's plans in History, the Church leaves the terrain open for the intellectual hypotheses of her children, safeguarded by the orthodoxy of the mentioned principles.

Thus, making use of this liberty, we present our thoughts on the matter.

D. Counter-Revolutionary Principles & Laws of the Philosophy & Theology of History

§ 9 The principles and laws[6] presented in this Letter D are a quick sketch of the counter-revolutionary thinking of Plinio Corrêa de Oliveira on the Philosophy and Theology of History, which I received from him in the more than 30 years that I was honored to accompany him in his fights, reflections and studies.

---

in its general lines and principal facts, of the combats and victories of the Church against Judaism, idolatry, the heresies, the schism and the apostasy, which would reach its apogee in the times of the Antichrist. …

"This second system, developed by La Chétardie, perfected by Holzhauser and in our days by Lafont-Sentenac, seems to be the one preferred by Drach."

"Drach evaluates: In brief, the system that sees in the Apocalypse, from chapters 6 to 19 inclusive, the principal phases of the History of the Church up to the second coming of Jesus Christ, seems to us the better one, although we recognize that it presents great difficulties that will only disappear when, after the predicted events have taken place, an exact idea of the ensemble of the march of the book can be made" (*ibid.*, pp. 602-603).

[6] The difference between principles, laws and plans that we adopt is based on good sense. A *principle* is a foundation of the religious, metaphysical or historical order from which other elements of these orders proceed. A *law* is a norm observed or to be observed in function of a presented ideal and as a consequence of accepted principles. A *plan* is constituted by an ensemble of intentions ordered in architectural form, according to the means of execution at hand, taking into consideration the admitted principles and the laws to which it is subject.

§ 10 The following summarized items do not obey any special order of theme. The topics – philosophy and theology – will appear as dictated by need in constructing a general view. Such an edifice departs generically from its chronological origins and universal concepts and adds, as it is built, more timely or complex data.

a. Axiological principle

§ 11 The guiding principle that commands History is what we call the *axiological principle*, that is, the principle by which the ensemble of the universe created by God is a worthy image and likeness of Him from the point of view of the *unum, verum, bonum* and *pulchrum*.[7] As such, it must fulfill the aim of glorifying God for which it was created.

The ensemble of the universe can be considered statically, i.e., the architecture of the cosmos and of the societies of angels, men and the Holy Church. It also can be considered dynamically, i.e., the movement of the cosmos, the relational life of men – either social or political – in the temporal and spiritual spheres, and also in History.

§ 12 By the force of the axiological principle, the ensemble of the universe has a background unity that glorifies God. The same principle is present in History, without impairing human liberty.

If this glorification were not to take place, Creation itself would be frustrated, which is tantamount to saying that God would not have made it since He is omniscient.[8]

---

[7] On the concepts of the transcendental principles of the *unum* (oneness), *verum* (truth), *bonum* (goodness) and *pulchrum* (beauty) see Vol. VII, *Destructio Dei*, Chap. III §§ 146-154, 222, 223, Note 164.

[8] a. We find this principle mentioned in the words of Pius XII: "The Catholic Church knows that all events take place according to the will or the permission of Divine Providence and that God achieves His goals in History. As the great St. Augustine said with classical concision: What God proposes, '*hoc fit, hoc agitur; etsi paulatim peragitur, indesinenter agitur*' [this is done, this is executed, and although it is completed gradually, it is continuously in action] (*Enarration in Ps 109*, n. 9, in PL 37, 1952). God is truly the Lord of History" ("Per il X Congresso Internazionale delle Scienze Storiche," in *Discorsi e Radiomessaggi di Sua Santità Pio XII*, Poliglotta Vaticana, 17, p. 2120).

b. St. Pius X alludes to the same principle here: "Man, abusing his liberty, can violate the right and the supreme authority of the Creator; but the victory always belongs to the Creator" (Encyclical *E Supremi Apostolatus*,Vozes: Petrópolis, 1958, n. 7).

b. Principle of the good & bad angelic action

§ 13 The next principle is the principle of the good and bad angelic action. After creating the Angels as the most elevated part of the universe and giving them a most clear intelligence and an irreversible will, God invited them, by means of a trial,

---

c. Based on St. Thomas, Max Seckler makes some observations that approximate the axiological principle: "If the thesis of the similarity between the effect and the cause (*omne agens agit sibi simile* – every agent produces an effect similar to himself – *Summa Theologiae* I, q. 4., a. 3) is not only a [static] verification of a state of affairs, but also the expression of a law determining a whole process of events moving in a certain direction (*effectis tendit in similitude agentis* – the effect tends to become like the agent – *Contra Gentilis*, III, 19), it implies, at the same time, that the similarity between the creature and the Creator is not only in the *form* of similarity or likeness, but also in the way its process of assimilation develops.

"The historic event, then, clearly signifies, as an *event*, a similarity with God, to the point that the most elevated form of similarity in man does not consist in a static reproduction, but in a dynamic image of activity, either in knowledge or in love" (*Le Salut et l'Histoire – La Pensée de Saint Thomas d'Aquin sur la Théologie de l'Histoire*, Paris: Cerf, 1967, p. 51).

Further on, Seckler explains another consequence: "The thesis of the similarity between effect and cause finds its most central and interesting application for the Theology of History, according to St. Thomas, in the domain of the doctrine of Creation: The world was created in the image and likeness of God (cf. *Summa Theologiae* I, q. 4, a. 3; *Contra Gentiles* I, 29; II.II, prolog). Going beyond the relationship of cause and origin, he says here about Creation that the Creator 'reflected himself' in it as the model (*causa exemplaris*). This is valid both for the different traits of similarity in the details and for the total image of the world (cf. *Contra Gentiles*, II, 39-45)" (*ibid.*, p. 73).

According to Seckler, St. Thomas alludes to the figure of the circle as an expression of perfect movement: "By becoming aware of that which is 'pre-drawn' in the eternal model regarding a temporal event, that event can complete itself, closing the circle: *Universum perficitur in coniunctione ultimi ad principium primum* [The universe perfects itself when the last principle connects to the first] (*III Sententiarum* d.1, q. 1, a. 3, ad 1)" (*ibid.*, p. 83).

He also explains the role of man's free will: "Seen in its ensemble, the world is perfect because its 'return' [to the starting point] is not a natural process, but a freely-consented to act, i.e., the free acts that are the foundation of History lead to the process of assimilation and complete the figure of this world (cf. *Contra Gentiles*, II, 46)" (*ibid.*, p. 93).

to give their adhesion to the plan of glory He had established for them and the rest of the universe. As it is habitually believed, one third of the Angels defected and were thrown into Hell (cf. Apoc 12: 3-4, 8-9; 2 Pet 2:4).

§ 14

According to the *axiological principle*, for the plan of God to be accomplished regarding the ensemble of the Angels, it would be necessary for other intelligent and free creatures to come and fulfill the angelic vocations left unaccomplished. Hence, some Doctors teach that the Blessed in Heaven have the mission to fill the thrones of the fallen angels.[9]

c. Principle of the fight between good & evil

§ 15

Due to the initial rupture among the angels, the *principle of the good and bad angelic action* is projected over the whole created universe. The good Angels sustain and direct the uni-

---

[9] Commenting on this verse of the Apocalypse – "and his [the dragon's] tail swept a third of the stars out of the sky and flung them to the earth" (12:4) – Cornelius a Lapide affirms: "St. John alludes here to the first sin of pride of Lucifer who, as Vittorino teaches, after revolting against God, convinced and solicited those who followed him – his tail, made of a third part of the stars, that is, the angels.

"Therefore, when, it is said that men will take the places of the fallen angels to compensate for their fall, this must be understood in a general and non-defined way, and not in a singular and defined way. That is, it must be understood that the group of the elect among men will succeed the group of fallen angels, although the former is much less numerous than the latter" (*Commentaria in Apocalypsim*; cf. St. Thomas Aquinas, *II Sententiarum*, d. 1, q. 2, 3, c).

In our opinion, admitting the *laws of Christocentrism and Mariocentrism* (see below §§ 16, 17), even if the angels had not fallen, the creation of man would have taken place. Hence, it seems to us that men have a mission different from that of the angels and that, by assuming the mission of the fallen angels, men do so in a cumulative way, taking it up along with another mission that God gave to them. To confirm this thesis we can quote a Lapide: "Primarily God created, destined and called all men, as well as all angels, for their end, that is, for salvation and eternal life; and He would have created, destined and called them even if no angel had fallen" (C. a Lapide, *ibid.*).

Admitting this hypothesis, we remove ourselves from the discussion of the number of the elect – whether it will be larger or smaller than the vacant places of the angels. We only affirm that the criterion of the places of the angels is not the exclusive criterion to determine the mission of men.

verse for the greater glory of God from the vantage points of the *unum*, *verum*, *bonum* and *pulchrum* (oneness, truth, goodness and beauty). The bad angels do exactly the opposite.[10] The *principle of the angelic action* has, therefore, as an indispensable corollary the *principle of the fight between good and evil*. This fight will have consequences on all of History.

d. Law of Christocentrism or Christ Pantocrator

§ 16 Given that God resolved to create a universe composed of spiritual and material beings, the best synthesis of it is man, who by his nature has both elements, and not the Angel, who has only the noblest element.[11] Since God wanted to take the glori-

---

[10] "The fallen angels conserved a part of the government of the material world that remained to them. Their power over it is such that 'if God were not to retain their fury,' says Bossuet, 'we would see them tossing and turning this world as easily as we play with a little ball'" (Henri Delassus, *La Conjuration Antichrétienne*, Lille: Desclée de Brower, 1910, vol. 3, pp. 779-780).

[11] St. Thomas Aquinas: "For this reason man is called microcosm (*minor mundus*) because all creatures of the world are to be found in him in some way" (*Summa Theologiae*, I, q. 91, 1).

Further on, he returns to the same thought: "In some way all things are found in man ... There are in man four elements to be considered: to wit, the reason by which he is harmonized with the Angels; the sensibility by which he is harmonized with the animals; the natural forces by which he is harmonized with the plants, and his body by which he is harmonized with inanimate things" (*ibid.*, I. q. 96, a. 2).

However, this synthesis of Creation found in man does not make him *ipso facto* the best image of God. In this regard St. Thomas distinguishes: "We can speak of the image of God in two ways: *First*, referring to that which we consider to be the reason of the image, that is, the intellectual nature. In this sense, the image of God is found more in the Angels than in men, because in them the intellectual nature is more perfect, as said above (q. 58, a. 3; q. 75, a.7, ad 3; q. 79, a.8).

"*Second*, we can consider the image of God in man regarding how that image is secondary, that is, by the fact that in man is found a certain imitation of God, consisting in the fact that man proceeds from man, in the same way that God proceeds from God. Also, because man's whole soul is found in his whole body and in every part, in the same way God is found in the world. In these and other similar things, the image of God is found more in man than in the Angels.

"However, in this second way, the reason why man is His image presupposes the first way, which is by reason of the intellectual nature.

fication of the whole universe to its apex and simultaneously to redeem original sin, it was convenient for Him to unite himself hypostatically to a man and not to an Angel.[12] The revelation of such a plan and the humble acceptance of the hypostatic union of God with a Being of a nature inferior to theirs constituted the essence of the angelical trial. [13]

Otherwise, even the brute animals would be considered the image of God. Therefore, by the fact that by the intellectual nature the Angel is more the image of God than man, simply speaking [*simpliciter*] we must concede that the Angel is more to the image of God than man is; however, in a certain aspect [*secundum quid*] it is man that is" (*ibid.*, q. 93, a. 3).

[12] The Council of Cologne (1860) affirms: "If God wanted to demand a full satisfaction for sin, which would be at the same time a manifestation of His mercy and justice, no one could do this unless He would be at the same time God and Man" (p. 1, c. 18, *apud* Santiago Ramirez, *Introductión General al Tratado del Verbo Encarnado de Santo Tomás de Aquino*, Madrid: BAC, 1960, vol. 11, p. 36).

The following differentiations made by Fr. Santiago Ramirez confirm our affirmation about the glorification of God in the ensemble of the universe: "The objective aims of the Incarnation are varied and ordered among themselves: the near or immediate aim, the remote or mediate aim, and the final aim. The near or immediate aim is the objective redemption. The remote or mediate aim is threefold: the complement of the universe, the consummation of the supernatural order and the universal primacy of Jesus Christ over all things. The absolute last aim of the Incarnation is the same as its efficient cause, that is, the glory of God manifested through it by the way of divine mercy" (*ibid.*, pp. 44-45).

[13] "Lucifer saw that, in order to enter into union with God and receive the supernatural life from this union, he would have to bow before a Being inferior to himself in one of the two natures of which His Person should be composed, the Son of God made Man, made head of all Creation; and he must do the same before the Woman who, cooperating with the Incarnation of the Word, would merit to share His royalty over the universe, heaven and earth" (H. Delassus, *La Conjuration Antichrètienne*, vol. 3, p. 770).

In the same sense St. Thomas Aquinas declares: "About the mystery of the Incarnation of Christ we can speak in two ways: One, in general, is the way it was revealed to all the Angels from the beginning of their blessedness. The reason for this is, that this mystery is like a general principle to which all the mysteries of the Angels are ordered: 'All are ministering spirits, sent to minister for those who shall receive the inheritance of salvation' (Heb 1:14), and this is brought about by the

This Man-God, Jesus Christ Our Lord, is, therefore, the center of the divine plan of Creation. To Him everything must be ordered as the end and subjected to as the means.[14] This is

---

mystery of the Incarnation. Hence, it was necessary for all the Angels, from the beginning, to have a general knowledge of this mystery.

"Another way we can speak of the mystery of the Incarnation regards its special conditions. In this way, it was not known by all the Angels from the beginning" (*Summa Theologiae*, I, q. 57, a. 5, ad 1).

Cornelius a Lapide points out the most probable opinion of the Doctors when he comments on this passage of St. Peter: "For God spared not the angels that sinned, but cast them down to Hell and delivered them into chains of darkness" (2 Pet 2:4). His comments follow:

"It is probable what Francisco Suarez says that the angels ambitiously desired the hypostatic union with the Word in such a way that it would be granted to one of them, that is, Lucifer their prince, and not to a man, that is, Christ. In effect, Lucifer seems to have been envious of Christ for this union, thus soliciting the other angels to join with him. The Apostle alludes to this when he says: 'And once again, when He brings the First-begotten into the world, He says: And let all the angels of God adore Him' (Heb 1:6). The same opinion regarding this passage is maintained by Catharin, Tertullian (*Lib. de Patientia*), St. Basil (*Homil. de Invidia*), St. Cyprian (*Tract. De Zelo et Livore*), St. Bernard (*Serm. 1 de Adventu*), Rupert (in Jn 8:5) and others" (*Commentaria in II Epistola S. Petri*, Cap. 2).

[14] That all must be subject to Our Lord Jesus Christ as the means and oriented to Him as the end is a logical consequence of His primacy. In this regard the comments of Fr. Santiago Ramirez in the Introduction to Part III of *Summa Theologiae* are opportune:

"The primacy of Jesus Christ can be considered in four ways: in the ontological order or order of perfection, in the order of causality, in the order of dignity and in the order of the glorious exaltation. In all of them St. Thomas elevates and exalts Him more than any other above all created things.

"a. In the *ontological order*: Jesus Christ as man has an absolute primacy over everything created because of the hypostatic union. This union, according to St. Thomas, is the most intimate and profound of any that God can establish with creature (III, q. 2, a. 9) …

"b. In the *order of causality*: When we consider the *final cause*, in the Thomistic conception, all things … are absolutely ordered toward Jesus Christ. By this, we mean that the whole order of nature, including the Angels and the order of grace with the redemption of man, are ordered toward Jesus Christ as their end, and they must have a true subordination toward Him, even as Man, because of the hypostatic union. The objective redemption, the proximate aim of the Incarnation,

the *law of Christocentrism* or the *law of the Christ Pantocrator*. Christ is the center regarding the history of the Angels and men, as well as of the irrational universe: the animal, vegetal

---

as well as man himself along with all natural and supernatural orders of grace … are ordered toward the glory of Jesus Christ. …

"Regarding the *efficient cause*, the primacy of Jesus Christ is manifest, given that He is the Redeemer of mankind, by the actions of His most holy life. … We should add that, in this way, the last end of the creation of the world is absolutely realized by Jesus Christ. For, in the present state of things, this last end is nothing other than the supreme manifestation of God's goodness through His infinite mercy. This end is reached principally through the Incarnation ordered toward the redemption of man. ..

"Regarding *exemplar causality*, Jesus Christ as man also enjoys the primacy of sanctity by the grace of union, by the absolute plenitude of habitual grace (III. q. 7. a. 1) and by His absolute impeccability (*III Sententiarum*, d. 12, q. 2, a. 1, 2; d. 13, q. 18, a. 1, as 4). …

"c. *The primacy of dignity* of Jesus Christ is manifested, as Redeemer of mankind, as the universal Head of man and of the Angels and as the Judge of the living and the dead. …

"d. Jesus Christ also has *the primacy of glory* as Man, not only in His Soul, but also in His Body: In His Soul by reason of the hypostatic union and of the absolute plenitude of grace. Just as it is not possible that a greater degree of grace could exist more than in Jesus Christ (III, q. 7, a. 12), so also there could not exist a more perfect vision of the divine essence than what His human Soul enjoys (q. 10, a. 4c, e ad 3). Jesus has this primacy of grace and glory from the first instant of His conception by virtue of the hypostatic union and, therefore, without merit (III. q. 19. a. 3). …

"Conversely, He possesses the glory of the Body after He merited it. For He could not have it from the beginning because this is incompatible with the passion and death of Jesus Christ presupposed by the same motif as the Incarnation. Jesus Christ merited His glorification and exaltation in Heaven by His passion and death. …

"From all this it results that the Thomistic conception of the proper motif of the Incarnation, far from diminishing or perverting the primacy of Jesus Christ, on the contrary, exalts it and perfects it. In it, Jesus Christ is constituted in the center and apex of all the works of God *ad extra*. He is not only the *exemplar* and *efficient cause* of our predestination, but also the *final cause*" (S. Ramirez, *Introduction to Part III of Summa*, pp. 55-59).

and mineral kingdoms, including the cosmos – *Ecce coelum et terra clamant quod fact sint* (Behold heavens and earth glorify the One who made them).[15]

e. Law of Mariocentrism

§ 17

For God to unite himself with a perfect Man, it would be better that such a union should take place in the first instant of the life of this Man and not afterwards. Otherwise, this Man would not be entirely perfect from the first instant, but would tend to perfection afterwards, and only then would He be able to unite with the Second Divine Person. Therefore, it would be more convenient for God that this Man be perfect from His conception.

For this to happen, it would be indispensable for His Mother to be a perfect creature.[16] Our Lady appears, therefore, as a condition for the Incarnation and, as such, with a mission indissoluble from that of Our Lord Jesus Christ.

---

[15] St. Augustine, *Confessions*, book 11, c. 4. 6, in PL 32, 811.

[16] Commenting on the Apocalypse: "And a great sign appeared in heaven: a Woman clothed with the sun, and the moon under her feet, and on her head a crown of 12 stars" (12:1) – Cornelius a Lapide refers to the opinions of St. Bonaventure and St. Thomas on the perfection of Our Lady:

"Therefore, she is a great sign because, as St. Bonaventure says: 'She is the one whom God could not make greater: God could have made a greater world or a greater heaven, but God could not make a greater mother than the Mother of God' (*Speculum B. Virginis*, chap. 7).

"St. Thomas asks whether God can make things better than what He made and answers that He can. He makes three exceptions, however: Christ, the Blessed Virgin and our created bliss. He explains: 'The humanity of Christ [could not be greater] because it is united to God; our beatitude because it is the enjoyment of God; and the Most Holy Virgin because she is the Mother of God. These three things have a certain infinite dignity for the infinite good which is God' (I, q. 25, a. 8 ad 4)" (*Commentaria in Apocalypsim* 12:1).

Regarding the incomprehensibility of the perfection of Mary, Pius IX adds something more to the opinions of the those great Saints and Doctors: "Therefore, far above all the Angels and all the Saints, so wondrously did God endow Mary with the abundance of all the heavenly gifts poured from the treasury of His Divinity, that this Mother, being entirely free of any stain of sin, all fair and perfect, would possess that plenitude of innocence and sanctity which, below God, one cannot conceive anything greater and which no one, except for God, can fully comprehend" (Bull *Ineffabilis Deus*, *Acta Pii IX*, pp. 597-598, *apud Catolicismo*, Campos, December 1954).

§ 18 Under this title, as a mere creature, below the human nature of Christ Our Lord, it is she who summarizes the synthesis of the created universe. She is, therefore, Queen of the Universe. To her everything must be subordinate as the means to attain the end, which is Our Lord.[17]

---

[17] In this regard, in the Encyclical *Octobri mense* of September 22, 1891, Leo XIII affirms: "When – for the redemption and glory of man – the eternal Son of God wished to take on human nature and by this means establish with mankind a mystical union, He did not do so until the one who was chosen to become His Mother gave her free consent. She represented, in a certain manner, all human kind, according to the illustrious and just opinion of Aquinas: 'In the Annunciation the Virgin, representing all human nature, was besought to give her consent' (*Summa Theologiae* III, q. 30, a. 1).

"Hence, it is licit to affirm, most properly and truly, that from this great treasure brought by the Lord … nothing is distributed to us except by Mary, because God so desired it. Thus, as no man goes to the supreme Father except by the Son, so in a similar way does no one go to Christ except by His Mother" (DR 1949a; cf. Encyclical *Fidentem* of September 1896; St. Pius X, Encyclical *Ad diem* of February 2, 1904).

Thus, we see that the universal mediation of Mary is fully sufficient to demonstrate the need for Mariocentrism. The solemn words of Pius XII officially declaring the Virgin the Queen of the Universe further confirm this: "From the first centuries of the Catholic Church, the Christian people have raised prayers of petition and hymns of honor and devotion to the Queen of Heaven. … And never has that hope wavered that they placed in the Mother of the Divine King, Jesus Christ; nor has that faith ever failed by which we are taught that the Virgin Mary, Mother of God, reigns over the universe with a maternal heart, and is crowned in celestial happiness with the glory of a Queen. …

"As we have indicated before, venerable brethrens, the principal argument upon which the royal dignity of Mary is based is without a doubt her Divine Maternity, which is already evident in the documents of ancient tradition and in the books of the Sacred Liturgy. …

"In fact, in the Sacred Scriptures it is affirmed of the Son Who will be born from the Virgin: 'He shall be called the Son of the Most High and the Lord God shall give unto Him the throne of David His father, and He will reign in the house of Jacob forever, and of His Kingdom there will be no end' (Lk 1:32-33). Mary is also proclaimed 'Mother of the Lord' (Lk 1:43). From this it logically proceeds that she herself is a Queen, since she bore a Son Who, at the very moment of the conception by virtue of the hypostatic union with the Word, was also as a man King and Lord of all things.

"Thus, St. John Damascene writes with good reason: 'When she became Mother of the Creator, she truly became Mistress of all creation'

We are, therefore, before the *law of Mariocentrism* in the universe and in History as a consequence of the *law of Christocentrism.*

f. Law of Ecclesiocentrism

§ 19 The lordship of Our Lord Jesus Christ and His glorification by the entire universe supposes that this be made principally over men and by men. Hence the necessity appears for a first circle of men to constitute the court of Christ Pantocrator from which His powers and mercies are distributed to the ensemble of men. Through this circle, also, the honor and glory paid by men should ascend to Him. This is the mission of the Catholic Church. We are in presence of the *law of Ecclesiocentrism* as a necessity for the glorification of the Man-God in the entire universe and as a fundamental law in History.[18]

(*De Fide Orthodoxa*, book 4, c. 14, PG 94, 1158-1159). …

"But, the Blessed Virgin Mary should be proclaimed Queen not only because of her Divine Maternity, but also because God willed her to have the special role that she played in the work of our eternal salvation. …

"Now, in the accomplishing of this work of redemption, Mary Most Holy was most closely associated with Christ; and so it is fitting to sing in the Sacred Liturgy: 'Near the cross of Our Lord Jesus Christ there stood, oppressed by sorrow, the Blessed Mary, Queen of Heaven and Mistress of the World' (*Festum septem dolorem Beata Maria Virgo*, Tractus.).

"Hence a pious disciple of St. Anselm wrote in the Middle Ages: 'Just as … God, by creating everything through His power, is Father and Lord of everything, so also Mary, by repairing all with her merits, is Mother and Queen of everything. For God is the Lord of all things because by His command He made each of them; and Mary is Queen of all things because she restores each to its original dignity through the grace which she merited' (Eademrus, *De Excelentia Virginis Mariae*, c. 11, PL 94, 508). …

"For just as Christ, the new Adam, must be called a King not merely because He is Son of God, but also because He is our Redeemer, so also, in a certain way, one can affirm that the Blessed Virgin is Queen not only because she is Mother of God, but also because, as the new Eve, she was associated with the new Adam" (Pius XII, Encyclical *Ad coeli Reginam* of November 11, 1954, in *L'Osservatore Romano,* October 24, 1954, *apud Catolicismo*, Campos, December 1954)

[18] Blessed Pope Boniface VIII teaches these principles that are directly applicable to *Ecclesiocentrism*: "It does not conform to the order of the universe that all things be led back to order equally and immediately, but that order be established by the action of the intermediate

over the lowest, and the higher over the lower. Hence, we ought the more openly to confess that the spiritual exceeds any earthly power in dignity and nobility, as spiritual things surpass the temporal ones. ...

"Thus is accomplished the prophecy of Jeremiah concerning the Church and the ecclesiastical power: 'Behold, today I have placed you over nations and over kingdoms,' and the rest. Therefore, if the earthly power errs, it shall be judged by the spiritual power; but if the lesser spiritual power errs, it shall be judged by a superior spiritual power; but if the supreme power errs, it can be judged only by God, and not by man, according to the testimony of the Apostle: 'The spiritual man judges all things, but he himself is judged by no one': (Bull *Unam Sanctam* of December 18, 1302, in Giorgio Balladure Pallieri & Giulio Vismara, *Acta Juris Genium Pontificia*, Milan: Società Editrice Vita e Pensiero, 1946, p. 8, n. 27, *apud Catolicismo* June 1954).

The doctrine of the sun and the moon by Pope Urban IV offers similar principles regarding the central role God reserved to the Church and her relationship with the temporal order:

"The One Who rules Heaven and earth, that is, the One Who knows the order of Heaven and can establish on earth the image of the heavenly order, can also derive from the higher things examples for the lower. Thus, just as He placed in the celestial firmament two great luminaries to alternately illuminate the world, so also on earth in the firmament of the Catholic Church He instituted higher luminaries, to wit, the Priesthood and the Empire, for the complete governance of spiritual and temporal things, in such a way that the functions of both powers, by their complementation, never contradict one another. Rather, in the exercise of their offices, they are united in their ends. Thus, the undeniable advantage of harmony between the two will provide both mutual defense and benefits, and will more freely maintain justice and peace, and assure tranquility and union for the world.

"Indeed, it is by the spiritual authority that the Empire is oriented toward salvation and, assisted by its protection, immediate unrests are calmed and the Empire becomes tranquil and stable. The Priesthood, in its turn, must find secure and pious shelter in meekness and veneration of the Emperor. Ruling over the vastness of the Roman Empire, he must play the role of a special advocate and the first defender of the Church. His strong arm must defend her liberties, extirpate the heresies, extend the cult of the Christian Faith, extinguish her enemies, and conserve the Christian people in the harmony of peace and a repose in opulent tranquility" (Letter *Apud urbem veterum* to Richard King of the Romans, August 27, 1263, in *ibid.*, p. 7, n. 24, *apud ibid.*).

Leo XIII also offers a solid argument in favor of *Ecclesiocentrism*:

"For what did Jesus Christ Our Lord seek in establishing and maintaining His Church? Only one thing: to transmit to the Church the same mission and the same mandate that He himself received from His Fa-

§ 20 These three laws – *Christocentrism, Mariocentrism and Ecclesiocentrism* – were presented, we believe, by God to the Angels at the moment of their trial.[19]

§ 21 From what was explained so far, the two principles – the axiological principle and that of the angelic action – are consequences of the created order; the three laws – *Christocentrism, Mariocentrism* and *Ecclesiocentrism* – are ideals of the moral and institutional order of History.

g. Principle of double gradualism

§ 22 God created man in such a way that his intelligence comprehends things step by step, his sensibility experiences by degrees what is presented to his senses, and his will adheres or rejects gradually what his intelligence and sensibility offer it.[20]

---

ther, so that they should be perpetuated. This is what He clearly resolved to do; this is what He actually did. 'As My Father has sent Me, so I send you' (Jn 20:21). 'As You sent Me into the world, I also have sent them into the world' (Jn 17:18).

"Now, it is in the mission of Christ to redeem from death and save 'that which has perished,' that is, not only some nations and cities, but the whole human race, without distinction of time or place. 'The Son of man came so that the world might be saved by Him' (Jn 3:17). For 'there is no other name under Heaven given to men whereby we must be saved' (Act 4:12).

"The mission of the Church, therefore, is to spread far and wide among all men and to transmit through all the ages the salvation worked by Christ and all the blessings flowing from this. Wherefore, by the will of her Founder, it is necessary that this Church should be one in all lands and at all times" (Encyclical *Satis cognitum*, Petropolis: Vozes, nn. 8-9).

These principles are confirmed by Pius XII: "The principal meaning of the supra-nationality of the Church is to perennially give figure and form to the basic structure of human society, above all the diversities and beyond the limits of space and time" (Speech *La Elevatezza*, February 20, 1946, Petrópolis: Vozes, n. 22).

[19] Someone could imagine we are admitting the eternal presence of Christ, Mary and the Church before the Creation of the universe. He would be mistaken. We strongly deny this supposition. We have already clearly stated our rejection of such a progressivist utopia in Vol. VIII, *Fumus Satanae, passim*, especially in Chapters IV and V. The only thing we admit is that God could have given knowledge of His plan to the Angels before Christ, Mary or the Church had real existence.

[20] St. Thomas confirms *regarding the intelligence*: "The human intellects obtain their perfection in the knowledge of truth by a kind of movement and discursive intellectual operation; that is to say, as they advance

§ 23 Correspondently, the created universe is one and varied. The element that harmonizes its variety is hierarchy, making it tend toward unity. By being hierarchical, it is ordered by degrees or gradually.[21]

§ 24 Thus, to the gradualism of the universe presented to man for his contemplation of God as the *exemplar cause*, we find a corresponding gradualism of the knowledge, feelings and adhesions or rejections in human nature. This is *the principle of double gradualism*. It is the foundation for the notion of the process of the ascent or descent of man, society and History, as we will see further on.

h. Principle of human liberty; law of *natura integra* & law of *natura lapsa*

§ 25 Under the action of the three mentioned principles of the created order – the *axiological, the action of the angels* and *double gradualism* – God submitted man to his trial. Thus, the *principle of human liberty* enters Creation, which, by the choice of the free will, shall condition all of human History. With original sin, nature suffered its consequences: Human intelligence became subject to error, the will was weakened and turned toward evil, and the sensibility became dispersive and corrupted.[22]

By the effect of free will, History left the governance of the *law of natura integra* (perfect nature) and was hurled into

---

from one known thing to another" (*Summa Theologiae*, I, q. 58, a. 3)

Regarding the senses: "As the intellect proceeds from potentiality to act, the same order of knowledge appears in the senses. For by sense we judge of the more common before the less common, in reference both to place and time; in reference to place, when a thing is seen afar off it is seen to be a body before it is seen to be an animal; and to be an animal before it is seen to be a man, and to be a man before it is seen to be Socrates or Plato. The same is true regarding time, for a child can distinguish man from no-man before he distinguishes this man from that man. ... Thus, it is evident that indistinct knowledge is midway between potentiality and act" (*ibid.* q. 85, a. 3).

Regarding the will: "To choose is to desire something for the sake of obtaining something else: wherefore, properly speaking, it regards the means to the end. Now, in matters of knowledge, the principles are related to the conclusion to which we assent on account of the principles, just as in appetitive matters the end is related to the means, which is desired on account of the end" (*ibid.*, q. 83, a. 4).

[21] See in this Chapter Note 39.

[22] Cf. Vol. X, *Peccatum – Redemptio*, Chap. I.2, 3.

the *law of natura lapsa* (corrupted nature). Man became capable of affronting the divine plans and of attempting to accomplish others opposed to them.

i. Law of love for the Cross

§ 26 Since the human will became unstable after original sin, its adhesion to evil is susceptible to regret. This is the reason God did not condemn Adam straight to Hell, but to a life of suffering and combats.

Men can return to the initial plan God designed for them by means of the punitive, expiatory or redemptive suffering. We have the Cross that is set as a road for men to return to truth and goodness and the criterion for their judgment: This is the *law of love for the Cross*.[23]

j. Principle of the fight between the two races

§ 27 After the original sin, Adam gave birth to two different progenies: a good one having as its ideal a return to the primeval situation with the Cross as the means to achieve this; and a bad one opposed to the first. Such progenies were prophesized by God himself when He issued the curse against the serpent: "I will put enmities between you and the Woman, and between your seed and her seed. She shall crush your head, and you shall lie in wait for her heel" (Gen 3:15). We have, then, *the principle of the fight between the two races* projected inside History.[24]

---

[23] "This Cross [of Our Lord Jesus Christ], dispersed into so many places over the earth, will be brought together and transported to Heaven. The Cross, shining with radiant brilliance, will judge, by its sight, the living and dead. It will claim revenge against its enemies, joy and leniency for all its friends. It will give glory to all blessed and will sing its victory on earth and in Heaven" (St. Louis Grignion de Montfort, *Carta-Circular aos Amigos da Cruz*, Rio de Janeiro: Ed. Santa Maria, 1954, p. 70).

[24] • "God has established one sole enmity – but it is an irreconcilable one – which will not only last, but will go on increasing to the end of time. That enmity is between Mary, His worthy Mother, and the Devil, between the children and servants of the Blessed Virgin and the children and followers of Lucifer. Thus, Mary is the most terrible enemy that God has set up against the Devil" (St. Louis Grignion de Montfort, *Tratado da Verdadeira Devoção à Santíssima Virgen*, Petrópolis: Vozes, 1961, pp. 54-55; cf. pp. 56-57).

• "It is true, great God, that the world will set, as You predicted, great traps at the heel of this mysterious Woman, that is, for the small Com-

§ 28 Thus, the *principle of angelic action*, which is synonymous with the fight between the good and bad angels, finds a similar action in human History. It is in History, therefore, that men and angels fight for the installation either of the Kingdom of God or, conversely, of the kingdom of the Devil.

Thus, after the original sin, human History unfolds under the symbols of the Cross and the sword.

k. Law of the tendency to reach the summit

§ 29 The free will of man obeys the *principle of double gradualism*. The dynamism of its process, however, relies on the force with which it tends towards its end. In the case of the good, this force proceeds from the will strengthened by grace and helped by the Angels, and in the case of the evil, from the will subjected to the dynamism of vice, accelerated by the action of the devils.

The aim toward which the good man tends is, thus, the apex of good – union with God. On the contrary, the goal of the process of the evil man is the apex of evil – union with the Devil.

---

pany of her children who will appear near the end times. It is true that there will be great enmities between this blessed posterity of Mary Most Holy and the cursed race of Satan. But this enmity is entirely divine, it is the only one of which You are the Author: *Inimititias ponam* [I will place enmities]" (*ibid.*, pp. 305-306).

Leo XIII confirms the principle of the fight between the two races: "From the moment that the Devil, moved by envy, miserably separated himself from God, to whom he owed his existence and his supernatural gifts, mankind divided itself into two enemy camps that never cease to combat one another: one that contends for truth and virtue, the other for everything that is contrary to virtue and truth. The first is the Kingdom of God on earth, namely, the true Church of Jesus Christ, whose members, insofar as they desire to belong to her from the bottom of their heart and attain salvation, must necessarily serve God and His One Son with their whole mind and will. The second is the kingdom of Satan. Under his empire and in his power are all those who, following the sinister example of their chief and of our first parents, refuse to obey the divine law and multiply their efforts to ignore God or to act directly against Him.

"These two kingdoms were seen and described by St. Augustine with great discernment under the form of two cities, opposed to one another in their laws and ideals. With an ingenious simplicity, he stressed the constitutive principle of each with these words: 'Two loves gave birth to two cities: The earthly city proceeds from the love of self even to the disdain of God; the celestial city proceeds from the love of God even to the disdain of self' (*De Civitate Dei*, book 14, c. 17)" (Encyclical *Humanum genus*, Petrópolis: Vozes. 1960, n. 1; cf. n. 2).

This is the *law of the tendency to reach the summit*, which is an indispensable corollary of the *principle of double gradualism*. Both are summarized in the words of Juvenal: *Nemo summus fit repenter, nemo pessimus fit repenter* (no one becomes either extremely good or bad suddenly). "[25]

l. Law of processivity or the process

§ 30 These two factors allow us to define the *law of processivity* or the *process* in the will of man and in History. The *law of processivity* or the *process* is the dynamic enchainment of causes and effects whereby each effect becomes the cause of the subsequent phase with a growing acceleration of speed. This *process* tends toward a final end, which is already foreseen in each of its phases.[26] Scripture alludes to the process of evil when it affirms: *Abyssus abyssum invocat* (One abyss calls for the other) (Ps 41:8).

m. Law of the tendencies

§ 31 According to the *law of processivity*, before acts of the intelligence and the will are clearly formed, there are already tendencies in which future ideas and deliberations are in a stage of germination. Although sub-conscientious, such tendencies have a considerable influence on the course of the life of men and societies. These characteristics follow the *law of the tendencies*, correlated to the *law of processivity*.

---

[25] Juvenal in V.A., *Phrases e Curiosidades Latinas* (Rio de Janeiro, 1955), p. 455.

[26] Regarding the revolutionary process that shook Medieval Christendom, Plinio Corrêa de Oliveira presupposes the elements of the above definition: "This crisis is not a spectacular, isolated fact. It constitutes, on the contrary, a critical process of five centuries. It is a long chain of causes and effects that, having originated at a certain moment with great intensity in the deepest recesses of the soul and the culture of Western man, has been producing successive convulsions from the 15th century to our days. …
"This process should not be viewed as an altogether fortuitous sequence of causes and effects that has taken place unexpectedly. Already at its inception, this crisis had all the necessary energy to carry out all its potentialities. It is still strong enough to cause, by means of supreme convulsions, the final destructions that are its logical outcome" (*Revolution and Counter-Revolution*, York, PA: The American Society for the Defense of Tradition, Family and Property, 1993, Part I, chap. III. 5).

Besides the normal process of the birth of the tendencies, it is indispensable to refer also to the disordered process, which is the consequence of original sin. Situated principally in the sensibility and the will, the mechanism of the disordered passions has a marked, even determinant, influence on the sprouting and development of certain bad tendencies. When they are not combated by vigorous discipline and asceticism, such disordered tendencies often play a relevant role in the history of individuals as well as of peoples in determining mentalities, deliberations and thoughts.[27]

n. Laws of divine economy in History: Law of primitive revelation, law of written revelation & law of grace

§ 32

By the ministry of the Angels, throughout History God preserved in man the ideal he should fulfill by means of three communications, which, in turn, gave rise to the three *laws of divine economy in History.*

First, there was the *law of primitive revelation,*[28] which

---

[27] "These disorderly tendencies by their very nature strive for realization. No longer conforming to a whole order of things contrary to them, they start by modifying mentalities, ways of being, and artistic expressions and customs, without immediately touching directly – at least habitually – ideas" (*ibid.*, Part I, chap. V.1).

[28] What we present as the *law of primitive revelation*, Bossuet describes as the *phase of tradition*: "Imagine, therefore, a world that is still new and, so to speak, still soaked by the waters of the Deluge, when men, still so close in time to the origin of things, had need of nothing but tradition, which had been conserved in them since Adam and Noah, to know the unity of God and the service owed to Him. This tradition conformed so closely to the lights of reason that it seemed that a truth so clear and important could never be obscured or forgotten. This was the first state of religion, which lasted until Abraham. In it, in order to know the greatness of God, men had only to consult their reason and their memory.

"But reason was weak and corrupted. As men moved farther away from the origin of things, the ideas they had received from their ancestors fell into disarray. The children, unruly and coarse, no longer wanted to believe their elders, whom they hardly knew after so many generations had passed. The brutalized human mind could no longer elevate itself to the high intellectual things. And since men now desired only what they could see, idolatry spread over the whole world" (J.B. Bossuet, *Discours sur l'Histoire Universelle*, Paris: Garnier-Flammarion, 1966, chap. 2, pp. 164-165).

Further on, he returns to this thought as he describes the institution

was present in the memory of men regarding that primeval stage from which Adam had fallen and the initial relations he had with God. Those happy memories and wise rules were transmitted orally from father to son.

§ 33 *Second*, when primitive revelation was forgotten by men because of their infidelities over time, Divine Providence established the *law of written revelation* and chose the Hebrew people to be the guardian of such revelation.

§ 34 *Third*, when, after the fidelities and infidelities, after the victories and defeats of the children of God, the time of this law was completed, the Divine Word took flesh with the *fiat* of the Virgin Mary. From Him the Catholic Church would be born: God established the *law of grace*.

After the Redemption of sin was accomplished, the *law of grace* not only restored the noblest part of the ideal that Adam knew, but far surpassed the primeval stage. Our Lord Jesus Christ – the New Adam and Man-God – defeated the Devil, broke the scepter of power he held over the world (cf. Jn 12:31; 16:11; 1 Jn 3:8) and established the Kingdom of God on earth.

§ 35 The cumulative ideals of *Christocentrism*, *Mariocentrism* and *Ecclesiocentrism* became a reality: an indisputable reality in the spiritual realm – the Church, the Kingdom of Christ[29]

---

of the written law: "Amid such great ignorance, man reached the point of adoring the work of his hands. Thus he believed he could imprison the divine spirit in his statues. He had so profoundly lost the notion that God had created him that he believed he himself could make a god. Who could believe this, if experience did not show us that such a stupid, brutal error was not only the most universal of errors, but also the most deeply rooted and incorrigible in men?

"Thus, we must recognize that, to the great confusion of mankind, the original truth ... which deeply impressed the human mind, became the furthest removed from the sight of men. The tradition that conserved this truth in their spirits, although still clear and sufficiently present if attention were paid to it, was on the brink of vanishing: Prodigious fables, abounding with impiety and extravagance, took its place. The moment had arrived when the truth, poorly guarded in the memory of men, could no longer be conserved without being written. Thus, God decided to form His people in virtue by means of explicit and numerous laws that would be left written for them" (*ibid.*, chap. 3, p. 175).

[29] St. Thomas Aquinas teaches that the Church is the Kingdom of Christ by antonomasia (cf. *IV Sententiarum*, d. 49, q. 1, a. 2, q. 5, c. St. Augustine peremptorily affirms: "Henceforth, the Church is the

– and a political and social reality still in germination. This seed would develop in the course of a history of sufferings and fights until, with the graces emanating from the Catholic Church, the ensemble of peoples and nations would form medieval Christendom.[30] With this, the Kingdom of Christ was established also in the temporal order, and the initial plan of God was fulfilled.[31]

o. Plans to impede order & to establish an anti-order

§ 36

If the ideal of the offspring of the children of the Virgin is to establish the Kingdom of Christ over all peoples and nations, an aim desired by the three centrisms – *Christocentrism,*

Kingdom of Christ and the Kingdom of Heaven" (*La Cité de Dieu* (Paris: Jacques Lecoffre, 1854), vol. 3, p. 298.

[30] The Catholic Church also inspired many ancient Catholic Kingdoms, such as the Armenian and Ethiopian, and even ensembles of Kingdoms, such as the Western Roman Empire from Constantine to Romulus Augustus. She principally inspired the Byzantine Empire or the Eastern Roman Empire, which lived much longer than its Western counterpart.

However, those Western and Eastern Christendoms became paralyzed and lost their flux of life, caused by a hyper-valorization of the role of the temporal authority – the Emperor or King – and the incorrect idea that the Pope should depend on it. In them the Church never had the autonomy and liberty she had in the West after the conversion of Clovis. Perhaps for these reasons, those first Christendoms did not produce the full harvest of temporal fruits that Western Medieval Christendom did. This is why we consider that only when Medieval Christendom grew and expanded throughout Europe did the Kingdom of Christ in the temporal sphere assume its full meaning. It became the Christendom *per antonomasiam*.

[31] Leo XIII confirms this thesis: "However, triumphing over all the obstacles, violence and oppressions, always spreading out her pacific tent, the Church, by safeguarding the glorious patrimony of the arts, sciences and letters and by making the spirit of the Gospel penetrate deeply into human society, formed a civilization that was called Christian. It brought to those nations that did not obstruct her beneficial influence equity of law, elevation of customs, protection of the weak and unfortunate, and respect for the rights and dignity of all. Furthermore, as much as it is possible in view of human inconstancy, she brought to civil life peace, which derives from the perfect harmony between liberty and justice" (Encyclical *Parvenu*, Petrópolis: Vozes, 1952, n. 8; cf. *Immortale Dei*, Petrópolis: Vozes, 1954, n. 28; St. Pius X, Apostolic Letter *Notre Charge Apostolique*, Petrópolis: Vozes, 1951, n. 2).

Mariocentrism and *Ecclesiocentrism* – and maintained by the three laws of divine communication, the ideal of the offspring of the Serpent is precisely the opposite.

That is, what the Devil wants is to prevent the plan of God from being realized and to accomplish the opposite. His aims are, respectively, the *plan to impede order* foreseen by God and the *plan to establish an anti-order*. Anti-order in its full meaning is the Kingdom of the Devil.[32]

p. Principles of the conspiracy & of the action of the Secret Forces

§ 37 The ideal of the children of the Serpent cannot be presented in the light of the day. This is because it is born from the vices of pride against God and hatred for the children of the Virgin. Such characteristics make it infamous. This causes it to hide its ideal in the darkness and keep its members unknown.[33]

---

[32] This visualization is ratified in part by these words of Leo XIII: "In effect, who can ignore the immense conspiracy of hostile forces that today aims to shake and demolish the great work of Jesus Christ, attempting with relentless pertinacity to destroy in the intellectual order the treasure of celestial doctrine and to subvert in the social order the most holy and healthy Christian institutions?" (Encyclical *Parvenu*, n. 2).

The Pope generically confirms the plan of the children of the Devil to destroy the work of God: "The world is always the same. The satellites of this great enemy of mankind, who rebelled against the Most High from the beginning and is called in the Gospel the Prince of this World, constantly work against the children of God. For this reason, in face of the law and the one who presents it in the name of God, the world revolts with an immense pride and spirit of independence to which it has no right. Ah! How many times, in more tempestuous days, have the enemies of the divine joined together, with unheard of cruelty and true injustice, with the aim of madly destroying the divine work, with evident damage to social communion!" (*ibid.* n. 6)

[33] See Vol. VIII, *Fumus Satanae*, Chap VII §§ 27-30, 33-35.

Additionally, Leo XIII explains why the members of the secret forces are obliged to remain occult. He is referring directly to agents of diverse sects analogous to Freemasonry:

"Those who are affiliated [to those secret sects] must promise blind obedience and follow without discussion the desires of its leaders and masters; they must be always ready – at the least notification and slightest expression of their will – to execute their orders; otherwise, they are submitted to the most rigorous penalties, including death. In fact, it is not rare that this ultimate penalty is inflicted on them when they are judged to have betrayed some secret of the sect or to have

We have, then, the *principle of conspiracy* of the children of darkness against the children of light. We also have, as its indissoluble corollary, the *principle of the action of the secret forces* throughout History, which promotes and pushes forward the kingdom of the Devil.

q. Plan of the Revolution

§ 38

Taking into consideration that the Kingdom of Christ had already been established in the Church and overflowed from her to the European peoples to form Medieval Christendom, that is, the temporal Kingdom of Christ, the Secret Forces and the Devil felt themselves defeated. In effect, that triumph represented the initial plan of God accomplished in the most important part of the world.

The first *plan to impede order*, the ideal of the Secret Forces, had been defeated by the expansion of the ideals of the good and by the preponderance of *the law of grace*. Therefore, that plan of evil should be replaced with another, the *plan of the Revolution*, which would attempt to invert the order of the Kingdom of Christ in the Church and in Christendom, to destroy it and to establish the Kingdom of the Devil.[34]

---

resisted the commands of their masters. This is done with so much audacity and dexterity that, in the majority of the cases, the executor of such sentences of death escapes [civil] justice, which was established to oversee crimes and take revenge for them.

"Behold some of these monstrous practices condemned by nature itself: to live in dissimulation and act in darkness; to reduce men to slavery by binding them [to the masters] in the tightest bonds without knowing beforehand to what they have committed; to use these passive instruments enslaved to the will of another for all kinds of assaults; to arm men's hands for bloodshed after securing impunity for the crime" (Encyclical *Humanum genus*, n. 8).

[34] a. These words by St. Pius X confirm the amplitude of the effort of the evil against the order desired by God: "In our days it is undoubtedly true that 'the nations have raged and the people imagined vain things' (Ps 2:1) against their Creator; and this cry of His enemies has become frequent: 'Depart from us' (Jn 21:14). It ensues from there that there is a complete rejection of all respect to God in the majority [of men]. From this it results that public and private customs of life were adopted that take no account of the sovereignty of God. What is more, every effort and every artifice is employed to utterly abolish the memory of Him and even the notion of Him.

"Whoever weighs these things has good reason to fear that this great perversity is the beginning of those evils announced for the end times, and that there may already be present on the earth that 'son of perdition' of whom the Apostle speaks (2 Thes 2:3). Such, in truth, is the audacity and wrath employed everywhere in persecuting Religion, in combating the dogmas of the Faith, in the brazen effort to uproot and annihilate all relations between men and the Divinity!

"As the Apostle says, the distinguishing mark of the Antichrist is that, with an infinite temerity, man puts himself in the place of the Creator, elevating himself 'above all that is called God.' And this in such a way that, although he cannot completely extinguish in himself the notion of God, man, however shakes the yoke of His Majesty and, as it were, makes of the world a temple wherein he himself is to be adored. 'He sits in the temple of God, showing himself as if he were God' (2 Thes 2:2)" (*E supreme apostolatus*, nn. 5-6).

b. Leo XIII points to Freemasonry as the principal agent for the realization of the inversion of the Kingdom of Christ:

"The facts that we have just summarized shed sufficient light on the inner constitution of the Freemasons and clearly show the road they tread to reach their aim. Their principal dogmas are so greatly and manifestly at variance with reason that nothing can be more perverse. Actually, is it not the summit of madness to wish to destroy the Religion and the Church established by God himself and insured by Him of perpetual protection, in order to re-establish among us, after a lapse of 18 centuries, the customs and institutions of the pagans? But, what is neither less horrible nor more supportable is to see the repudiation of the benefits mercifully acquired by Jesus Christ, first for the individuals, and second for men grouped in families and nations. ... Surely, in this insane and wicked endeavor we may recognize the implacable hatred and spirit of revenge with which Satan is inflamed against Jesus Christ" (Encyclical *Humanum genus*, n. 19).

c. Pius IX also describes the plan of the Revolution: "Each of you has noticed, Venerable Brethren, that in these our disastrous times a very bitter and fearsome war is being unleashed against all that is Catholic by men bound together in a perverse society. These men are imbued with a perverse doctrine, having closed their ears to the truth, and encouraged and disseminated among the people all kinds of false doctrines that proceed from error and darkness. We are horrified and our heart is filled with sorrow when we consider their monstrous errors and their many harmful methods, plots and contrivances. These men use these means to spread their hatred for truth and light. They are experienced and skillful in deceit, which they use to set in motion their plans to extinguish all piety, justice and virtue; to corrupt customs, to step on divine and human rights, to weaken the Catholic Religion and civil society and even overthrow it, if it were possible" (Encyclical *Qui pluribus*, Petropolis: Vozes, 1960, n. 2).

r. Revolution or revolutionary process

§ 39 The *principle of conspiracy* gives birth to another reality, the *Revolution* or *the revolutionary process,*[35] which brings together what is worst and most dynamic in evil and in the secret forces to fight against the Church and Christendom. Henceforth, the *plan to impede order* and the *plan to establish an anti-order* are encompassed by the *plan of the Revolution.*

s. Principle of the action in the tendencies, ideas & facts

§ 40 In order to implant itself in the human soul and in society, the *revolutionary process* starts to act in the tendencies. It is the *principle of the action in the tendencies* that characterizes the *Tendencial Revolution.* This opens the doors for the *principle of action in the ideas*, which characterizes the *Sophistic Revolution* or the *Revolution in the Ideas*.

This *Revolution in the ideas* ferments in spirits until it precipitates the *Revolution in the Facts.* The *Revolution in the facts* – in ambiences, customs and institutions – will constitute the landmark for a new development of tendencies, ideas and facts.[36] Thus is the enchainment of the *revolutionary process.*

t. Counter-Revolution or counter-revolutionary process

§ 41 In opposition, the birth of the Revolution produced in the Church Militant the *counter-revolutionary process* or *Counter-Revolution.* It is the order of the Kingdom of Christ in a state of counter-attack.[37]

Thus, *Revolution* and *Counter-Revolution* are the two processes that synthesize in History the *principle of the fight between the two races* on earth and the *principle of the fight be-*

---

[35] Regarding the Revolution, Plinio Corrêa de Oliveira states: "Its principal objective is not the destruction of certain rights of persons and families. It desires far more than that. It wants to destroy a whole legitimate order of things and replace it with an illegitimate situation. And 'order of things' still does not say it all. It is a vision of the universe and a way of being of man that the Revolution seeks to abolish with the aim of replacing them with radically opposed counterparts" (*Revolution and Counter-Revolution*, chap. VII.1.c).

He further affirms: "If this is what order and legitimacy are, one easily sees what the Revolution is, since it is the opposite of that order. It is disorder and illegitimacy *par excellence*" (*ibid.*, chap VII.2.E).

[36] Cf. *ibid.*, part I, chap. V.

[37] Cf. *ibid.*, part II, chap. II.1,2.

tween good and evil in the angelic sphere in their most expressive and dynamic aspects and in their general movement toward their apexes.

Both processes develop to establish their ideals in the ensemble of peoples and nations. The fight *Revolution versus Counter-Revolution* is situated, therefore, at the center of History.[38]

u. Law of the glory of God manifested by the ensembles

§ 42 The mention of the ensemble of peoples and nations leads to the consideration of the vocations of these social bodies and the analysis of their constitution or, in other words, to the *law of the glory of God manifested by the ensembles*, a consequence of the *axiological principle.*

§ 43 If, from the perspective of the *axiological principle*, God receives and will receive the glory He foresaw in His initial plan, this will take place principally regarding the ensemble of men, that is, in society, and in society as its exists throughout time, that is, in History.

Something analogous occurs regarding each people and nation that God created: analogous because of the *principle of liberty* that permits an entire people, similar to an individual, to accept or reject God's plan for that people.

§ 44 The human ensembles are called to glorify God in a special manner. In effect, it is through these ensembles, when they are faithful to grace and submissive to the beneficial influence of Holy Church, that Catholic civilization and culture come to light.

Through civilization a political-social order that is hierarchical and harmonic, just and merciful, solemn and accessible, glorifies God by its whole structure, by the good relationship of its parts and by the end it strives to reach. Through culture, knowledge and the arts, all sing the glory of God.

§ 45 In an organic society the intermediary ensembles between the State and the individual play an important role. These intermediary ensembles – the nobility, the military orders, the diverse bodies that compose the State, the professional guilds, the institutions of charity, the groups of professors and disciples in the universities, the artisanal guilds and, finally, the families – embroider from top to bottom the rich fabric of the social body and glorify God, each in its own way, by tending toward the elevated aim it pursues and with its proper dignity.

---

[38] Cf. H. Delassus, *La conjuration antichrètienne*, vol. 3, pp. 837-844.

From this order come private laws (*privilegia*), customs and ceremonies that characterize each intermediary society, powerfully contributing to the advance of the civilization and culture of a people.

§ 46 Upon creating each people in History, God gives it a particular vocation to reflect His glory. In function of this major vocation, He gives minor vocations to each of the more restricted ensembles that compose the State and society of this people.

If this is the case regarding a people or nation, with more reason is it so in what concerns the ensemble of peoples. The vocation of such an ensemble is the establishment of the Kingdom of Christ on earth, obeying the laws of *Christocentrism*, *Mariocentrism* and *Ecclesiocentrism*.

v. Principle & law of hierarchy

§ 47 In society, as well as in the whole universe, the best reflection of God is found in the inequality of the multiple elements and in the factor that orders and unifies them all: hierarchy. The *principle of hierarchy* – the element that gives unity to the variety of the universe – and the *law of hierarchy* – the ideal to which men must be subjected – constitute the best reflections of God in Creation.[39]

---

[39] a. St. Dionysius the Areopagite gives us the following definition of hierarchy, which confirms what we said about the *principle of hierarchy* and the *law of hierarchy*: "Hierarchy is, I believe, a sacred order, a science, an activity which, so far as is attainable, is similar to the form of God, and, according to the illuminations God gives it, it elevates itself to the degree of its own forces to the imitation of God. …

"Thus, when I speak of hierarchy, I want to signify a certain sacred disposition, image of the splendor of God, which completes the mysteries of its own illumination in the orders of hierarchical knowledge, and is similar, as much as possible, to its proper Principle [God]" (*La Hiérarchie Céleste*, Paris: Cerf, 1970, pp. 87-90).

b. As far as we know, St. Thomas Aquinas does not apply the word hierarchy to the ensemble of the created universe, although at various times he teaches that inequality is the best reflection of God: "Now, the form of the universe consists in the differentiation and order of its parts. … That which is good and excellent in the universe consists in the mutual order of its parts, which cannot exist without differentiation. For it is by this order that the universe is established in its wholeness and in this its excellence consists" (*Summa Contra Gentiles*, II, chap. 39).

c. "The differentiation of the parts of the universe and their order is the

w. Principle & law of sacrality

§ 48

The splendor of hierarchy is sacrality,[40] *i.e.*, it is the atmosphere which, on the one hand, encompasses and, on the other hand, emanates from the various elements that are harmonically related and hierarchically ordered as they tend toward the summit of good. The apex of good in the social-political ambit is

---

proper effect of the first cause" (*ibid.*, chap. 49).

d. "Created things cannot reach a perfect likeness to God if they are limited to only a single species of creatures. For, since the cause exceeds the effect, that which is in the cause, simply and in a united way, exists in the effect in a composite and multiple fashion. ... It was therefore opportune to have multiplicity and variety among created things so that a perfect likeness to God be found in them, each in its own way" (*ibid.*, chap. 45).

e. "God is the first exemplar cause of all things. To understand this we must consider that if for the production of anything an exemplar is necessary, it is so that the effect may have a determinate form. For an artist produces a form determined by the exemplar he looks at. ... Now, it is obvious that natural things have determinate forms. This determination of forms must be reduced to their first principle, to Divine Wisdom, Who devised the order of the universe, which is based on the differentiation of things" (*Summa Theologiae*, I, q. 44, a. 3).

f. "The order of the universe, which shines both in natural beings and in those who have a will, demonstrates the justice of God" (*ibid.*, I, q. 21, a. 1).

g. However, St. Thomas applies the word hierarchy to the social body: "A hierarchy is a principality, that is, a multitude uniformly ordered under the rule of a prince. Now, such a hierarchy would not be ordered, but confused, if it were not composed of different orders. Therefore, the proper character of a hierarchy requires diversity of orders" (*ibid.*, I, q. 108, a. 2).

[40] The two following examples express the difference between hierarchy and sacrality. If we consider a pine tree, one aspect is the hierarchy we find in the arrangement of its branches from bottom to top; another aspect is the shade it projects and the aroma it expels. Sacrality is the protective atmosphere we feel sitting under the tree that gives forth the freshness of its shade and the perfume of its foliage.

If we consider a cathedral, the hierarchy is expressed by the structure of the building; the sacrality is the atmosphere we feel inside it that derives from imponderable elements, such as its blessed peace, its welcoming silence, the internal twilight that envelops everything, the light-filled colors that filter through its stained glass windows, the lingering aroma of incense burned in an earlier ceremony, the sonorous notes of an organ that descend from the choir loft, etc.

the service to and the exaltation of the Catholic Church and the establishment of the Kingdom of Christ through Mary; the apex of good in the private ambit is fidelity to grace, holiness and the salvation of the soul.

Insofar as it is a transcendent element present in irrational beings, sacrality constitutes a principle – the ***principle of sacrality***. Insofar as this transcendent element relies upon man's free will, we have the ***law of sacrality*** that should rule all the peoples.

x. Law of voluntary dependence or law of alienation

§ 49 In a hierarchical and sacral society men have inter-relationships where some are superior and others inferior. This is what gives birth to the protection-service bond: protection by the superior and service from the inferior in the practical order and the tenderness-veneration bond in the affective order.

The superior not only protects the inferior because of a contract they have entered into, but sees in him a reflection of Our Lord Jesus Christ. This conviction generates the affection of the father for the son, of the strong for the weak, of the grand for the small. It is the sentiment of tenderness. For an analogous reason, the inferior sees in the superior not only the creditor in a social pact, but respects him as a reflection of Our Lord for his superiority. From this bond the sentiment of veneration is born.

We can, thus, say that society, insofar as it is hierarchical, is founded on the protection-service bond and, insofar as it is sacral, it is founded on the tenderness-veneration bond. These two bonds constitute the essence of the *law of dependence* or *law of alienation*, which is the fundamental law of the Kingdom of Christ on earth and, consequently, the basic law of History.[41]

---

[41] The voluntary dependence of the inferior upon the superior constitutes an act of supreme liberty and indisputable lucidity. It is *supreme liberty* because, in the exercise of his liberty, the inferior lacks the conditions to achieve by himself the aim the superior naturally achieves; therefore, it constitutes a supreme use of his liberty – defined as the choice of the proper means to attain a determined end – for the inferior to voluntarily abdicate his liberty and subordinate himself to the superior to reach an end more elevated than what would be proportional to the inferior.

Analogously, such an attitude of alienation constitutes an act of *supreme lucidity* because, by uniting himself to the superior, the inferior saves his own efforts by allowing the superior to lead him to the goal

---

he desires, like a passenger of a ship who entrusts himself to the nautical skills of a commander in order to reach his desired destination. This same principle is praised in the *chanson de geste*: "*Aquel que a buen señor sirve, siempre vivie en paraíso*" (One who serves a good lord always lives in paradise) (Anonymous, *Poema de Mio Cid*, Madrid: Aguilar, 1969, *Cantar Primero*, 45, p. 95). The dependence of the inferior on the superior, however, is just one aspect of the question.

More arduous, on the other hand, is the alienation of the superior regarding the inferior. For, since the superior does not depend on the inferior except accidentally, he can always dismiss or replace him. The voluntary dependence the superior assumes toward the inferior is composed of two fundamental elements:

First, of the love for the common good that the superior will only realize with the harmonic collaboration of his subjects;

Second, of the goodness and disinterested attention shown by the superior for the particular good of the inferior. For, since the particular subordinate is not necessary for the superior, the maintenance of that bond of dependence assumes a gratuitous character, in other words, one of goodness. It is more difficult to accept the sacrifices imposed in the name of the common good and someone else's interests than those demanded by one's own interest. Therefore, the dependence of the superior on the inferior is more arduous and, for this reason, more meritorious.

Historian Marc Bloch describes in practical terms the birth of this kind of voluntary dependence in the Middle Ages as the mold for the civilization that came forth:

"To seek a protector or to find satisfaction in being a protector – these things are common to all ages. But we seldom find them giving rise to new juridical institutions save in civilizations where the rest of the social framework is giving way. Such was the case of Gaul after the collapse of the Roman Empire.

"Consider, for example, the society in the Merovingian period. Neither the State nor the family provided adequate protection any longer. The village community was barely strong enough to maintain order within its own boundaries; the town community scarcely existed. Everywhere, the weak man felt the need to look for the support of someone more powerful than himself. The powerful man, in his turn, could not maintain his prestige or his fortune, or even ensure his own safety, except by securing for himself … the support of subordinates bound to his service.

"On the one hand, there was an urgent quest for a chief; on the other hand, there were usurpations of authority, sometimes in a brutal way. And as notions of weakness and strength are always relative, in many cases the same man occupied a dual role – as a dependent of a more powerful man and a protector of humbler ones. Thus, there began to

§ 50 The Devil, the Secret Forces and the Revolution always try to abolish the *law of alienation* by stimulating in society the vice of pride – opposed to hierarchy – and the vice of sensuality – opposed to sacrality. From this constant effort derive their egalitarianism and liberalism. The struggle to abolish the *law of alienation* is an echo in History of Lucifer's cry: *Non serviam*.

Our Lady, the Church and the Counter-Revolution always stimulate the *law of alienation* as a response to revolutionary action. It is the echo of the angelic shout of St. Michael: *Quis ut Deus?*

*

§ 51 Even though the Kingdom of Our Lord Jesus Christ was installed in the temporal ambit in the Middle Ages and, thus, in essence the demand of the *axiological principle* was somehow accomplished, it is also true that Medieval Christendom did not extend throughout the entire world. In this sense, the demand of the *axiological principle* for a complete victory was not satisfied.

§ 52 Further, soon after the apogee of that Christendom, the *revolutionary process* started, which today boasts its victory everywhere.

§ 53 Therefore, by the demand of the glory of God and the full accomplishment of the *axiological principle*, we have a moral certainty – confirmed by the prophetic message of St. Louis Marie Grignion de Montfort – that the Revolution will be smashed by the action of the counter-revolutionaries assisted by the Most Holy Virgin. From this victory will come an age of great glorification of the Holy Church. [42]

---

be built up a vast system of personal relationships whose intersecting threads extended from one level of the social structure to another" (*La Société Féodale*, Paris: Albin Michel, 1970, pp. 212-213).

[42] In his "Fiery Prayer," St Louis Maria Grignion de Montfort speaks of the Apostles of the Latter Times and mentions the victory against the Revolution to which we referred:

a. "But above all, [God of goodness] remember Your beloved Son: *Respice in faciem Christi tui*. Look upon the face of Your anointed One, the Agony He suffered, the shame He endured, the loving complaint He made in the Garden of Olives when He said: *Quae utilitas in sanguine meo?* [Of what use will be My Blood?] His cruel death and the blood He shed, all these cry out to You for mercy, so that, by means of this Congregation, His Kingdom may be established over the ruins of the empire of His enemies" (*Tratado da Verdadeira De-*

§ 54 In this era to come, the demands of the glory of God in History will be accomplished. We will see shining as never before throughout the entire world, in the Church and the State, the *law of hierarchy* and the *law of sacrality* substantiated in the *law of alienation*. This will be the golden clasp that will close History. After that, what will remain will only be the terrible and final defection from the Faith, which will call for the presence of the greatest saints to face it. They will be the worthy court of nobles and heralds that will precede the coming of the King of Kings and Lord of Lords (Apoc 19:16) in order to annihilate the Antichrist and initiate the Last Judgment.

*

§ 55 Therefore, human History, viewed from its noblest and amplest aspect, is an extremely rich, complex and subtle reality wherein quite varied factors concur, with different degrees of influence over the individual free will, which is the determinant factor in human events.

It is not my intention to make an exposition here of all the principles of Theology and Philosophy of History, along with the correlated principles of psychology, sociology and politics that I received from my Master. I leave, registered in this book, only a quick overview of the ensemble as a point of reference for an appraisal of other systems of Philosophy and Theology of History.

*

2. Critique of Various Presentations of Philosophy & Theology of History

§ 56 Let us *first* analyze the revolutionary presentations, and *second,* the Catholic presentations.

---

voção à Santíssima Virgem, p. 302).

b. "Did You not give, beforehand, to some of Your friends a vision of the future restoration of Your Church?" (*ibid.*, p. 303).

c. "*Accendatur*. Let this divine fire that Jesus Christ came to bring to earth be enkindled before the all-consuming fire of Your wrath comes down and reduces the whole world to ashes. *Emitte Spiritum tuum et creabuntur et renovabis faciem terrae*. Send to the earth, O God, this fiery Spirit to create fiery priests by whose ministry the face of earth will be renewed and Your Church reformed" (*ibid.*, p. 307).

A. Revolutionary Presentations of Philosophy & Theology of History

§ 57 Some presentations of History pretend to be philosophical, like those of Condorcet, Sainte Croix and Bertrand Russell, but are atheistic. Because they deny the existence of God, they consequently do not consider the role of grace and of the Church in History. They further deny the influence of the Angels on human action. Those who defend such systematizations are like students of architecture who would obstinately deny the existence of roofs, pillars of foundation and columns in buildings. They are, at the most, dilettante admirers of the ruins of façades. No serious discussion about History can be made based on them.

§ 58 Others frontally deny the role of the *axiological principle* in the universe, replacing it with a tragic fatalism. This appears to be the fundamental error of Vico, who saw the nations "going round and round without ever leaving the circle of the divine, heroic and human ages," and imagined "an eternal circle of an ideal history in which the histories of all the nations – with their birth, progress, decadence and end – revolve throughout time."[43]

Michelet also supposed "a regular rotation of the natural and civil worlds where, under the eyes of Providence, all the peoples make an eternal chorus of life and death."[44] In his analysis of society, Ballanche declared that God placed in it "something inexorable similar to the fatality of the tragic poets."[45] However, the most characteristic author of this tragic fatality, in our opinion, is Hegel, who imagines History as an eternal conflict between the idea, nature and the spirit.[46] In order to explain the life of the peoples, both Hegel and Vico "adopt the symbol of the Phoenix, which dies and is reborn from its ashes."[47]

§ 59 There are still others who, in the extremely subtle equilibrium between the *axiological principle* and the *principle of human liberty,* force the plates of the scale to one side or the

---

43 Henri de Lubac, *La Posterité Spirituelle de Joachim de Flore* (Paris: Lethielleux, 1979}, vol. 1, p. 230; cf. Humberto Padovani & Luís Castagnola, *História da Filosofia* (São Paulo, Ed. Melhoramentos, 1967), p. 348.

44 H. de Lubac, *La Posterité Spirituelle*, vol. 1, p. 231.

45 *Ibid.*, p. 315.

46 Cf. F. Klimke, *História de la Filosofia*, pp. 505-506.

47 H. de Lubac, *La Posterité Spirituelle*, vol. 1, p. 362.

other. As they look for laws to orient the course of History in a certain supposedly infallible way, they overreach the legitimate search for the central plan of God dictated by the *axiological principle*. They fall into historical determinism. They establish ecclesiological, metaphysical or scientific laws that would fix an invariable direction to History.

§ 60 Campanella imagined that the life of the Church would be regulated by the circular movement of the stars.[48] Spinoza, Leibniz and, after them, Lessing established a "law of development" in the universe that would determine History.[49] Herder pretended to glimpse everywhere – in stars, animals and civilizations – a "fundamental law of nature," which would consist in "composing a being from many beings and in smashing multitudes of diversified organizations by the wheel of creation – always moving and destroying. From this destruction would come less numerous creatures, but always finer forms of life."[50] Generally speaking, the Philosophies of History professing Evolutionism follow a similar determinism.

§ 61 Placed in a symmetrical disequilibrium, other authors consider only human liberty, without taking into account the *axiological principle* or other factors that strongly influence History toward good or evil. However, since the most important principle of History is that *of human liberty*, these authors in fact are not fundamentally wrong. For this reason, their conception is objective in its nucleus and their conclusions are generally consistent. However, given that the conception is incomplete, it is subject to distortions.

---

[48] *Ibid.*, p. 217.

[49] The historical vision of Leibniz, dynamic and optimistic, is clear in his *New Essays*. Commenting on this viewpoint, Victor Delbos states: "Everything that occurs in mankind as in nature, necessarily expressing God, constitutes an order, not immobile and abstract. but mobile and alive. Everything that comes from it is subject to a law of development.

"This idea of development, which Spinoza proposed without fully acknowledging it, had just brilliantly appeared in German thought with the *New Essays* by Leibniz, released not long before. It was linked to a determinist conception of things, to the principle of continuity and to the idea of a moral end for the universe. Lessing fully assumes it and rigorously deduces all its consequences" (*Le Problème Moral dans la Philosophie de Spinoza et dans l'Histoire du Spinozisme*, Alcan, 1893, p. 239, *apud* H. de Lubac, *La Posterité Spirituelle*, vol. 1, p. 276).

[50] H. de Lubac, *La Posterité Spirituelle*, vol. 1, p. 282.

§ 62 Starting principally with Kant, we find visualizations of History based no longer on free will but rather on an intuition of the human spirit. Such an intuition or internal sentiment would exercise a determinant influence over the will and would cause man, society and History to follow a certain determined course. With this, we have a determinism of the sentiment, and, therefore, a falsification of the *principle of the human liberty* and its importance in the historic development.[51]

§ 63 Schelling encouraged the sentimental admiration man has for nature, poetry and beauty: Thus German Romanticism sprouted. Schleiermacher saw in the internal sentiment, transposed to religion, the vehicle through which God revealed himself to man. This conception found success later when it was adopted by Catholic theologians in Germany and France and constituted one of the principal tenets of Modernism. The historical criticism of the modernists and, after it, that of the progressivists, considered man's internal sentiments for God as the foundation of the History of Salvation.[52]

§ 64 If we can say that in Romanticism the role of the sentiment characterizes determinism, with more reason can we accuse Modernism and Progressivism of the same; for, to the certainty proceeding from the human sentiment, modernists and progressivists added the certainty proceeding from divine revelation, which supposedly takes place through that sentiment. Here we find a double determinism that blatantly violates the *principle of human liberty*.

§ 65 The large majority of the Philosophies of History become entangled when they deal with these two fundamental principles – the *axiological principle* and the *principle of human liberty*. At times, they conceive History and Creation as being moved by a tragic fatalism in opposition to the *axiological principle*, which supposes the victory of God manifested by the ensemble of History; at times, they exaggerate the unity of the ensembles to the detriment of liberty; at yet other times, they replace liberty with

---

[51] This supposed determinant influence of the intuition or internal sentiment on the will would apply *mutatis mutandis* to those who defend the determinism of reason. They are the rationalist followers of Descartes (cf. Vol. VI, *Inveniet Fidem?* Chap. III §§ 38-44) and Pascal.

[52] Cf. §§ 101, 116-122 of this Chapter.

a determinism of the sentiment or of reason; finally, there are others that correctly understand the place of the will, but forget the role of the ensembles for the glorification of God.

B. Great Catholic Systematizations of History

§ 66 In his *The Reign of Jesus Christ in History,* Fr. Henri Ramière, S.J., criticizes the great work of St. Augustine that summarizes all of History as a confrontation between the City of God and the City of Man. Ramière points out that the Bishop of Hippo failed to consider the collective role of the individual in society and the plan of God for the ensemble of peoples. This supposed lacuna would make St. Augustine the most illustrious and respectable representative of an incomplete Philosophy and Theology of History[53] since he would not have taken into account the *law of the glory of God manifested by the ensembles.*

In making this criticism, Ramière states: "We confess, however, that even regarding facts of the past, the theory of St. Augustine contains a considerable lacuna. He tells us nothing about which law governs the collective destiny of the peoples. The formula he presents to differentiate the two Cities is perfectly correct when it assigns each man his individual place in the great plan of Providence. But, beyond this individual action, which constitutes the moral value of each man, there is a collective action that he exercises along with those who belong to the same political society. …

"His explanation of the growth of the Roman Empire can help us understand what he thinks is this providential action over societies, but no where does he give us a more complete theory on this topic. In his book we can clearly see the two Cities developing together and advancing toward opposite aims, but he does not sufficiently show the influence one exerts on the other and the unity of the divine plan that regulates their developments."

§ 67 Those who pass through this first sieve – the role of the *axiological principle,* the *principle of human liberty and the law of the glory of God manifested by the ensembles* – as in the case of Bossuet, seem, however, to have difficulty in discerning the action of evil in History in all its amplitude.

---

[53] We have at hand a typed copy of the *Le Règne de Jésus-Christ dans l'Histoire* that the eminent Jesuit used at the seminary in Vals, France in the 19th century. The criticism above can be found in *Douzième Leçon – Vraie Science de l'Histoire – Doctrine de Saint Augustin, VII.*

§ 68 Although Bossuet, in his work *Discourse on Universal History* (1681), analyzes History from the moral point of view, takes into consideration the *law of Ecclesiocentrism*[54] and recognizes the nefarious action of the Jews[55] and heretics[56] against the true Religion, he does not make explicit the *principle of angelic action* and the consequent *principle of the fight between the good and bad angels*. He also does not see in History the *principle of the fight between the two races*.

§ 69 In his remarkable study, Fr. Henri Ramière adapts the notion of the two Cities of St. Augustine to Bossuet's view of ensemble and, thus, conceives History as a fight between two Churches: the One of Our Lord and the one of Satan.[57] He includes, therefore, the principles that Bossuet missed. However, Ramière merely alludes to the existence of a conspiracy among the evil without giving too much attention to it.[58] Therefore, in

---

[54] Cf. Jacques Benigne Bossuet, *Discours sur l'Histoire Universelle*, part II, *passim*.

[55] Cf. *ibid.*, part II, chaps. 21 to 24.

[56] Cf. *ibid.*, part II, chaps. 25, 26.

[57] H. Ramière, *Le Regne de Jésus-Christ, Septième Leçon, le Plan Satanique, passim*.

[58] "As soon as the Church of Jesus Christ was constituted, the Church of Satan, in its turn, established itself in those abominable sects, which under diverse names have perpetuated themselves until our days" (*ibid., Sèptieme Leçon*, III, § 5).

In this fleeting allusion to the past of the Church, the illustrious Jesuit does not specify whether those sects acted separately against the Church or were joined together in a conspiracy. In view of this omission, we cannot know what degree of importance he confers to the Church of Satan. We do not know whether it is just a general spiritual point of reference or an articulated movement with agents, plans of action and the means to execute the destruction of the Catholic Church and install in its place the worship of the Devil.

Further on, he makes a clear allusion to the conspiracy without, however, entering into details on such an important matter:

"In our days also, this army practices a discipline that until now was unknown. It is easy to see that, from one side of Europe to the other, this army obeys with surprising punctuality its orders, either remaining still, retiring from the field or launching forward with furious impetuosity. All the newspapers that are loyal to it, like well-commanded artillery, thunder their cannons simultaneously and attack unremittingly the posts assigned to them. From where come the immense resources at this army's disposal? Who can tell? (*ibid.*, § 8).

his criteria the *principle of the action of the Secret Forces*, the *plan of the Revolution* and, consequently, the notion of the *revolutionary and counter-revolutionary processes* are not stressed. It is hard to understand how Ramière, who criticized St. Augustine for not considering the ensembles, did not present a vision of the ensemble of evil among men.

§ 70 We see, therefore, that the amplitude of the action of the evil is the second sieve of analysis through which the Philosophies and Theologies of History conceived by the most laudable authors, whose works have done a great good for the Church and Christian Civilization, will not pass. In particular, we note the *City of God* of St. Augustine, which sealed the death of the Classical World and was one of the principal sources of inspiration for the formation of the Middle Ages.

C. A Particularly Good Counter-Revolutionary Presentation

§ 71 In our opinion, the author who more closely visualizes the action of evil throughout History is Msgr. Henri Delassus in his work *La Conjuration Antichrétienne*, praised by Cardinal Merry del Val on behalf of St. Pius X. In it we find the consideration of almost all the principles and laws we mentioned above. This makes his study one of most extensive and efficacious works for the defense of the Holy Church and Christendom against the Revolution.

§ 72 If someone were to ask us to point out what is missing in the magnificent exposition of Msgr. Delassus, we would list three points:

§ 73 *First*, Delassus establishes as the first fundament of History man's predisposition to realize his own happiness – like Bossuet and Ramière.[59] Now then, although we consider this ap-

---

[59] a. Based on Bossuet, Delassus comments on happiness as being the last end of man: "Why are these two civilizations [Christian Civilization and Modern Civilization] different? It is because of the different conceptions they have of the last end of man and the diverse and opposed effects that each produces in the social and private order. 'The chief aim of man in life is to be happy' says Bossuet (*Méditations sur l'Evangile*). For man this is appropriate; it is the objective toward which all minds tend without exception. The great orator also does not fail to note 'Intelligent natures have neither will nor desire except for their own happiness,' and he adds: 'Nothing is more reasonable, because what can be better than to desire the good, that is, happiness?'

petency a very important factor, it is not properly speaking the initial fundament, but a consequence of it. Actually, an analysis of the human psychology shows that what is innermost in man's constitution is his contingence.

It is because of his contingence that the initial necessity to complete himself in the Absolute sprouts in man. The thirst for the Absolute is, therefore, the first fundament of human psychology and of History, and not his appetency for happiness. The latter seems to be merely the consequence of the former.

§ 74 Hence, St. Augustine is more correct than the other three authors when he points to the precedence of the quest for the Absolute over happiness: "Thou hast made us for thyself, O Lord, and our heart is restless until it finds its rest in Thee."[60]

§ 75 St. Ignatius also shows that human happiness is nothing compared with the service to God:

"What end did God desire for us when He gifted us with such high prerogatives? Was it by chance for us to become great lords, great scholars, great entrepreneurs on earth? Was it by chance for us to harvest the sweetest flowers of earthly pleasures? For us to acquire great fame and renown in the world?

"Certainly it was for none of these reasons, as natural reason and the divine Faith teach us. Temporal things cannot

---

("Sermon pour la Toussaint" in *Oeuvres Oratoires de Bossuet*, Édition Critique et Complete par l'Abbé J. Lebarq, v. 325).

"Thus, we find in the heart of man an invincible impulse that drives him toward the quest for happiness. Even if he wished, he could not change it. It is behind all his thoughts and the great driving force of all his actions. Even when he takes his own life, it is because he is convinced that he will find in nothingness a fate preferable to the one he presently has.

"Man can be fooled, and in fact he very often makes mistakes in his quest for happiness, in his choice of the path to lead him to it. Bossuet also says: 'To find happiness where it is, is the source of all good; the source of all evil is to find it where it is not' (*Méditations sur l'Evangile*). This is as true for society as it is for the individual man" (H. Delassus, *La Conjuration Antichrètienne*, vol. 1, pp. 10-11).

b.Ramière also defends man's quest for happiness: "Man in society, like the individual man, seeks only one thing, happiness, and even more when he finds himself supported by his neighbors than when he is abandoned to himself" (*Le Règne de Jésus-Christ, Cinquième Leçon, Le Plan Divin Étudié dans la Nature de la Société*, III, § 3).

[60] St. Augustine, *Confissões* (Porto: Livraria Apostolado da Imprensa, 1948), book 1, chap. 1.

be the final end of an eternal soul. The miniscule dimension of these goods cannot be the final happiness of a creature, which has sculpted in itself the image of the Creator. If these pleasures, richness and honors were our end, we should live on earth forever. Another life would not exist for us, because once the ultimate end is reached, nothing better can come after it. … We were uniquely created, therefore, to praise, serve and love God. …

"We will become similar to God when we see Him as He is, because just as God has no other bliss or end beyond himself, so also He does not want us to have a lesser end than God himself, nor a lesser happiness than His own bliss."[61]

§ 76 Further, he makes it clear that the love of the Absolute – that is, the love of God independent of recompense or felicity – has primacy over the enjoyment of eternal bliss itself:

"If God would have created you only to serve and honor Him, without expecting any other recompense afterwards, would not God be most worthy of your slavery and service because of His infinite excellence as well as the infinite debt you have for being His creature? Could you deny Him what is His without being guilty of enormous ingratitude and blatant injustice? Should you not consider yourself greatly honored to serve Him and dispose all your affections to accomplish His most just and most holy will?"[62]

§ 77 To this premise he legitimately adds the desire for eternal happiness:

"What, then, is your obligation when the infinite goodness of God desires with so much charity that your end is not only to serve Him, but also to enjoy a bliss similar to His own glory and equal to His own eternity? Without a doubt, man should have no other desire than to attain such an elevated end."[63]

§ 78 Just as those who are good thirst for the true Absolute, which is God, those who are evil construct false absolutes for themselves. Adam sinned when he believe the false absolute that the Devil promised him: "*Eritis sicut dii*" (You will be like gods) (Gen 3:5). This explains why the Revolution has a metaphysical and religious ideal and not just a hedonist one, as would be the case if happiness were the first driving force of human psychology.

---

[61] St. Ignatius of Loyola, *Exercícios de Santo Inácio e Leituras Espirituais* (Porto: Ed. A.J., 1934), pp. 272-275

[62] *Ibid.*, p. 275.

[63] *Ibid.*, pp. 275-276.

§ 79 *Second*, in his description of the revolutionary conspiracy, Delassus does not seem to have his eyes particularly turned toward how the revolutionary action exploits the gradual appetency that man has for the plenitude of evil. In other words, he does not consider the *principle of double gradualism* and the *law of the tendency to reach the summit*.

In his description, the Revolution appears more as a plan imposed by external agents, without emphasis on how it installs itself inside man by enticing his bad side. And, to the degree that the Revolution penetrates the human soul, it makes of its victim an accomplice who can easily become a new willing agent of the forces of evil. In Delassus' work, the Revolution is excellently described as a historic-theological phenomenon and less well portrayed as a psychological-sociological process.

§ 80 *Third*, as a consequence of the lacunae pointed out above, in diverse parts of his extraordinary work the author analyzes the Revolution in customs, ideas and institutions,[64] but he does not pay attention to the revolutionary action over the disordered tendencies of the human soul and society.[65]

However, before a custom is established or an idea formed, a good or bad tendency already existed in which the custom and the idea germinated. The action in the tendencies of man and society is the most powerful driving force of the Revolution[66] as well as the Counter-Revolution.[67] By not considering the *Tendential Revolution* or the *law of action in the tendencies*, Delassus fails to point out the most dynamic element of the *revolutionary process*, whose general lines he described admirably.

§ 81 The great profundity of revolutionary action in the human soul and society is, therefore, the third sieve of analysis for us to evaluate the Philosophies and Theologies of History.

---

[64] Cf. H. Delassus, *La Conjuration Antichrètienne*, vol. 1, chaps. 3-5l, vol. 2, chaps. 28-37.

[65] It seems to us that the only mention of the disordered passions appears when he asks what would be the future of the Church and her image in society: "We know, however, that God frequently leaves to the unbridled passions and to the Devil himself the task of executing His will and of accomplishing His eternal designs" (*ibid.*, vol. 3, chap. 40, p. 835).

[66] Cf. Plinio Corrêa de Oliveira, *Revolution and Counter-Revolution*, part I, chap. VI.1.A.

[67] Cf. *ibid.*, part II, chap. IX.1, 2; chap. X.

3. Progressivist Conception of History

§ 82 The expositions in the previous Items of this Chapter provide enough foundation for us to understand the progressivist conception of History.

A. Aims Progressivism Pursues in History

§ 83 With regard to History, Progressivism aims, *first* and foremost, for the destruction of the Catholic doctrine on Creation.[68] Toward this end, it changes the traditional Exegesis of the Scripture and, consequently, the dogmas of original sin, Redemption, the mission of the Church, the end of the world and eternal life. The principal goal of progressivist Historicism is, therefore, the subversion of all of Exegesis and Dogmatic Theology.

§ 84 *Second*, Progressivism aims to terminate that which it calls "*borné* thinking," which would be the traditional thought, and to establish broader horizons, which are supposedly the progressivist horizons. Progressivists accuse Catholic traditional thinking of being narrow-minded, turned exclusively to its own glorification and interests. According to them, the Holy Church would have obliterated the presentation of the historic reality by teaching only what was convenient for her, leaving aside the history of peoples and religions extraneous to her. This would constitute a lack of objectivity that should be remedied. This, then, would be the second objective of Progressivism regarding History.

§ 85 This second reason is unjust and has a false foundation. It is unjust because the broadness of vision of Catholic thinking has always been one of her dominant characteristics.[69] From the beginning, Holy Mother Church always carefully considered the vocations of other peoples,[70] and this interest only increased with

---

[68] Cf. in this Volume, Introduction §§ 15-20, Chap. I §§ 15, 24, 40.

[69] The criticism we presented before of some Catholic visualizations of History does not aim to attribute a lack of horizon to them. On the contrary, we looked for the three more universal Catholic conceptions only to compare them with a model ideal. The lacunae they may have in comparison with that model does not invalidate or devalue the broad world views of their authors.

[70] This is what St. Paul did in dealing with the vocations of the Jews and the Gentiles (Rom 1:16; 2:10-11; 3:27-30; 11: 11-28); likewise, for all the Catholic exegetes who commented on him. This is what St. John did in the Apocalypse, mysteriously describing how the accomplishment of the vocations of all peoples glorifies Our Lord Jesus Christ. The saints and authors who wrote about the Apocalypse can easily fall

time. Incidentally, it could not be otherwise. Since she received from Our Lord the mandate to evangelize all the peoples (cf. Mt 28:19; Mk 16:16), and effectively did so as much as she could, how can she be accused of disinterest regarding other peoples?

§ 86 Besides being unjust, this allegation is baseless because it supposes that the Catholic Church should give the same consideration to those peoples who adhered to the Catholic Faith as well as to those who rejected it and, furthermore, to those who still have not received it. It is likewise baseless because it also supposes that she should consider herself as essentially equal to the false religions. Now, this implies the denial of the divine plan for Creation, the denial of the *principles of Christocentrism and Ecclesiocentrism* and, in final analysis, the denial of the true Faith. It is, therefore, a false and inadmissible conception.

Since the Holy Church considers the vocations of the peoples ordered hierarchically in relation to Our Lord and to herself, she sees the vocation of each people in the most elevated and most objective perspective possible.

To deny this visualization implies assuming religious indifferentism.

B. Reasons Progressivism Alleges to Achieve its Aims

§ 87 The reasons alleged by Progressivism to achieve these objectives allow us to make a more accurate analysis of its conception of History. In effect, Historicism presents them in three different facets: theological, philosophical and scientific. To each facet there is a corresponding alleged reason.

a. Theological reason or 'Trinitarian conception of History'

§ 88 When we try to comprehend the expression "Trinitarian conception of History" used by Progressivism. we come up against a difficulty, which often is not analyzed in depth, but just glossed over by most persons. The difficulty is to know how, for progressivists, History can represent the Trinity.

---

within the realm of the Theology of History. This list includes St. Justin and St. Iranaeus in the 2nd century, St. Dionysius and St. Methodius in the 3rd century, St. Basil and St. Gregory Nazianzenus in the 4th century, St. Ambrose, St. Augustine, St. Jerome and St. Cyril of Alexandria in the 5th and 6th centuries, St. Bede and Alcuin in the 8th century, Rabano Maurus and Aretas in the 9th century, St. Anselm in the 11th century, Rupert and Richard of St. Victor in the 12th century, St. Albert the Great and St. Thomas in the 13th century, St. Antoninus in the 15th century, Bossuet in the 17th century, Bartholomew Holzhauser in the 19th century, Delassus and Balthasar Pereira in the 20th century.

§ 89 Progressivism imagines History as a reflection of the Trinity based on two foundations:

First, it is based on Rahner's idea that the "Immanent Trinity" would be identical to the "Economic Trinity." That is, the Trinitarian life would be identical in God and in Creation and History. In other words, there would be no substantial difference between God and the universe He created, which is tantamount to affirming that God would be immanent in the universe and History.[71]

If we presuppose this doctrine, the entire progressivist conception of History becomes consistent: History would be a march of the liberation of the Trinitarian immanence in Creation throughout the ages. Thus, we could have the age of the Father, of the Son and of the Holy Spirit, according to the various manifestations of God. This is all the more comprehensible in the doctrine of Rahner since he considers that the Three Persons are actually not Persons, but mere manners of existence of God.[72] It is understandable, thus, that this visualization of History is evolutionary and demands the destruction of the traditional conception of Creation and all of Catholic Dogma.[73] Everything is coherent and completely anti-Catholic…[74]

§ 90 *Second*, Progressivism tries to base its Theology of History on the doctrines of Joachim of Fiore (1130-1202). In effect, this medieval Abbot divided History into three ages, assigning each age to one of the Divine Persons: The age of the Old Testament is the Kingdom of the Father; the age of the New Testament is the Kingdom of the Son, and the new era that he imagined had started in his time would be the Kingdom of the Holy Spirit.

He affirmed that the era of the Father was characterized by the relationship of God with the Chosen People (conjugal state); the era of the Son was marked by the relationship of God with the institutional Church (clerical state), and the era of the Holy Spirit would be characterized by the relationship of God with spiritual men or monks (monachal state).

---

[71] Cf. Vol. VII, *Destructio Dei*, Chap. III §§ 41-43, 58, 103-105, 110-115; about the immanentism of God in man and the universe defended by other progressivist authors, see also Chap. IV §§ 54-89.

[72] Cf. *ibid.*, Chap III §§ 110-115.

[73] Cf. *ibid.*, Chap. III §§ 63-65.

[74] Cf. *ibid.*, Chap. III §§ 116-130.

§ 91 Describing his "third kingdom" or "third era," the Calabrian monk used many metaphors that modernists at their time and progressivists today apply to "justify" the destruction of the institutional Church and Christendom and to advocate the installation of the "New Church," which would be the realization of the visions of Fiore and the consummation of History.

§ 92 Thus, we find the modernist Ernesto Buonaiuti re-editing the *Tractatus Super Quatuor Evangelia* (*Treatise on the Four Gospels*) by Joachim of Fiore, in which the institutional Church is compared to the aged Simeon who sees the new ecclesiastical order – the infant – being presented to him; then he blesses it and prepares himself to die. In the work of Cardinal Henri de Lubac on the thinking of Fiore, we read:

"But, why is this Gospel called the *Gospel of the Kingdom* by the Lord and *Eternal Gospel* by John except because the Gospel that was given to us by Christ and the Apostles, according to the faith of the sacraments, is transitory and temporal regarding these same sacraments, while the Gospel that is sacrificed (signified)[75] by them is eternal? Therefore, when such an infant will manifest himself in the Church of God – an infant who is contemplative, just, wise, spiritual, able to succeed to the order of Bishops, which was established by the Lord to follow Him in His active life just as King David was succeeded by Solomon, and Peter, Prince of the Apostles, succeeded John the Evangelist, and further, John the Baptist was succeeded by Christ – then, the Roman Pontiff, joyful and comforted, will bear with a calm heart the torments inflicted on him by the Antichrist,[76] knowing that the Lord told him in the person of Peter: 'When you grow old, another one will gird you and lead you where you do not want to go.'

"The aged Simeon, then, will somehow receive the infant in his arms while the successors of Peter, who received the prerogative of faith and the gift of discerning between the holy and the profane, will see that this order follows faithfully in the footsteps of Christ in full spiritual force. He [Simeon as the figure of the Pope] will support it with the weight of his authority, confirm it by his words and his testimony, announcing that in

75 The parentheses are by de Lubac, who reproduces the translation published by Buonaiuti; the brackets are ours.

76 Joachim of Fiore supposed that this Antichrist would not be the final Antichrist, but one who would come before the "third kingdom" (cf. H. de Lubac, *La Posterité Spirituelle*, vol. 1, pp. 50-51, 81).

this infant the oracles of the prophets will be fulfilled, which say: 'The kingdom under the whole heaven shall be given to the people of the saints of the Most High' (Dan 7:27). He could not mourn its disappearance, since he will recognize that a better succession will come.

"We know, in effect, that if one order is established in the predecessor and another in the successor, this does not come from a difference in faith, but from a particularity in religion.[77] For when an order starts to establish itself, it conserves the same name insofar as the one that succeeds it still has the same form. But, if an order coming from it has a better form and changes for the better, then we do not say that it is the same order, but rather that it is another which proceeds from it.

"But can the one who sees such a fruit that comes from it complain because a particular perfection ceases to exist in it in order to give forth a universal perfection? *Absit! Absit hoc!* [God forbid! God forbid this!].

"No, this is not how it should be in the succession of Peter!

"It should not be jealous regarding the perfection of the spiritual order, an order that it will see only as having the same spirit of its God; that it will see walking according to its doctrine in the pathways of its commandments.

"On the contrary, it will exult and, overflowing with joy, say: 'Now, Lord, let Your servant go in peace according to Your word, for my eyes have seen the salvation that You prepared for all peoples;' and, with joy, he added: 'it is a light to illuminate the Gentiles, and the glory of Your people Israel' (Lk 2:29-31)."[78]

§ 93 Commenting on the changing of water into wine, which Fiore predicts should happen in the Church, de Lubac approvingly asserts:

"A 'mutation' must indeed take place – the word is very strong – that is, progress with a radical change, just as in Cana the water was mutated, 'converted' into wine."[79]

---

[77] De Lubac observes that "Joachim conceived a change in the entire Church" (*ibid.*, p. 397, note 1).

[78] *Ibid.*, vol. 1, Appendix A, pp. 396-397. This expression in Latin is in the original of the *Tractatus,* pp. 86-89.

We note here what seems to be more than a coincidence: that the principal document of Vatican II, its Dogmatic Constitution *Lumen gentium,* has the same title alluding to the same episode.

[79] H. de Lubac. *La Posterité Spirituelle*, vol. 1, p. 397, note 3.

§ 94 In a commentary on the *Expositio in Apocalypsim* by the medieval monk, de Lubac further observes:

"But none of these statements signifies that the role of the Roman Church and the service that is due to her should last forever."[80]

§ 95 Returning to the *Tractatus*, de Lubac comments on the "New Church of the religious":

"For the entire people of God, it will be a great 'sabbatical,' a state of extreme exhilaration after the many works, miseries and ruins that will abound in the sixth age of the world. 'O! How blessed that time will be!' After the times of Judah and of Benjamin, that is, of the Father and of the Son, it will be the time of Levi, who was the closest to Joseph, the 'perfect figure of the Holy Spirit.'

"In that epoch, the repose will be such that the saints will no longer need to write books: *quiescent ab opera scribendorum librorum*. If we are tempted to smile at this observation, it is because we do not understand it: It means that the time of the Word will have passed: The nourishment for the whole soul will be the celestial manna received directly from the Spirit.

"This obviously supposes a profound change in our spirits and in our hearts. We will no longer be what we have been, but will have started to be others. How could we not desire such a change? Who, then, would dare to maintain that the present state of time is sufficient for us, as if the spiritual doctrine that we possess were luminous enough, and as if it could unfold in its plenitude the splendor of its rays over the whole world?"[81]

§ 96 Analyzing the epoch in which Fiore lived, de Lubac imagines him to be opposed to Scholasticism:

"But, he [Joachim of Fiore] undoubtedly considered the invasion of the Scholasticism as causing a return to the ancient past, opposed to the new spirit inaugurated by Christian revelation. That type of knowledge, which sought the favor of Fiore's contemporaries, certainly appeared to him to paralyze thought in a rational immobilization, rendering it incapable of understanding conflicting thoughts and be open to a still unformulated future, even while it aspires, at least in its sub-consciousness, to release from it a driving force."[82]

---

[80] *Ibid.*, p. 56.

[81] *Ibid.*, p. 60.

[82] *Ibid.*, p. 16.

§ 97 Following in the footsteps of Fiore, Pope Benedict XVI, then theologian Joseph Ratzinger, alludes to this new historical era:

"Joachim, verifying that, after Christ, human History developed in a unsatisfactory way, apparently deprived of salvation, comes to the conclusion that a truly salutary and good history is still to come on earth."[83]

§ 98 Cardinal Hans Urs von Balthasar finds a basis for his *Theology of History* and his singular notion of "qualitative time"[84] in the thinking of the Calabrian monk and his Franciscan followers:

"The tendency of Joachim and especially of his Franciscan followers[85] … gives occasion to make conscious the subjacent category of theological qualitative time in its successive developments: the time of creation, of sin, of revelation and of the Church."[86]

---

[83] Joseph Ratzinger, *Le Dieu de Jésus-Christ* (Paris: Fayard, 1977), pp. 109-110, *apud* H. de Lubac, *La Posterité Spirituelle*, vol. 1, p. 61.

[84] What von Balthasar calls "qualitative time" here is essentially the same as his "subjective time," "concentrated time" or " time of grace," which we have analyzed in detail in Vol. VIII, *Fumus Satanae*, Chap. IV, 1; see also in this Vol. IX the explanation of the link between "subjective time" and "qualitative time" (cf. §§ 118-121).

[85] Von Balthasar's mention of the Franciscan followers of Joachim of Fiore is curious. In fact, it was principally among the Franciscans that the Calabrian monk found ardent adepts. These followers applied his prophecies to the Order founded by St. Francis (1212) shortly after Fiore's death (1202). His ideas had so much influence that Gerald of Borgo San Donnino, a Franciscan, wrote the controversial *Liber Introductorius in Evangelium Aeternum* (Introductory Book to the Eternal Gospel) in 1254 (cf. H. de Lubac, *La Posterité Spirituelle*, vol. 1, pp. 80-81). In this work, he proposed the prophecies of Fiore as the Franciscan ideal. At the Council of Arles, both his theses and those of Fiore were condemned as heterodox (cf. *ibid.*, Appendix B, pp. 400-405).

Later, the theses of Fiore were also censured by the IV Lateran Council (cf. DR 431). Even one of the first Superiors General of the Franciscan Order, John of Parma, supported Gerald and the proposals of Fiore, which contributed to his dismissal and the election of St. Bonaventure as Superior of the Order (cf. H. de Lubac, *La Posterité Spirituelle*, vol. 1, p. 82-83).

Von Balthasar's mention of the "Franciscan followers" of Joachim of Fiore, without any restrictions, permits us to think that he endorses their errors.

[86] Hans Urs von Balthasar, *De l'Intégration*, p. 148.

§ 99 We would say that in von Balthasar's unrestricted mention of the followers of Joachim of Fiore, he seems to include himself:

"The third kingdom of Joachim is an eschatological religious state (after the conjugal state of the first and the clerical state of the second), and here we find a Metaphysics of History typical of the way of thinking of religious orders. It goes beyond the *fraticelli* and Cola di Rienzo, beyond the secret orders behind Hieronymus Bosch, the brothers of the Spirit in the Renaissance, and even the Rosicrucians, the Freemasons of the Enlightenment and the 19th century, up to groups like those of George and Guénon, the projects of orders of Derleth and the Nazi Ordensburgen. In all these movements a wind of the Apocalypse blows, moving toward a final kingdom in History."[87]

§ 100 It is also in Joachim de Fiore that von Balthasar pretends to find the origin of evolutionary thinking and, consequently, of the historicity of dogma. He also defends that the difference between sacred and profane History ended as a late fruit of Fiore:

"In fact, during the 19th century and in the whole movement of thought related to evolution, the concept of evolution burgeoned – as a late orthodox fruit of Joachim of Fiore – in theology itself. Today we speak normally of the evolution of dogma, and we mean by this the unfolding of 'all the hidden treasures of wisdom and knowledge' (Col 2:3) contained in the deposit of revelation entrusted to the Church. The Church brings forth this unfolding under the enlightening guidance of the Holy Spirit.

"In this regard, it suffices to note that this progress is no longer itself (objective) revelation like that of the Old Testament. In the Old Testament the tendency to an objective revelation, consistent in itself, was part of a succession of phases. But now, since the absolute plenitude [of revelation] has already been given, the interpretation can move freely without the need for development, turning over on itself like infinite waves. …

"In its essence, the life of the Church, like that of her glorified Head, is situated above the plane of progress. …

"The content and heart of the Church, which transcend History, are the supreme gift of the Creator to human history, bringing her to her own realization by liberating herself from within. Objective revelation presents itself, therefore, under

---

[87] *Ibid.*, p. 146.

the pattern of a diptych: 'polarity and ascension,' that is to say, 'progress' (Old Testament) and 'overflowing plenitude' (New Testament). And this diptych becomes the fundamental historical pattern that spreads out, from this center, in a network of analogical tensions that depend on and refer back to that center. …

"The 'wall of separation' (Eph 2:13-14) between secular and sacred history falls at the point where the Word no longer descends prophetically from heaven, but becomes flesh, that is, man (perhaps it was Hegel who understood this more profoundly). For once God, the most unique Being, chooses to express himself entirely through the language of his highest creature – man – and no longer to one people [the Jewish] but to mankind, so the Word can only be entirely assumed from within, proved and rescued in 'His flesh,' in a 'body' (Eph 2:12-16). …

"The 'fall of the wall of separation' means suppressing the difference between the history of particular salvation (historical salvation, literally) and a universal and secular history. From Christ onward, all of history is fundamentally 'sacral' and, above all, by the presence of the Church of Christ as testimony in the boson of the total history of the world."[88]

§ 101 Numerous less important theologians linked to charismatic movements consider that the coming of the Kingdom of the Spirit, or simply the Kingdom, is an indisputable reality that is already knocking at the door. It is a mystical, not dogmatic, certainty that moves them. It is caused by a certain emotional vibration, which constitutes the driving element of the charismatic movement, be it in the exclusively religious ambit – the Communities of Jerusalem (based in the Paris Church of Saint Gervais), underground churches or movements that contest the Hierarchy – or in the socio-political ambit – liberation theologies, feminist theology, homosexual theology or black theology.

In all of its various springs the charismatic movement has longings for the Kingdom. These longings, more or less explicitly, presuppose the voluntary or compulsory destruction of the Kingdom of the Son in the Church and in Christendom.[89] Such a conception is linked, either closely or remotely, to the Trinitarian visualization of History of Joachim of Fiore.

---

[88] H.U. von Balthasar, *Théologie de l'Histoire*, pp. 165-168.

[89] This affirmation by Fiore is quite expressive: "*Necesse esst enim ut transeat significatum Petri et maneat significatum Joannis*" (It is necessary for Peter's importance to depart and for John's to remain), *apud*, H. de Lubac, *La Posterité Spirituelle*, vol. 1, p. 52.

§ 102 Therefore, these progressivist theologians – both major and minor – who base themselves on Joachim of Fiore all have the presupposition that the destruction of the Petrine Church, that is, of the institutional and hierarchical Church, must precede the Kingdom of the Spirit. Consequently, they also want to destroy the temporal institutions that are reflections of the Christendom of a bygone era.

§ 103 These are the principal practical consequences that come from the progressivist "Trinitarian conception of History."

The immanentism of God in Creation and the destruction of the Catholic Church and Christendom are, therefore, the doctrinal and practical outcomes of the progressivist conception of History from its theological perspective.

b. Philosophical reason or historical evolutionism

§ 104 Although in History, the theological and philosophical perspectives normally interweave, and, in the case of the progressivist conception of History, it is rare to differentiate the theological focus from the philosophical one, we will do so here for the sake of clarity in the exposition of the matter.

The criterion we will follow is established by the actual foundations adopted by the progressivists. We say that the reason is theological when the foundation for the analysis of History is either revealed truths or the exegesis of such truths, as in the case respectively of Rahner or of the progressivist interpretations of Joachim of Fiore's works. We say that the reason is philosophical when the foundation is accessible to natural reason. We say that the foundation is scientific when it is an empirical datum, as in the case of the next Letter c.

§ 105 It seems to us that, from the philosophical point of view, the progressivist interpretations of History can be classified by two matrices.

The **first matrix** considers History as a spiral of evolutionary cycles that ascends organically from the less to the more noble until it reaches a final plenitude. The role of evil and suffering is considered accidental. They would be blind forces established in the universe as hindrances to the evolutionary process, just as weight, friction and obstacles in a road can slow the acceleration of an inert body that is being put into movement. These hindrances lose their negative effects insofar as the process gains speed and draws near its end.

§ 106 In this conception, man's free will occupies a clearly secondary place. When man chooses evil – when he sins – he does so because of ignorance, a lack of conscientiousness. Such ignorance is generally attributed to the slowness of the process. Therefore, guilt in the proper and absolute sense does not exist, but only in an analogical and relative way.[90]

---

[90] This first matrix of the progressivist Historicism is expressed, for example, in the visualization of Fr. Maurizio Flick, S.J., professor at the Gregorian University in Rome:

"The vision of the world inspired by the sciences teaches us that the universe is an 'evolutionary system' in which the more complex and structured phenomena come later in time and are fruits of less complex and structured phenomena. Human sciences, in their turn, present man as a 'historical being,' who, challenged by external and internal situations, transforms himself – his thinking, his own affectivity, his body – creates cultures and organizes the material world for his own service, survival and development. This image of man is linked to the conviction that 'mankind not only can and should increasingly reinforce its dominion over creation, but also must establish a political, social and economic order that increasingly serves man better and helps individuals and groups to affirm and develop their own dignity' (GS 9). …

"The phenomenological reality exists by continuously surpassing its own previous phases. The self-surpassing of the creature is not accomplished in a univocal way, but adapts itself to the plans of the being: the development of biological life, History, and the growing insertion in Christ are analogous processes. The role of creatures as instruments of God in the evolutionary creation of the universe can be verified in the more perfect world, in the historical dimension of human existence. For this reason, the Genesis revelation, presenting man as created in the image of God, describes him as an interlocutor with God in a dialogue, who was given the alternative of either accepting the invitation of God to collaborate with Him or to refuse it and, thus, destroy himself. …

"Now, evolutionary creation is inseparable from evil, which is a dimension inseparable from existence, either of the just or the sinner. …

"It is tautological to say that the world we build is not exempt from evil: In fact, whatever is in movement is evidently far from the goal. Speaking of human history, this 'evil of indigence' must also be felt as such, that is, it must be painful, because in this phase of development evil is not only the inevitable metaphysical reversal of the progress toward good, but also the challenge that stimulates self-construction. …

"The 'evolutionary evil,' which results from a deficiency in the creature,

§ 107 Thus, a man is "guilty" or a "sinner" when he prevents others from walking in the direction of evolution; he is "faithful" when he marches in that direction; he is a "prophet," a "saint" or a "hero" when, in one stage of the process, he foresees the next one and gives, by his personal action, a new acceleration to the ensemble; he is a "martyr" when, while living in an ambience that is outdated by its own "guilt," he tries to maintain the speed of the process, but is persecuted. In this case, he is considered a "prophet" who is not understood by the "faithful" of his time. "Guilty" or not, men follow the march of the evolutionary process and, thus, History moves, irremediably, following this law.

We see, therefore, that this is an obliteration of the *axiological principle* that violates the *principle of human liberty* and is transformed into historical determinism.

§ 108 Such is the description of the **Monist Evolutionism** or **Organic Evolutionism** that can be presented as the first matrix of the progressivist Philosophy of History.

§ 109 However, in this analysis we have thus far found only the description of the evolutionary march, which must correspond to a conception of the being. In effect, how could the being gradually change from one stage to another until it becomes essentially different from what it was in the beginning, except by a change in the very notion of being?

This ontologically mutable being is no longer a **being**, but a **being-in-evolution** or a **coming-into-being**. The progressivists who defend this position effectively abolish all of Ontology and replace it with Phenomenology, that is, by the study of

---

invades not only the sphere of 'nature,' but, what is more, that of the person. When the cooperation of many persons is needed, there will always be those who – either through involuntary errors or a refusal to freely collaborate – will cause delays and deviations. ...

"If God wants to give His creature the dignity of a dynamic (evolutionary and historical) self-realization, He cannot spare him from evil, although painful. Often development takes place, above all in human history, precisely when one faces pain. ...

"The historical dimension of man, thus, prevents us from issuing a definitive value judgment on each one of the stages of evolution, history and human sanctification, leaving out the prior stages that they supersede and the next stages for which they are preparing" (Maurizio Flick & Zoltán Alszeghy, *Il Mistero della Croce - Saggio di Teologia Sistematica*, Brescia: Queriniana, 1978, pp. 275-277).

the being *hic et nunc* (here and now), as it presents itself in the present phase of the evolutionary process, and no longer the being in itself, as Catholic Philosophy always did.[91]

§ 110 The presupposition of this position, which rarely is found explicated, is that the being-in-evolution of the progressivists is driven by a mysterious latency that makes it start from the stage of brute matter. It goes through the stage of animated matter, of spiritualized matter – man – heading toward the stage of the spirit – the "new man" – and toward a final reintegration in the plenitude. This plenitude, then, was already present in the beginning of the process, germinating and growing in its various phases. In other words, the plenitude is immanent in the being. Thus, the progressivist notion of the **coming-into-being** or **being-in-evolution** is a philosophical diversion to avoid touching the heart of the question, which is Immanentism.

§ 111 Now then, Immanentism presupposes that when the Initial Principle – be it called the Creator, God, the Demiurge, Archonte, Schekinah, Malkhouth or other such names – gave origin to the cosmos, the latter emanated from the former. That is, Immanentism presupposes Emanatism. Thus, a philosophical analysis of historic evolutionism brings us to an initial conception of God himself. Behind the progressivist Philosophy of History, its Cosmogony appears.[92]

§ 112 These are the philosophical foundations of the **Historic Evolutionism** of Progressivism following its **monist matrix**.

§ 113 To this conception, fundamentally philosophical, some progressivists have added the names of God, Christ and the Church, as well as religious concepts and moral notions. This

---

[91] In an article tilted "Fé en la Creación y Teoria Evolutiva" (Faith in Creation and Evolutionary Theory), Joseph Ratzinger describes the evolutionary position, confirming what we just affirmed: "Philosophically, therefore, we could say that the evolutionary concept bases itself on the phenomenological plan and that it encounters different particular forms existing *de facto* in the world; while the creationist faith develops on an ontological plan, behind the particular things, admiring the marvel of the being itself" (in V.A., *Es Esto Dios?*, p. 233).

Shortly before, referring to evolution, he states: "The fundamental understanding of reality changes: The future, the coming-into-being replaces the being, evolution replaces Creation, ascension replaces the Fall" (*ibid.* p. 232).

[92] Here we see that the progressivist philosophy and theology *a propos* Creation is entirely linked to its strange theogony and cosmogony, already studied throughout Vol. VIII, *Fumus Satanae*.

gave birth to the *Cosmogenesis* of Teilhard de Chardin, the principal representative of this conception. And, from there, a new religion followed.

§ 114 The **second matrix** of the progressivist interpretation of History is also cyclical. But, different from the first, the historical cycles now proceed from one another through conflicting shocks. Each cycle has a dominant unity, but, alongside it, the opposite principle is developing in a stage of latency. Hence, at the end of each cycle, a shock is produced between the weakened dominant element and the growing dominated one. The oppressed principle liberates itself, and will dominate the next cycle. The same sequence repeats itself throughout History. However, insofar as the process advances, the ensemble grows in quality, that is, it evolves. It tends, thus, to the final plenitude. It is, therefore, a tragic process of successive dilacerations, which tends toward an apparently happy denouement.[93]

The role of evil in this process follows the dialectical seesaw. What is good in one cycle becomes evil in the next.[94]

We have, therefore, a relativist notion of evil.

§ 115 We see that this second matrix of the progressivist Evolutionism is dualist in its method. and, although relativist, it is still dualist in its conception of good and evil. We call it, therefore, the **dualist matrix** or **Dialectical Evolutionism**.

§ 116 Since the procession of History is dialectical and the notions of good and evil are contradictory, it becomes extremely difficult to objectively situate the direction of this process. For a man to know if he is in tune with History, he should search in himself for the latent signs of evolution. However, evolution does not manifest itself uniformly in all persons since not only the evolutionary process varies according to the different influences and vicissitudes of the times, but also the experiences and reactions of each man are different.

---

[93] We say "apparently happy" because, in the most frequent version of this matrix, the progressivists suppose an eschatology with a positive outcome so that it can be more easily assimilated to Catholic teaching on the end times and the celestial bliss that follows. However, we have already seen that such an outcome, in opposition to the apparent general reconciliation preached by the "theology of love," in fact implies a tragic "war of gods" (cf. Vol. VIII, *Fumus Satanae*, Chap. VI).

[94] Thus, for example, the law and justice that represented good in the Old Testament would become bad in the New Testament, replaced by love and mercy.

§ 117 Thus, there can be countless experiences of evolutionary latencies. While some will believe that History is following a certain course that is good, others will think the opposite. We have, then, completely fragmented philosophical criteria as fundamental elements of this matrix of progressivist Evolutionism.

To unify these almost infinite fragments, an a-religious, a-philosophical and a-moral love is offered as a solution.[95] It is love raised to the position of philosophy... The "philosophy of love," which aims to transcend all the philosophies...[96]

§ 118 Trying to present a more solid philosophical foundation than this merely affective inclination, the partisans of this conception go on to modify the notion of time. They imagine a new concept of time that would "unify" the various phases of the evo-

---

[95] This is the perspective of von Balthasar's work *Das Ganze im Fragment* (*The All in the Fragment*), which was translated to French with the suggestive title of *L'Intégration* (Integration).

[96] In Vol. VII, *Destructio* Dei, Chap. III §§ 179-228, we analyzed the philosophical system of the "theology of love." There we saw that von Balthasar establishes a new personalist perspective of love, which pretends to unify and replace all philosophical systems. This philosophical reflection of his "theology of love" can well be called a "philosophy of love."

According to von Balthasar, it is not philosophy but love that shall unify all fragmentary knowledge: "**It is not question of any philosophical conception of God, but it is in this mystery of love that all fragmentary views are accomplished and fulfilled**. Otherwise, the formal breath of the philosophical idealizations can favor the theologian, the exegete and the believer to center only on the historic aspect of Christ's Revelation as the most important thing, overlooking the Holy Spirit" (H.U. von Balthasar, *Solo l'amore è credibile*, Turin: Borla, 1965, p. 147).

In another work he affirms philosophy must renounce itself and assume the mystery of love: "**If philosophy does not want to speak abstractly about the being and think concretely about what is on earth and in the world (and nothing else), it must first divest itself from itself**, in order to know 'nothing, save the crucified Jesus Christ' (I Cor 2:2). Then, departing from there, it would be able to announce 'the wisdom of God, mysterious and secret, that He destined for our glory before the world began' (I Cor 2:7). But, **then this announcement will stream from a much more profound silence and from a much darker abyss than anything a simple philosophy could ever know**" ("Mysterium Salutis," in *Misterium Paschale, Compêndio de Dogmática Historico-Salvífica*, Petrópolis: Vozes, 1974, p. 43).

lution in which men find themselves. Time would no longer be a clear and objective measurement that relies on the movement of matter, but a measurement of the movement of the spirit.[97]

They defend that there would be a subjective time or punctual time, rather than the current concept of objective or chronological-linear time. According to this idea, each man, depending on the degree of his awareness and love, would be situated in his own dimension of time, which would be "qualitative time."[98]

Would there be a special measurement for each individual, which would return us to the chaos of a complete subjectivism? Or would there be some underlying criterion to "unify" the various times of individuals and History? The adepts of this matrix respond that such a criterion does indeed exist. It would be love, measured by the particular phases of human love and, among these, principally love toward God.

§ 119 Thus, for these progressivists, there would be a time of creation, one of sin, another of revelation and still another of grace.[99] According to the degree of love they attain, peoples and individuals would be governed by one of these times. Therefore, various times would be ruling in a single historical epoch; this variety, however, would be included in one of the "types of time" mentioned above. This would be the philosophical criterion to give "unity" to the religious, philosophical and moral subjectivism regarding the past and the present.

§ 120 Regarding the future, however, the "unity" is more coherent. In effect, the progressivists imagine that the time ruling our universe is nothing but a degradation of eternity. This new "distended time" would be itself a part of evolution and would tend to ascend qualitatively until it reaches eternity. Hence, they imagine that, to the degree that the process of evolution draws

---

[97] The real and philosophical lack of foundation for this notion was already analyzed in Vol. VIII, *Fumus Satanae*, Chap. IV §§ 10-45.

[98] Above, in § 98 we presented an excerpt of von Balthasar in which he alludes to this matter.

[99] In this way, Dogma and Morals become diluted inside Philosophy by doing away with the boundaries between these fields of knowledge, thus producing another element of confusion.

Such a criterion of the distribution of time is not uniform among the progressivists. Often they refer only to "subjective time" and the "time of grace," encompassing all the phases of History.

near the end of History, the various times ruling the world will tend to become only one – by the force of the unifying love that an Ecumenical Church would bring to all the peoples and religions.

§ 121 Time should also follow the dialectical march of History, unfolding according to the successive shocks of the historical epochs. Thus, a more complete doctrine about progressivist time develops the "contractions" and "de-contractions" of "distended time" following the dialectical march of History.[100]

This would be the conception of time proper to the second matrix of progressivist Evolutionism.

§ 122 As the concept of time changes, all of philosophy changes with it, and also the concept of being. Just as in the monist matrix, this dualist matrix also conceives the being as **being-in-evolution** or a **coming-into-being.** The immanentist and emanatist consequences that we studied in the first matrix[101] also apply to this second matrix.

In the second matrix, however, the consequences go further. In effect, since here History develops in a dialectical march along with time, the being also must necessarily have within itself those two antagonistic principles. We have, then, a dualist conception of the being. This projects a dualist conception inside God himself.[102]

These are the philosophical foundations of the **dualistic matrix** of the progressivist **Historical Evolutionism.**

§ 123 This dualistic matrix violates the *axiological principle.* Its deceitful supposition of a happy outcome for History[103] does not satisfy the demands of this principle regarding the glory of God. For the hypothetical "happy ending" they propose would be the glorification of religious, philosophical and moral relativism, which is the exact opposite of the glory of God. If we were to admit the attainment of such a utopia, it would be better to speak of an anti-axiological principle and the glorification of an anti-God. Therefore, this conception is actually tragic and not happy, which corresponds to the determinist fatality of its dialectic laws.

§ 124 The *principle of human liberty* is also transgressed by this conception. *First,* it is violated by the determinism of the

---

100 Vol. VIII, *Fumus Satanae*, Chap. IV, §§ 20-31, 58-70.

101 Cf. §§ 105-113.

102 This corresponds to the dualistic conception of the Trinity analyzed in Vol. VIII, *Fumus Satanae, passim.*

103 Cf. above, § 114, Note 93.

dialectical procession of History. *Second*, to present love as the center of History does not attenuate this violation, as it could appear by the fact that love is an act of the will, but makes it graver.

Indeed, if we analyze this love, we see that it does not imply a sound act that tends toward good and to the actualization of the volitive faculty, but rather moves toward the ablation of true desire, which is replaced by a conformism with a Buddhist hue[104] in accordance with the tragic fatality of historical dialectics. It represents a self-immolation of the will,[105] not its fulfillment.

Such a "love" implies, as we have already studied, the denial of the primacy of the intelligence over the will, as well as the denial of the very notion of contingence of the being.[106] Furthermore, this love would not be substantially different from Divine Love,[107] which is tantamount to denying the essential difference that exists between God and the creature. That is, it would be the immanentism of God in man. Therefore, the concept of love presented by the progressivist dialectical Evolutionism is predatory of the human will under these various titles.

§ 125 These are the principal points of criticism regarding the Philosophy of History of the dualistic matrix defended by countless progressivists, among whom the most expressive is the Cardinal Hans Urs von Balthasar.

*

§ 126 We see, therefore, that none of the philosophical matrices of Historical Evolutionism complies with the equilibrium that must exist between these theories and the *principle of human liberty*. Both matrices are determinist. They are, therefore, false Philosophies of History.

Further and above all, both matrices are immanentist, proponents of a religious, philosophical and moral relativism, damaging to a healthy Philosophy and sound Catholic Morals, and akin to all forms of evil. Such is the doctrinal outcome of the progressivist conception of History considered from its philosophical perspective.

---

[104] Cf. Vol. VII, *Destructio Dei*, Chap, III § 197.

[105] Cf. *ibid.*, Chap. III §§ 198, 207-211, 215.

[106] Cf. *ibid.*, Chap. III §§ 185-188, 207-215.

[107] Cf. *ibid.*, Chap. III §§ 191, 194, 201, 214..

c. Scientific reasons

§ 127 Along with the alleged theological and philosophical reasons, progressisivist Historicism also employs false scientific reasons to attack the traditional conception of Creation and to oppose Catholic doctrine.

First, progressivists affirm that the Church must change her doctrine on Creation because of the **scientific character of History**, which would have been indisputably demonstrated in the 19th century.[108] Now, when we analyze this supposedly "indisputable demonstration," we find very few positive supportive facts. Indeed, the most that we find in the 19th century are countless authors who, more or less clearly, apply the criteria of the philosophers of the Enlightenment and German Idealism to History, principally Hegel and Schelling. Regardless of how these systems and authors vary, they generally fall into one of the two matrices we analyzed in Letter b: that is, into a cyclical conception of History of a monist type – Organic Evolutionism – or into a cyclical conception of a dualistic nature – Dialectical Evolutionism.

In what sense are these conceptions scientific? In theory, they could be considered scientific in the modern meaning of the word[109] if their laws were susceptible to a precise and infallible application, like the experimental laws of physics. Now, the two matrices of 19th century Historicism, as well as today's progressivist Historicism, suppose historic determinism. Then, their scientific character should be verified by the inexorability of the application of their laws to History. This seems to have been the pretension of Marx when he defended his "Scientific Socialism" as a necessary consequence of the march of History.

§ 128 However, when we consider the fundaments upon which such laws are established, we find little verification in experience. On the contrary, we find their denial by experience, like Marx' Communism, which has proved to be a flagrant failure in the political, social and economic fields. The foundations of such laws are exclusively philosophical. Therefore, since today science is based almost exclusively upon the experimental verification of its laws, those conceptions of History cannot be considered scientific in the modern sense of the word.

---

[108] Cf. in this Vol. IX, *Creatio*, Chap, I. §§ 75-77.

[109] Cf. in this Vol. IX, Chap. II § 87.

§ 129 Would they, perhaps, be scientific in the philosophical sense?

In our opinion, for a Philosophy of History to be considered a science, it must have a perfect correspondence with reality, an internal coherence in its own ambit and a harmonic relationship with all the other fields of human knowledge.[110]

A considerable part of the 19th century as well as contemporary Philosophies of History sin against a proper correspondence with reality as well as a harmonic relationship with the other fields of knowledge. In effect, regarding reality, these currents of thought obliterate the role of human liberty since they are, in general, determinist. They present evolutionary conceptions of the being and of ontology contrary to good sense and Scholastic teaching. For example, the notion of *being-in-evolution* or *coming-into-being* is out of line with both experimental reality and theoretical teaching. Consequently, they present an entirely false notion of the Absolute Being. Thus, they ravage both Philosophy and Theology and cannot be considered philosophical sciences in the proper sense of the term.

§ 130 The name philosophy is given to them only to situate the ambit of their cogitations and because some of them have an internal coherence within the false perspectives they adopt. Should someone, however, deem to use the name of science to refer to one of these philosophies, he is adopting an improper and analogical meaning.

§ 131 We see, therefore, that the mentioned Philosophies of History cannot be considered sciences either in the modern sense of science or in the normal meaning of philosophy.

§ 132 ***Second***, some progressivists, perhaps realizing the fragility of presenting Historicism as "scientific," avoid using this category directly and appeal to another: They present **historical criticism as an acquired patrimony of modern science**,[111] that is, as a consummate fact to be accepted without discussion.

They, then, conclude by arguing for the need to incorporate this historical criticism into the theological interpretation of Creation, to modify the exegesis of Genesis, etc.

§ 133 Without a doubt, historical criticism used as an instrument against the Catholic interpretation of the Scriptures is a fruit of modern revolutionary thought. Incidentally, it is actually

[110] We infer these conditions from the exposition on science by St. Thomas Aquinas, cf. Chap. II §§ 49-60.

[111] Cf. Chap.I §§ 15, 38.

not so modern. Luther already applied the same criticism to the interpretation of the Sacred Letters and called it the method of free examination of the Scriptures. This was a manifestation of revolt and pride against the tutelage of the Magisterium over the interpretation of the revealed truths contained in the Scriptures.

The difference between free examination and historical criticism is not, therefore, in the aims both seek or in the means they employ. The difference lies exclusively in the departure points they adopt. Free examination affirms that each man has the necessary lights, acquired by divine infusion, to know Scripture; historical criticism says that each man has the necessary lights, transmitted to him by modern science, to know what is right and wrong in History.

§ 134 Historical criticism cannot receive the name of scientific for the same reasons that disqualify the Philosophies of History, from which it proceeds. Thus, once the historic-scientific foundation is removed from historical criticism, it finds itself reduced to what it really is: a subjective exegetical criticism. We return, then, to just another type of free examination.

§ 135 ***Third***, other progressivists allege the **scientific character of Evolutionism as Natural History**. We have already sufficiently studied the fallacies of this argument.[112] It is interesting to note, however, that although the scientific failure of Evolutionism has been clearly demonstrated, the progressivists still do not abandon it, which proves their bad faith.[113]

---

[112] Cf. Chap. II.

[113] Cf. Chap. I §§ 41-62 on how countless theologians have taken this position.

Another confirmation is found in this text by Joachim Illies, German biologist and author, in his collaboration to the work *Bilan de la Théologie du XXe Siècle*: "The evolutionary doctrine of Lamarck, the model of his system established by Darwin, and the discoveries of genetics transformed the static image of a world created just once, and henceforth conserved without change, into a dynamic image of species that develop from one another. **Dealing with the origin of multiplicity, we indicated how in our century this doctrine of evolution became an indubitable scientific acquisition of Biology and how we cannot exclude man himself from this rationally irreproachable description of reality**. [Our observation: in neither the mentioned page, nor chapter, nor in the entire essay does the author offer any evidence leading to the conclusion that the evolutionary doctrine is an

§ 136 Still other authors, more cautious, recognize that Evolutionism is just a scientific hypothesis. They invent, however, a new artifice. They simply state that evolution is an "indubitable acquisition of science" and term it the "fact of evolution," but without ever explaining for sure what this "fact" is. Based on this "fact," they advocate the same changes in the Catholic conception of Creation. When we analyze what they understand by "fact," we see that it is not that different from "dogma." It would be the "dogma of evolution" that must be accepted now, no longer for scientific reasons but for reasons of faith.

*

§ 137 Throughout this analysis, we did not find foundation for the progressivist conception of History in any of their theological, philosophical or scientific reasons.

Nor did we find any reason whatsoever to modify the Catholic conception of Creation.

We found, however, countess proofs that demonstrate the progressivist conception of History is an evolutionary theory with emanatist and immanentist roots.

Further, it was also demonstrated that this insidious doctrine aims at the destruction of the traditional doctrine of Creation and, further on, of all of Catholic Dogmatic Theology.

* * *

"indubitable scientific acquisition of Biology."]

"This de-mythification of man from the perspective of his origin, this 'natural history of Creation' that replaced the biblical testimony of Genesis, obliges theology in our century to rethink and re-evaluate its position" (J. Illies, "Biologie et Théologie au XXe Siècle," in V.A., *Bilan de la Théologie du XXe Siècle*, vol. 1, p. 168).

CHAPTER V

DIVINE IMMANENCE, SUBSTRATUM OF THE PROGRESSIVIST DOCTRINE OF CREATION

§ 1 Divine immanence is the *leitmotiv* of the progressivist theology of Creation. It underlies not only this part of progressivist doctrine, but its whole conception of God, man and the world, as we have seen in various parts of the Collection *Lamma Sabacthani?*[1] However, since it also appears in its doctrine of Creation, let us dedicate some pages to this topic in order to complete the theme of the Theology of Creation.

§ 2 In dealing with the subject of Creation, the progressivists add another line to their defense of Immanentism, which follows logically from their notion of a continuous Creation or a Creation in evolution.

§ 3 Teilhard de Chardin's thesis of a *Cosmogenesis*, a "baptized" evolution applied to ecclesiology and History, is immanentist. Indeed, according to this theory, Creation would proceed from the divine *Logos* (the *Alpha* point), and would bear in itself the latent energies that were actualized during the evolution of

---

[1] In Vol. VI, *Inveniet Fidem?*, Chap. III, we considered the immanentist foundation of Modern Philosophy and its acceptance by conciliar Progressivism.

In Vol. VII, *Destructio Dei*, Chap. II §§ 55-84, we explained the immanentist notion of God professed by the progressivists. Further on, in Chap. III, we analyzed their two principal systems regarding the Triune God, and we concluded that both are immanentist. In Chap. IV, while studying the concept of God as transcendent, we presented texts of progressivist authors defending God as immanent in man (§§ 56-69), in Creation (§§ 70-84) and in History (§§ 85-89). Also in Chap. IV, while studying the denial of God as Personal, we saw that the progressivist notion of person is immanentist (§§ 316-320) and also in its application to God (§§ 321-328).

Throughout Vol. VIII, *Fumus Satanae,* in which we presented the strange progressivst Trinitarian conception, we demonstrated that at its base is divine Emanatism, with a consequent divine Immanentism in the universe.

In this Vol. IX, we alluded to Immanentism when we presented a synopsis of the progressivist doctrine of Creation (Chap. I §§ 63-71), and when we analyzed the two matrices of historical Evolutionism (Chap. IV §§ 105-124).

organic matter (*Biogenesis*) and of human thought (*Noogenesis*). With the coming of the historical Christ, it would have become clear that evolution had been tending toward Christ (*Christogenesis*).

Thenceforth, the number of those who have become aware of this process would have been continuously increasing through the action of the Church. And today, with the advent of the modern era, that awareness would be on the brink of becoming universal through the action of ecumenism. Once there is universal recognition that evolution and a universal religion are interchangeable, we would be rapidly reaching the end of History: the immersion of mankind into Christ (the Omega Point).

§ 4 Creation presents itself as a fundamentally immanentist reality, given that it initially emanated from the *Logos,* has Him latent in its ontological reality and tends to accomplish itself in Christ by the emanation of universalizing energies. This is an inevitable consequence of the philosophical-theological principles adopted by the progressivist current.

§ 5 Thus surfaces the weak point of the progressivist doctrine, which leaves it quite vulnerable because the condemnation of Pantheism issued by the ecclesiastical Magisterium can be applied directly against it.[2] This is why it was indispensable for the progressivists to conceal its pantheistic character.

§ 6 With this aim, the progressivists launched their new concept of personalization.

The artifice is tricky since one of the principal objections against Pantheism is that it annihilates the person. In effect, when Pantheism considers man as just a particle of a divine All, his individuality loses its meaning, and, therefore, he becomes depersonalized.

While maintaining the immanentist character of their doctrine of Creation, the progressivists nonetheless affirm that their doctrine serves to stimulate the process of personalization. Thus, they try to escape the accusation of favoring Pantheism.

The concepts of person and personalization become, therefore, the center of the question.

§ 7 According to Catholic Doctrine, as we have seen,[3] the notion of person indissolubly implies the notion of individual.

---

[2] Cf. Chap III § 11, Notes 10, 17.

[3] Cf. Vol. VII, *Destructio Dei*, Chap. IV §§ 171-183.

And the latter, in its turn, supposes the incommunicability of the essence of every man.[4]

§ 8 According to the progressivist doctrine, on the contrary, the notion of individual is denied. The person would be fundamentally a dialogical reality, which would find the realization of itself not in itself, but in someone else. The person would be, therefore, essentially communicable.[5]

§ 9 While the battle between Catholic doctrine and Pantheism can be focused on the concept of person – the former stimulating personalization, the latter destroying it – the battle between the same Catholic doctrine and Progressivism must be centered on the concept of the incommunicability of the person.

§ 10 The progressivists suppose that the substance of each individual is realized only in a dialogue with someone else, and that when the two enter into a relationship they constitute the initial cell of the "person." Thus, there would be no individual in the person, but a duo or a couple.

Is this duo or couple communicable or incommunicable?

If it were incommunicable, we would have a "mono-nuptial-person" as the foundation of human reality. In this hypothesis, each individual would be dissolved in the other of the duo. We would have, then, a dissolution of individuality similar to the one that takes place in Pantheism, with the difference being that such a dissolution would be operated by couples. It would be, then, a variant of Pantheism, a "Pantheism by twos."

If it were communicable, the initial couple would transmit its substance to others: It would be a "pan-nuptial-person." It would thus be Pantheism as we know it.

Therefore, the progressivist concept of person presents itself as a mere windscreen to hide its pantheistic notion of the communicability of being.

With this summary of the progressivist theory about person and personalization, the Reader can more easily discern the pantheistic doctrine in excerpts by progressivist authors.

§ 11 We will find, first, Fr. Teilhard de Chardin condemning Catholic doctrine when it indissolubly links the individual and the person:

---

[4] Cf. St. Thomas Aquinas, *Summa Theologiae,* I, q. 13, a. 9c; III, q. 77, a. 2, c; *II Sententiarum*, d. 3, q. 1, 4; *De Causis*, 10, 4, c, 3.

[5] Cf. Vol. VII, *Destructio Dei*, Chap. IV §§ 180-183, 189-199, 241-270.

"The only error of egoism, which takes it completely astray from the good path, is to confuse individuality with personality. In trying to separate itself as much as possible from others, the element individualizes itself. But, in doing so, it falls back and tries to drag the world backwards toward plurality, toward matter. What really happens is that it diminishes itself, it loses itself.

"To be fully ourselves, we must advance in the opposite direction, toward a convergence with all the rest, toward the other. The aim of ourselves, the apex of our originality, is not our individuality, but our person, and, according to the evolutionary structure of the world, we can only find our person by uniting with one another. There is no spirit without synthesis. … The true ego grows in inverse proportion to 'egoism.' Like the Omega that attracts it, the element can only become personal by universalizing itself."[6]

§ 12 Teilhard goes on to address the question of how the being dissolves in Pantheism. He tries to escape the accusation of being a Pantheist by stating that the dissolution of the being in the Omega is just a "super-centralization," which he understands as personalization:

"In any domain where union may occur – whether it be the cells of a body, the members of a society or the elements of a spiritual synthesis – it differentiates. The parts fulfill and complete themselves in every organized whole. It was because we forgot this universal rule that so many Pantheisms were led astray to the cult of a Great All in which individuals would be lost, would dissolve themselves like a drop of water or a grain of salt in the ocean.

"Applied to the case of an addition of consciences, however, the law of union frees us from this perilous and recurrent illusion. No, following the confluent orbits of their centers, the grains of conscience do not tend to lose their contours and blend with one another. … To the contrary, the more they become the other all together, the more they find 'themselves' as self. How could it be otherwise, since they penetrate in the Omega? Could a center dissolve? Better said, would not its particular way of dissolving be to super-centralize? …

"If we try to apply logically the notion of collectivity to an ensemble of particles, the only image that appears is that of a grouping in which the personalization of the all and the person-

---

[6] P. Teilhard de Chardin, *O fenômeno humano*, p. 289.

alization of the elements reach their apex, without blending and simultaneously, under the influence of a focus of union that is supremely autonomous (the Omega Point)."[7]

§ 13 The same notion of conscience, now considered "centralization of consciences or awareness" appears in the text below. For us to understand what Teilhard affirms, we should consider that, for him, consciousness is a stage of the evolution of the universe. This stage would become increasingly more perfect to the degree men would become aware that evolution is a universal phenomenon tending to a final point, to a center.

Thus, the "centralization of consciences" would be a twofold movement: *first*, each man becomes aware that he is an element of the process; *second*, he tends to unite himself with all the other elements to speed the formation of the "center," which is the Omega Point. Such a movement would be the process of "personalization." We see, then, that Teilhard adopts the dialogical concept of person that we described above in § 8.

This is the text of Teilhard:

"Regarding the opposition between the All and the person, our difficulties and rejections would be dissipated if only we understood that, by its structure, the *Noosphere* [the sphere of human thought that would hover over the world], and more generally the world, represent a whole that is not only closed but also centered.

"Because it contains and engenders conscience [or awareness], space-time is necessarily convergent. Consequently, if we follow them [the *Noosphere* and the world] in the right direction, somewhere their extended layers must inflect forward to a point – let us call it Omega – which gives them their foundation and consummates them in themselves.

"No matter how immense the sphere of the world may be, it only exists and is finally perceptible in the direction in which its rays merge together ... Better still, the more immense this sphere is, the richer and deeper, and hence the more conscious is the point at which the 'volume of being' that it encompasses is concentrated. For, the Spirit, seen from our side, is essentially a potency of synthesis and organization.

"Seen from this aspect, the universe, without losing any of its enormity, decidedly grows in significance from the moment that to think it, to suffer with it and to act over it, we look *beyond*

---

[7] *Ibid.*, pp. 287-289.

our souls, and not the other way around. In the perspective of a *Noogenesis,* time and space become truly humanized, or better, super-humanized. The universal and the personal (that is to say, the 'centered') – far from excluding one another – grow in the same direction and culminate simultaneously in each other.

"It is, therefore, a mistake to look for the extension of our being or of the *Noosphere* in the perspective of the impersonal. The future-universal cannot be anything else but the hyper-personal at the Omega Point."[8]

§ 14 The immanentist character of Teilhard's conception becomes still clearer in the next text. In it he tries to shield himself against the label of Pantheist that comes to mind when we read his works. For this purpose he introduces the expression "incommunicable load of conscience or awareness" referring to the person. Nonetheless, the incommunicability of the person is totally denied in this excerpt, which proves that the expression is just another tactical artifice. We read:

"The universe is being built above our heads, in the inverse direction of matter, which dissolves itself: it is a collecting and conserving universe of the persons, not a universe of mechanical energies. All around us, one by one, like a continual effluvium, 'minds' liberate themselves, carrying upwards their incommunicable load of conscience; one by one, yet not in isolation.

"Since, due to the very nature of Omega, for each of them there can only be one possible point of definitive emersion: that point at which the *Noosphere,* under the synthesizing action that personalizes, will reach collectively its point of convergence – at the 'end of the world."[9]

§ 15 The same problem of this dialogical personalization appears when we consider the possibility of the existence of a "concrete universal," that is, of a person who would assume in his essence a part of the substance of the universe itself.

On this topic, Cardinal Henri de Lubac makes a comparative study of the thinking of Teilhard, Maurice Blondel and von Balthasar. The comments of de Lubac on the following citations try to deny they are Pantheists. We will analyze them further on. De Lubac writes:

---

[8] *Ibid.*, pp. 284-285.

[9] *Ibid.*, p. 300.

"Teilhard and Blondel both speak of a 'concrete universal.' Both give this expression the same fundamental meaning. Both, again, carefully distinguish the universal from the general. For Blondel, the concrete universal finds its full realization in the Being of God himself, which is supremely personal: 'True unity,' the unity which Pantheism seeks and fails to find, and to which Christianity leads us, 'consists, ' Blondel says, 'in the presence of the same real mediation in all and everything of a concrete universal, which, without mixing itself in the imperfections of creatures and their finite way of existing, nonetheless exists, everywhere and is entirely itself. …'

"More precisely, the Christian recognizes this concrete universal in Christ, the Man God, Who is the 'universal liaison, the *vinculum vinculorum* [the bond of bonds], the supreme and unique piece that contributes to the consolidation of everything else. …

"This is, fundamentally, what Hans Urs von Balthasar observes from a more historical point of view, when he speaks of the 'two great limitations that characterize the finite being:'

"'No individual being *per se* can be the universal; and no universal can be the individual being. But … in Christ it is God himself Who comes. Christ is neither one individual among others, because He is God in person, nor is He the norm in the sense of a universal, because He is an individual being entirely concrete… He is the 'universal concrete,' a 'concrete universal'… In philosophy we can affirm that the Phoenix is an impossibility, that is, an individual that in itself contains the whole species. Theology, on the other hand, departs from the Phoenix, Christ, Who as an individual being is universal, because He is the absolute Norm; Christ, Who as a contingent being in the bosom of History, is the necessary Law set above all History and all Nature.'

"For Teilhard, as well as for Blondel and von Balthasar, this notion of the concrete universal obviously presupposes a certain identification of the personal with the universal. At the same time, we must add that the identification is to be conceived in a precise sense: God is 'universal personality'; He is not a universal principle personalized by man; the 'universal-Personal is the supreme Personal.' Otherwise, the identification would replace the ontology of personal beings by a mythology of abstractions. It would generate another 'Gnosis.' …

"Understood in its true meaning, however, it constitutes an attempt to probe the mystery more deeply; it is a legitimate step towards 'understanding of the faith.' Now, in fact, the true meaning is not subjected to doubt. The doctrine of Teilhard, opposed to any 'Gnosis,' is realist and has 'personalist' realism. Certainly, Teilhard has a 'prevailing sense of the universal,' to the point that, as he himself tells us, 'he cannot appreciate anything except on the scale of the universal.' Everything he wrote, moreover, confirms it to us.

"Yet, his universe is still the 'personal universe.' This personal universe is in no way the abusive personalization (or the mythical personalization) of an impersonal. It is 'the centralization of the universe in a supreme Person,' in a 'supreme Someone': 'Common sense is right. It is impossible to give oneself to an anonymous number. On the contrary, the universe for us must assume beforehand a face and a heart, it must personalize itself, so to speak, not by becoming a person, of course, but by exercising in the very center of its development the dominating and unifying influence of a focus of energies and personal attractions. If this happens, the attractions of the elements will immediately blossom in the atmosphere created by this focus.'"[10]

§ 16 This comparative study by de Lubac seems to us illustrative for the topic we are addressing for various reasons:

First, because he brings together the thoughts of Blondel, von Balthasar and Teilhard, endorses them and, then, adds his own opinion to them. We have, therefore, a good example of the thinking of great exponents of the modernist-progressivist current.

§ 17 *Second*, because de Lubac presents Blondel and von Balthasar in a way that "justifies" Teilhard; and he presents the latter in a way to show the direction the two other authors normally travel. This allows us to analyze the three of them according to the same criterion.

§ 18 *Third,* entering into the merit of the question, because in the quoted passage of von Balthasar he pretends that what is an error in philosophy – the notion of universal individual – is a truth in theology.

Now then, this proposition is inadmissible because the Faith is a *rationabile obsequium* [a rational gift from the side of God, a rational homage from the side of man]. Therefore,

[10] H. de Lubac, *L'Eternel Féminin – Étude sur un Texte du Père Teilhard de Chardin* (Paris: Aubier-Montaigne, 1968), pp. 197-201.

theology must be rational, based upon sound philosophical reason. Nothing that is an error in philosophy can be admitted in theology. This, which is an imperative of good sense, was also condemned by the Church."[11]

§ 19 *Fourth*, because as de Lubac explains the thinking of Teilhard in the quoted text, he presents him from the exact same focus we are analyzing: that is, in order to save himself from the accusation of being a Pantheist, Teilhard shields himself behind the dialogical concept of person. De Lubac is so strongly aware of the weakness of his defense that he is obliged to argue *ad absurdum*: "This personal universe is in no way the abusive personalization (or the mythical personalization) of an impersonal."

---

[11] The Averroist thesis that a proposition can be true in theology and simultaneously false in philosophy and vice-versa was condemned by the Fifth Lateran Council in the Bull *Apostolici Regiminis* of December 19, 1513: "Since in no way can what is true be opposed to what is true, we define as absolutely false every assertion contrary to the truth of the revealed Faith and rigorously forbid that it be taught differently. We decree that all those who adhere to this error – since they dedicate themselves to sow the most reprehensible heresies everywhere – are detestable and abominable heretics or infidels who destroy the Catholic Faith and, as such, must be shunned and punished" (D 738).

Also Vatican Council I, in its Constitution *Dei Filius* on the Catholic Faith of April 24, 1870, in dealing with the impossibility of conflict between Faith and reason, affirms: "Although Faith is above reason, no dissension can ever occur between Faith and reason, because God himself, who reveals the mysteries and infuses the faith, placed inside the human mind the light of reason, and God cannot contradict himself, nor can the truth ever contradict the truth. Now, the vain appearance of such a contradiction arises chiefly from either the dogmas of Faith have not been understood and explained according to the mind of the Church, or deceitful opinions are considered as axioms of reason. Thus, 'we define as absolutely false every assertion contrary to the truth of the revealed Faith.'

"Further, the Church who, along with the apostolic mission of teaching, has received the mandate to guard the deposit of Faith, has also from Divine Providence the right and duty of proscribing *knowledge of false names* (1 Tim 6:20), *lest anyone be cheated by philosophy and vain deceit* (Col 2:8). For this reason, we not only forbid all faithful Christians to defend as legitimate conclusions of science those opinions known to be contrary to the doctrine of the Faith, especially if they had been condemned by the Church, but the faithful are also absolutely commanded to consider them as errors that have the cunning appearance of truth (D. 1797-1798).

To argue his point, de Lubac only quotes texts by Teilhard in which the latter says that the universe is "centered" in a person and that "it is impossible to give oneself to an anonymous number."

Now then, what is under discussion is not to know whether Teilhard uses or does not use the word person, whether he takes a position against the impersonal or not. The question under analysis, raised by de Lubac himself, is to know whether or not Teilhard abuses the term. Toward this end de Lubac failed to present any valid reason. This leads us to suspect that such reasons do not exist and that his appeal to the absurd is nothing but a tactical artifice to cover for the actual abusive use of the word person, as we have been showing in this Chapter.

§ 20 *Fifth*, although he tries to show that there is no Pantheism and Gnosis in the concept of concrete universal, de Lubac carefully avoids entering the heart of the question. In effect, if Christ were the concrete universal – as Blondel and von Balthasar affirm and Teilhard and de Lubac suppose – de Lubac should have shown how this coincides with Catholic doctrine.

According to Church teaching, Our Lord Jesus Christ is not a universal Person.[12] He is not a universal Person as a Man because, by being an essentially incommunicable individual (person)[13] of the human race, He cannot contain the universe in himself. He is not a universal Person as God because, since the Creator is substantially and infinitely above the universe and since the Three Persons are substantially incommunicable,[14] it is not possible that any type of universal Divine Person should exist representing an ontological confusion between God and the universe.

---

[12] The expression "universal person" can be understood in two ways:

First, from the ontological perspective, universal person would be that which has a substantial union with the universe.

Second, from the moral perspective, universal person would be that which, without an ontological link to the universe, would have greatly enlarged, by its own effort, the ambit of its thoughts and desires in such a way that they could be called universals. The first meaning is proper, the second is analogical. Here we are dealing only with the first, which is the only one that matters in studying the divine Immanentism professed by Progressivism.

[13] Cf. Vol. VII, *Destructio Dei*, Chap. IV §§ 164-179.

[14] Cf. *ibid.*, Chap. IV. §§ 184-187.

Now then, the Christ presented by de Lubac, Blondel, von Balthasar and Teilhard seems to be characterized by His ontological communication with the universe; hence, they qualify Him as the concrete universal. This is the Cosmic Christ of Teilhard de Chardin, analyzed various times in this Collection.[15]

We are dealing, thus, with an immanentist-pantheist conception of Christ and the universe. This differs from classical Pantheism only in a change of name: The pan-impersonal god of Pantheism becomes the Cosmic Personal Christ of Progressivism. The change of name, however, alters nothing in the essence of the concepts. It only shows the intent to deceive the careless.

§ 21

Sixth, the comparative study of Cardinal de Lubac reveals that the thinking of Teilhard de Chardin is consonant with those of Blondel, representing Modernism and of von Balthasar, representing Progressivism. It is, therefore, on a modernist-progressivist backdrop that we should understand the texts of Teilhard quoted in this Chapter.

We conclude this Chapter, having amply demonstrated that a divine immanence of a pantheistic hue is the last substratum of the progressivist theology of Creation.

* * *

---

[15] Cf. Vol. I, *In the Murky Waters of Vatican II*, Chap. IX § 75; Vol. III, *Animus Injuriandi I*, Chaps I Note 35, Chap. III § 33; Vol. IV, *Animus Delendi I*, Chap. IV, § 238, Chap V § 20; Vol. VI, *Inveniet Fidem?*, Chap V §§ 81-89, Chap. V §§ 111-116; Vol. VII, *Destructio Dei,* Chap. II §§ 10-23, Chap. III § 229; Vol. VIII, *Fumus Satanae*, Chap. I §§ 61-77, 92-110, Chap III §§ 27-36, Chap. IV § 161, Chap. VII §§ 119-121. In this Vol. IX, *Creatio*, Chap. I §§ 42, 43, 60, 61, 68; Chap. III § 31; Chap. V §§ 3, 12-14.

CONCLUSION

§ 1 Throughout this Volume IX of the Collection *Lamma Sabacthani,* we analyzed the progressivist conception of Creation in several of its important aspects:

- The genesis of its existence, its triumph in Vatican II and the endorsement it received from the principal theologians of the Council (Chap. I);
- § 2 Evolutionism as the nucleus of the new doctrine of Creation and its false scientific character (Chap. II);
- § 3 Lacking any serious scientific support, Evolutionism is nothing more than a hypothesis that assumes the characteristics of a true "dogma" of the new progressivist religion (Chap. III);
- § 4 Historicism is a close consequence of Evolutionism. For this reason, the progressivist conception of History was also analyzed and its principal currents summarized (Chap. IV).
- § 5 Finally, the metaphysical foundation of Evolutionism and Historicism has an immanentist conception with a pantheistic hue (Chap. V).

Having made this circumnavigation, we believe that we presented the more important points of this topic as well as its principal aim: the destruction of Catholic Exegesis and Dogmatic Theology on Creation.

§ 6 We did not deal here with specific themes referring to Creation such as, for example, how the creation of man took place and what was his situation in the paradisiacal state. We hope to address these topics in the next Volume when we will analyze original sin.

§ 7 Why did we not address these topics here? Basically, it was for a methodological reason. Normally the progressivists proceed from the particular to the general, from the less elevated to the more elevated, from the concrete to the abstract. This is a procedure that, in our opinion, aims to cover the weakest side of their thinking, which habitually lies in the general, the more elevated and the abstract.

To make it easier to denounce the weak points of Progressivism, starting with Vol. VI, *Inveniet Fidem?* we began to analyze the fruits and thinking of the Council starting from the more general and abstract perspectives. When we finally reach an analysis of the particular, the less elevated and the concrete, the Reader is naturally more familiar with the poison that each particular case can contain. Following this same method, several more specific themes related to Creation will be dealt with later.

§ 8 It is to the study of original sin and the Redemption in the next Volume that we invite the Reader who wants to know the fruits of the Council in these two important parts of Dogmatic Theology.

* * *

BIBLIOGRAPHY

(AAS) ACTA APOSTOLICAE SEDIS, Commentarium Officiale - Vatican City: Libreria editrice vaticana, 1909-. **ABBOTT, Walter M. and GALLAGHER, J.** - *The Documents of Vatican II,* Piscataway, NJ: New Century Publishers, Inc., 1966. **ALSZEGHY, Zoltán** - See Maurizio FLICK. **AQUINAS, St. Thomas Aquinas** - *De Anima,* Rome/Turin: Marietti, 1948; *De Potentia,* Rome/Turin: Marietti, 1949; *De Trinitate,* Rome/Turin: Marietti, 1954; *De Veritate,* Rome/Turin: Marietti, 1949; *Super Libros Metaphysicorum,* Rome/Turin: Marietti, 1950; *Sententiarum*, Paris: L. Lethielleux, 1933; *Super Libros Ethicorum,* Rome/Turin: Marietti, 1949; *Super Libros Posteriorum,* Rome/Turin: Marietti, 1955; *Summa Contra Gentiles,* Rome/Turin: Marietti, 1934; *Summa Theologiae,* Turin/Rome: Marietti, 1948, 4 vols. **ASHTON, John F.** - *In Six Days: Why Fifty Scientists Choose to Believe in Creation,* Green Forest, AR: Master Books, 2001. **AUBERTIN, Atanásio** - "A Evolução das Espécies: Apriorismos e Confissões Gnósticas," *Catolicismo* (Campos), January, 1962; "A Revolução, a Filogênese Humana e o Pe. Teilhard de Chardin (I-III), *Catolicismo*, May, July, September, 1963. **AUGUSTINE, St.** - *Confissões*, Porto: Livraria Apostolado da Imprensa, 1948; *La Cité de Dieu,* Paris: Jacques Lecoffre, 1854, 3 vols.

BALTHASAR, Hans Urs von - *De l'Intégration - Aspects d'une Théologie de L'Histoire,* Bruges: Desclée de Brouwer, 1970; *Le Coeur du Monde,* Paris: Desclée de Brouwer, 1956; *Mysterium Paschale,* in V.A., *Mysterium Salutis*; *Solo l'Amore É Credible,* Turin: Borla, 1965. **BLOCH, Marc** - *La Société Féodale*, Paris: Albin Michel, 1970. **BONIFACE VII** - *Unam Sanctam* of December 18, 1302, in Giorgio Balladure Pallieri & Giulio Vismara, *Acta Juris Genium Pontificia.* **BOSSUET, Jacques Benigne** - *Discours sur l'Histoire Universelle*, Paris: Garnier-Flammarion, 1966.

CABIBBO, Nicola - Article on Galileo, *30 Dias*, January 1993. **CASTAGNOLA, Luís** - see PADOVANI, Humberto. **CHARDIN, Pierre Teilhard de** - *Le Christique,* Paris: Seuil, 1976; *Le Coeur de la Matière,* Paris: Seuil, 1976; *O Fenômeno Humano,* Porto: Tavares Martins, 1970. **CHENU, Marie-Dominique** - "Les Signes des Temps – Réflexion Théologique," in Y. Congar & M. Peuchmaurd, *L'Église dans le Monde de ce Temps*; "O que Muda e o que Permanece," in V.A., *A Igreja e o Futuro.* **COLOMBO, Giuseppe** - "La Création," in V.A., *Bilan de la Théologie du XXe. Siècle.* **CONGAR, Yves** - *Théologie*, in DTC. **CONGAR, Yves & Marcel PEUCHMAURD**, *L'Église dans le Monde de ce Temps,* Paris: Cerf, 1967. 2 vols. **CUOZZO, Jack** - *Buried Alive: The Startling Truth about Neanderthal Man*, Green Forest, AR: Master Books, 2008. **CYPRIAN, St.** - *De Catholic Ecclesia Unitate,* in PL.

DARWIN, Charles - *The Origin of the Species,* London: John Murray, 1902. **DELASSUS, Henri** - *La Conjuration Antichrétienne*, Lille: Desclée de Brower, 1910, 3 vols. **(DR) DENZINGER, Heinrich & RAHNER, Carolus** - *El Magisterio de la Iglesia*, Barcelona: Herder, 1963, updated by

K. Rahner in 1946-1954. **(DS) DENZINGER, Heinrich & Schonmetzer, Adolphus** - the Denzinger collection with additions by A. Schonmetzer between 1955 and 1965, Friburgi/Brisgoviae/Barceinone: Herder, 1965. **(DTC) *DICTIONNAIRE DE THEOLOGIE CATHOLIQUE*** - A. Vacant and E. Mangenot, eds., Paris: Letouzey et Ane, 1923-1951. 15 vols. plus index. **DIONYSIUS THE AREOPAGITE, St.** - *La Hiérarchie Céleste*, Paris: Cerf, 1970. **DUQUESNE, Jacques** - *Jacques Duquesne Interroge le Père Chenu - Une Théologie en Liberté*, Paris: Centurion, 1975.

FERNANDO, A. - "Revelação Cristã e Iluminação Budista," *Concilium*, 2/1976. **FIELD, A.N.** - *The Evolution Hoax Exposed,* Rockfort, Il: TAN, 1971. **FLICK, Maurizio & Alszeghy, Zoltán** - *Il Mistero della Croce - Saggio di Teologia Sistematica*, Brescia: Queriniana, 1978. **FOULQUIÉ, Paul** - *Dictionnaire de la Langue Philosophique*, Paris: Presses Universitaires de France, 1962.

GODFREY, Laurie R. - see **PETTER, Andrew J. GOULD, Stephen Jay** - "The Return of Hopeful Monsters," *Natural History,* June/July 1977. **GUIMARÃES, Atila Sinke** - *Collection: Eli, Eli, Lamma Sabacthani?*: Vol. I, *In the Murky Waters of Vatican II,* Los Angeles: TIA, 2008, 3d ed.; Vol. II, *Animus Injuriandi-I,* Los Angeles: TIA, 2010; Vol. III, *Animus Injuriandi II,* Los Angeles: TIA, 2011; Vol. IV, *Animus Delendi I*, Los Angeles: TIA, 2000; Vol. V, *Animus Delendi II*, Los Angeles: TIA, 2002; Vol. VI, *Inveniet Fidem?*, Los Angeles: TIA, 2007; Vol. VII, *Destruction Dei*, Los Angeles: TIA, 2013; Vol. VIII, *Fumus Satanae.* Los Angeles: TIA 2014; Vol. XI, *Ecclesia,* Los Angeles: TIA, 2009.

IGNATIUS OF LOYOLA, St. - *Exercícios de Santo Inácio e Leituras Espirituais.* Porto: Ed. A.J., 1934. **ILLIES, Joachim** - in V.A., *Bilan de la Théologie du XXe Siècle.*

JOHN PAUL II (Karol Wojtyla) - *Insegnamenti di Giovanni Paolo II*, Lib. Ed. Vaticana, 1983, 18 vol.; Address to the Pontifical Academy of Sciences of November 10, 1979, *La Repubblica*, September 23, 1989; Address to the Pontifical Academy of Science on October 31, 1992, *L'Osservatore Romano*, November 1, 1992; "Messagio per la Celebrazione della Giornata Mondiale della Pace," January 1, 1990, n. 5. **JOURNET, Charles** - *L'Église du Verbe Incarné*, Desclée de Brouwer, 1955, 2 vols.

KLIMKE, F. - *História de la Filosofia,* Barcelona: Labor, 1947. **KLOPPENBURG, Boaventura** - *A Eclesiologia do Vaticano II,* Petrópolis: Vozes, 1971. **KÜNG, Hans** - *A Igreja,* Lisbon: Morales, 1970, 2 vols.

LALANDE, André - *Vocabulário Técnico y Crítico de la Filosofia*, Buenos Aires: El Ateneo, 1953. **LAMB, David** - *The Search for Extraterrestrial Intelligence: A Philosophical Inquiry,* NY: Routledge, 2001. **LAMBERTINI, Gastone** - "Quelli Errori Consueti del Neo-Evoluzionism," *L'Osservatore Romano,* August 19, 1989. **LAPIDE, CORNELIUS A** – *Commentaria in Scripturam Sacram,* Paris: Ludovicum Vivés Ed., 1874-1877, 24 vols. **LAVISSE, Ernest & Alfred Rambaud** - *Histoire Générale du 4eme Siécle à nos Jours,* Paris: Armand Collin, 1893-1901, 11 vols. **LEO**

XIII, Encyclical *Aterni Patris* of August 4, 1879, Petropolis: Vozes, 1956; Encyclical *Humanum genus*, Petrópolis: Vozes. 1960; Encyclical *Parvenu*, Petrópolis: Vozes, 1952; Encyclical *Satis cognitum*, Petropolis: Vozes, 1960. ***(L)'OSSERVATORE ROMANO*** - *Monitum,* July 1, 1962; Letter of Cardinal Agostino Casaroli praising Teilhard de Chardin, June 10, 1981. **LUBAC, Henri de** - *Catholicisme - Les Aspects Sociaux du Dogme,* Paris: Cerf, 1968; *La Posterité Spirituelle de Joachim de Flore,* Paris: Lethielleux, 1979; *L'Eternel Féminin – Étude sur un Texte du Père Teilhard de Chardin,* Paris: Aubier-Montaigne,1968.

MACCARRONE, MICHELE - *Atti del Convegno di Studio su Pio Paschini nel Centenario della Nascita 1878-1978, Udine:* Tip. Vaticana, 1981. **MESSORI, Vittorio** - Commentary on Galileo, *Avvenire*, October 19, 1989. **MEYER, Stephen C.** - *Darwin's Doubt,* NY: Harper Collins, 2013. **MILL, John Stuart** - *Auguste Comte and Positivism.* London: N Trübner & Co., 1865. **MOLARI, Carlo** - *La Problematica del Linguaggio Teologico*, Milan: Ancora, 1970. **MONTFORT, St. Louis Grignion de** - *Carta-Circular aos Amigos da Cruz*, Rio de Janeiro: Ed. Santa Maria, 1954; *Tratado da Verdadeira Devoção à Santíssima Virgen*, Petrópolis: Vozes, 1961. **MORTIER, Jeanne-M.** - *Avec Teilhard de Chardin - Vues Ardentes,* Paris: Seuil, 1967.

O'DONNELL, John - "Man and Woman as '*Imago Dei*' in the Theology of Hans Urs von Balthasar," *Clergy Review* (London) n. 78, 1983. **OLIVEIRA, Plinio Correa de** - *Revolution and Counter-Revolution*, York, PA: The American Society for the Defense of Tradition, Family and Property, 1993; São Paulo: Diário das Leis, 1982.

PADOVANI, Humberto & Luís CASTAGNOLA - *História da Filosofia,* São Paulo: Ed. Melhoramentos, 1967. **PALLIERI, Giorgio Balladure & Giulio VISMARA** - *Acta Juris Genium Pontificia*, Milan: Società Editrice Vita e Pensiero, 1946. **PASCHINI, Pio** - *Vita e Opera di Galileo Galilei,* Città del Vaticano: Pontificia Accademia delle Scienze, 1964, 1964. 2 vols. **PATROLOGIE LATINE (PL)** - pub. by Paul Migne, 161 vols. **PEREIRA, José Balthasar** - *Comentários sobre o Novo Testamento – Apocalypse,* Bahia: Typografia de São Francisco, 1912. **PETTER, Andrew J. & Laurie R. GODFREY** - *Scientists Confront Creationism: Intelligent Design and Beyond,* NY: W. W. Norton & Company, Inc., 2007. **PEUCHMAURD, Marcel** - see CONGAR, Yves & Marcel Peuchmaurd. **PHILIPS, Gérard** - *La Chiesa e il Suo Mistero - Storia, Testo e Commento della Lumen Gentium*, Milan: Jaka Books, 1982.

PIUS IX - Bull *Ineffabilis Deus, apud Catolicismo*, Campos, December 1954; Encyclical *Qui pluribus*, Petropolis: Vozes, 1960. **PIUS X, St.** - Encyclical *E supremi apostolatus* of October 4, 1903, Petrópolis: Vozes, 1958; Encyclical *Pascendi Dominici gregis* of September 8,1907, Petrópolis: Vozes, 1959. **PIUS XII, St.** - *Discorsi e Radiomessaggi di Sua Santità Pio XII*, Tipografia Poliglotta Vaticana, 1940-1959, 20 vols. plus index; Encyclical *Ad coeli Reginam* of October 11, 1954, in *L'Osservatore Romano,* October 24, 1954; Encyclical *Divino Afflante Spiritu* of September 30, 1943, Petrópolis: Vozes, 1950; *Humani generis* of August 12, 1950, Petrópolis: Vozes, 1961. **POUPARD, Paul** - Article on Galileo, *Corriere della Sera,* March 30, 1990; Study results on Galileo presented October 31, 1992, *L'Osservatore Romano*, November 2-3, 1992. **PUYO, Jean** - *Jean Puyo Interroge le Père Congar - Une Vie pour la Verité,* Paris: Centurion, 1975.

RAMBAUD, Alfred see LAVISSE, Ernest - *Histoire Générale du 4eme Siécle à nos Jours.* **RAMIREZ, Santiago** - *Introductión General al Tratado del Verbo Encarnado de Santo Tomás de Aquino*, Madrid: BAC, 1960, 16 vols. **RAHNER, Karl** - "La Cristologia dentro de una Concepción Evolutiva del Mundo," in V. A., *Escritos de Teología*; *Magistero e Teologia dopo il Concilio,* Brescia: Queriniana, 1967. **RAMIÈRE, Henri** - *Le Règne de Jésus-Christ dans l'Histoire,* unpublished. **RATZINGER, Joseph (Benedict XVI)** - *Fé e Futuro*, Petropolis: Vozes, 1971; "Fé en la Creación y Teoria Evolutiva," in V.A., *Es Esto Dios?; Le Dieu de Jésus-Christ*, Paris: Fayard, 1977; Speech on Galileo in Parma on March 15, 1990, *Corriere della Sera*, March 30, 1990.

SCHOONENBERG, Piet - no title, in V.A., *Cinco Problemas que Desafiam a Igreja de Hoje.* **SECKLER, Max** - *Le Salut et l'Histoire – La Pensée de Saint Thomas d'Aquin sur la Théologie de l'Histoire*, Paris: Cerf, 1967. **SEVERINO, Emanuele** - Article on Galileo, *30 Dias*, January 1993. **SUENENS, Leo Jozef** - "Co-responsibility: Dominating Idea of the Council and its Pastoral Consequences," in V.A., *Theology of Renewal.* **SUNDERLAND, Luther D.** - *Darwin's Enigma – Fossils and Other Problems*, San Diego, CA: Master Book Publishers, 1984.

V.A. (Various Authors) - *A Igreja e o Futuro*, Petrópolis: Vozes, 1973; *Bilan de la Théologie au XXe siècle*, Tournai/Paris: Casterman, 1970, 2 vols.; *Cinco Problemas que Desafiam a Igreja de Hoje,* São Paulo: Herder, 1970; *Es Esto Dios?* Barcelona: Herder, 1973; *Escritos de Teologia*, Madrid: Taurus, 1964; *Mysterium Salutis, Compêndio de Dogmática Historico-Salvífica,* Petrópolis: Vozes, 1974; *Phrases e Curiosidades Latinas*, Rio de Janeiro, 1955; *Poema de Mio Cid*, Madrid: Aguilar, 1969; *Theology of Renewal - Renewal of Religious Thought,* Montreal: Palm Publishers, 1968, *2* vols. **VIGANO, Mario** - "Galileo Ieri e Oggi," *La Civiltà Cattolica*, September 1984. **VISMARA, Giulio** - see PALLIERI, Giorgio Balladure.

* * *

SUBJECT INDEX

* * *

WORD INDEX

* * *